Withdrawn Stock
BCP Libraries

DAVID STEEL

DAVID STEEL

RISING HOPE TO ELDER STATESMAN

DAVID TORRANCE

Biteback Publishing

First published in Great Britain in 2012 by
Biteback Publishing Ltd
Westminster Tower
3 Albert Embankment
London SE1 7SP
Copyright © David Torrance 2012

ISBN 978-1-84954-140-4

10 9 8 7 6 5 4 3 2 1

For my aunt, Frances, and my late uncle, Andrew Bennie,
who were Liberals (and later Liberal Democrats)
through thick and – mostly – thin.

CONTENTS

ACKNOWLEDGEMENTS

A Whig is a perfectly sensible Conservative.
A Radical is a perfectly sensible Labourite.
A Liberal is anyone who is perfectly sensible.
John Maynard Keynes, 1926

I was born in the summer of 1977, a child of the so-called Lib–Lab Pact engineered by David Steel, the subject of this biography. Naturally, I remember nothing of that novel constitutional experiment. My childhood, however, was full of the lively politics of the late 1970s and 1980s. Although my father was a confirmed Scottish Nationalist, his sister and her late husband – to whom this book is dedicated – were active Liberals and, post-merger, devoted Liberal Democrats.

Frances had caught the political bug after witnessing a 'slight, dark, young man' (Steel) dashing in and out of his Peebles campaign headquarters during the 1965 Roxburgh, Selkirk & Peebles by-election, while later she was elected to Surrey Heath District Council as a Liberal representative. I knew Steel only as an image on my parents' television screen and, later, as a *Spitting Image* puppet. And even later, during my early years as a television reporter, I dealt with him when he was the Scottish Parliament's first Presiding Officer. My memory is of a rather aloof, intimidating figure.

As David Dutton observed in his history of the Liberal Party, 'David Steel has, so far, largely been his own historian.' Indeed, Liberals – including Steel – have charted their history at lengths inversely proportionate to their electoral strength and influence over the last century. Steel's 1989 memoirs (*Against Goliath*), however, were a rather disappointing addition to the Liberal library. 'It is journalistic in style,' judged Steel's Liberal colleague Archy Kirkwood in a perceptive review, 'and it lifts only tiny edges of the curtain on the innermost thoughts, only rare insights into the depths of the man.' The authorised biography, added Kirkwood, 'will eventually have to fill the gaps'.

Although this biography was not fully authorised, Lord Steel did co-operate fully and openly, responding to emails, lending me private source material and speaking to me at length about his life and career. If Steel and others are quoted in the text in past tense (i.e. 'said'), then it denotes a primary or secondary source, while if in present tense (i.e. 'says'), it indicates a fresh interview conducted for this book. I have avoided extensive footnoting, restricting this academic indulgence to primary archive sources only. Everything else – people, places and papers – is covered in a concluding bibliography.

I prepared most of this book at my two favourite research institutions: the British Library in London and the National Library of Scotland in Edinburgh. I also worked on drafts at my temporary berth in West Hampstead, for which I must thank my landlady Natasha Benenson for providing such a congenial environment (at a very reasonable rate), and also in my home city of Edinburgh, where one of my favourite Englishmen, Jason Orringe, generously hosted frequent research trips, often at short notice.

As ever, various friends, relatives and acquaintances (often new) kindly agreed to read all – or portions – of the typescript. In no particular order, Matt Cole, Duncan Brack, Hugh Andrew, John MacLeod, Jeremy Purvis, Ian Swanson, Willis Pickard, David Thomson and my brother Michael Torrance all provided frank feedback and suggested additions. I am also grateful to Michael Meadowcroft for lending me various sources and to David Thomson for giving me temporary custody of his comprehensive research notes for Steel's autobiography. Lord Steel said when I first contacted him two years ago that he would make no attempt to influence my analysis and, refreshingly, he was as good as his word. The usual caveat applies: any remaining errors of fact or interpretation are, of course, my own.

Without the generous support of the K. Blundell Trust, meanwhile, I would not have been able to consult the voluminous David Steel Papers at the London School of Economics as extensively as I did. Indeed, thanks to the passage of time and the careful acquisition policies of the UK's excellent network of libraries and universities, I was spoilt for choice when it came to primary archive material. Maria Castrillo at the National Library of Scotland was, as ever, not only friendly but highly professional, while I also owe thanks to the staff at the Wellcome Library, *The Guardian* Archives (particularly Susan Gentles), the University of Essex, Churchill College, Cambridge, and the University of Liverpool.

'I love deadlines,' quipped Douglas Adams, 'I love the whooshing noise they make as they go by.' And so it was with the present volume. For tolerating this, and other misdemeanours, with their usual good humour and professionalism I must end by thanking Iain Dale, Sam Carter, Hollie Teague, Aurélie Baudry and the rest of the team at Biteback, an imprint which goes out of its way to keep quality political publishing alive. For that, we should all be relentlessly grateful.

David Torrance
London, July 2012

FOREWORD

This is not the first book to chart the life of David Steel; he has penned one or two himself and others have been along this path as well. But it is surely a tribute to him as an individual and to his achievements in public life that his career remains of interest to anyone who follows politics in this country.

The reasons are not hard to find. First and foremost, David is associated in the public mind with his period as leader of the Liberals. Leading the third party in British politics is never easy, but his was a particularly challenging time. Over his twelve years in charge, he initially had to re-build a weakened party and then keep it relevant while British politics was polarising between a weakening, but increasingly hard-line, Labour movement and a resurgent right.

David showed he was not afraid to take risks, initially with the Lib–Lab Pact and later as he encouraged the development of the SDP, a new political force competing for votes in the same crowded, central space of British politics. Not every party member enjoyed the journey he took them on. But throughout a sometimes fraught period in British politics, he sustained his party's voice and carved an enduring role for himself in the nation's consciousness, as an articulate and effective advocate for liberal values and causes.

This is an important second dimension of his political life – his commitment to long-term campaigning on some of the biggest issues of the day. Some politicians may appear to arrive pre-packed with all the right views on the right issues at the right time. It has never really been David's approach. His upbringing as a son of the manse, his close family and his early experiences of Africa created a more broad-minded, liberal thinker than most.

He was not alone in fighting the anti-apartheid cause, but surely unusual in picketing a match in his own rugby-loving constituency when the Springboks came to play. And he was certainly not the only person outraged by the state of abortion law in the 1960s, but it took real courage and skill to pilot the Abortion Act through Parliament. In 1970 it was only when the postal votes were counted that he retained his seat.

Other battles have been less controversial, but required political stamina. His lifelong commitment to the creation of a Scottish Parliament was one such cause. Empowering individuals and devolving power from an over-centralised state have always been important liberal principles for David – and working across party lines to achieve consensus and secure political objectives something at which he remains very skilled.

His political principles and skills were vital to the cross-party efforts which secured the creation of the Parliament. So, it was fitting that he should be its first Presiding Officer when it was created in 1999, and that he should do so much to establish its place in the political consciousness of Scotland and the wider United Kingdom.

By the time David became leader of the Liberal Party in 1976 he had fought six elections in the Borders in a dozen years. In his remaining twenty-one years as a Member of Parliament he only had to fight four more elections, albeit three of them while also on the national stage. His roots as a local MP are another aspect of his political success and longevity. David has always been proud of campaigning in his own way (and delighting in not knowing what a political campaign manual looks like), but his sustained success as a constituency MP was built on those early years and the tough elections he fought.

He has always been an instinctive community politician – he knew the village postmasters, the parish ministers and the foremen in the mills. He rode the marches in the annual common ridings and knew when not to bluff a local farmer. That he and his wife Judy can still be seen at the Selkirk and Lauder common ridings each year, now watching their children and grandchildren as they ride across the moors, counts for a lot to those he last represented in Parliament fifteen years ago. His down-to-earth manner, basic decency and good humour continue to strike a chord wherever he goes.

Political leader, campaigner, statesman, family man – there are a lot of hats for David to wear and they all fit pretty neatly. As David's successor in the House of Commons, I owe him a significant debt of gratitude for my schooling in politics. As one of the first generation of Liberal politicians in a very long time to have had the chance to be in government at the UK level, I have good reason to reflect on, and be thankful for, the crucial role played by David (and others) over many decades.

His has been, and continues to be, one of the most diverse and important political careers of recent times – as the rest of this book will show.

Michael Moore
MP for Berwickshire, Roxburgh & Selkirk
Secretary of State for Scotland

RISING HOPE TO
ELDER STATESMAN

'You know there are times, perhaps once every thirty years, when there is a sea-change in politics,' James Callaghan told his adviser Bernard Donoughue shortly before the 1979 general election. 'There is a shift in what the public wants and what it approves of. I suspect there is now such a sea-change – and it is for Mrs Thatcher.'

'Sunny Jim', as he was known, was about to reach the end of three tumultuous years as Prime Minister. He was of course correct; the United Kingdom was soon to elect its first female premier and usher in a political era that, if anything, was to be even more eventful than what many saw as the low, dishonest decade preceding it.

Meanwhile David Steel, just a few days short of his forty-first birthday, was about to fight his first national election as Liberal leader. Dubbed 'the Boy David' following a memorable by-election victory in Roxburgh, Selkirk & Peebles fourteen years earlier, Steel soon made his mark by guiding a Bill to reform abortion law through the House of Commons. In 1976 he succeeded Jeremy Thorpe as Liberal leader and promised the Liberal Assembly of that year 'a bumpy road' ahead. Steel did not disappoint. In March 1977 he negotiated a 'Lib–Lab Pact' with Callaghan and, until July 1978, the thirteen-strong Parliamentary Liberal Party sustained a minority Labour government in office.

It had been a baptism of fire for Steel, albeit one of his own making. The effect on Liberal support had been immediate, with the party losing hundreds of councillors and by-election deposits across the country. The pact had also divided his party, between those who agreed with the logic of Steel's 'realignment' strategy, and those desperate to maintain the Liberals as an independent force untainted by association with the Labour Party. Thus the electoral outlook was, as Steel put it, 'bleak'. 'When we left the Liberal dining table for the last time,' he later recalled, 'we suspected that few of the fourteen [Liberal MPs] would be back.'

Callaghan's government had fallen in dramatic circumstances on the evening of Wednesday, 28 March 1979. Motivated by the failure of devolution referendums in Scotland and Wales, the Scottish National Party had initiated a censure motion, later taken up by Mrs Thatcher and turned into a motion of no confidence in Her Majesty's government. Callaghan had half-heartedly tried to cobble together a deal, but both Steel and the Scottish National Party (SNP) indicated their intention to vote with the Conservatives, thereby initiating an early dissolution of Parliament.

On the day of the debate, the House of Commons was packed and tense with expectation. Although the Leader of the Opposition's opening speech had not quite lived up to the occasion, the Prime Minister was on fine form. And while he had developed an avuncular interest in Steel since the early days of the Lib–Lab Pact in March 1977, this did not mean Callaghan was going to spare him his caustic rhetoric. Recounting recent events, the Prime Minister joked that in Mrs Thatcher's dealings with the Liberals and SNP, she had 'found the courage of their convictions'. He continued:

So, tonight, the Conservative Party, which wants the [Scotland] Act repealed and opposes even devolution, will march through the Lobby with the SNP, which wants independence for Scotland, and with the Liberals, who want to keep the Act. What a massive display of unsullied principle!

The minority parties have walked into a trap. If they win, there will be a general election. I am told that the current joke going around the House is that it is the first time in recorded history that turkeys have been known to vote for an early Christmas.

Even some Liberal MPs found Callaghan's 'turkey' line (first coined by the Liberal MP for Truro, David Penhaligon) amusing. Later in the debate it was Steel's turn to speak. 'Although the Prime Minister had his fun at our expense,' he told MPs, 'I have to make it absolutely clear … that there is no question, in our voting for a general election tonight, of appearing to be voting in any way for the Conservative Party.'

Steel then assessed his party's 'record' since March 1977. 'It is perhaps unusual for the leader of the Liberal Party in modern times to be talking of the record of the Liberal Party, but I intend to do so,' he said proudly, 'because I believe that the record shows that the period of greatest success in modern government was the period of the Lib–Lab agreement.'

First, during that period we had a Labour government in office, but left-wing socialism had to be abandoned for that period; therefore there was a degree of political stability and a process of government of this country from the centre. That in itself was beneficial.

Second, let us look at the figures of inflation … In the three months before the Lib–Lab Pact, inflation had gone up to 21 per cent, but it was during the Lib–Lab period of government that the inflation level came down to 7.4 per cent … I believe that the Lib–Lab Pact was important and provided a better way of running the country.

My third argument is that we saw in that period the start of some injection of Liberal influence for the first time into the government of the country.

In conclusion, Steel described a Parliament that found 'itself stuck on devolution, stuck on tax reform and stuck on pay policy, and on industrial relations policy it is not only stuck but is sub-contracting its responsibilities to groups outside Parliament' (a reference to the recent 'winter of discontent'). That, therefore, was the Liberal case for a 'fresh Parliament'. 'I believe that the electors of Liverpool Edge Hill will point to a better way tomorrow [in a pending by-election],' declared Steel. 'I think that there is a better way of running Britain, and the sooner the rest of the country is given the opportunity for it, the better.'

Finally, at around 9.30 p.m., it fell to the Leader of the House to wind up the debate on behalf of the government. Like Callaghan, Michael Foot had come to respect Steel as a result of their dealings during the Lib–Lab Pact, and he looked on the Liberal leader with a degree of affection. A talented parliamentarian, Foot's recap of the six-hour debate was an oratorical *tour de force*. Referring to the SNP, he said there had been nothing akin to the Nationalists' sudden affinity with the anti-devolution Conservatives 'since the armies of ancient Rome used to march into battle'. 'Hail Emperor,' said Foot as he looked in the direction of the SNP's Westminster leader, Donald Stewart, 'those about to die salute you.'

Foot then turned his gaze towards the leader of the Liberal Party:

> He knows that I would not like to miss him out. I am sure that I shall elicit the support and sympathy of the right hon. lady [Mrs Thatcher] when I say that she and I have always shared a common interest in the development of this young man ... I should very much like to know, as I am sure would everybody else, what exactly happened last Thursday night. I do not want to misconstrue anything, but did she send for him or did he send for her – or did they just do it by *billet-doux*?

This had the Conservative benches, and indeed the whole House, roaring with laughter. Foot, however, was not quite finished. 'What the right hon. lady has done today is to lead her troops into battle,' he continued, 'snugly concealed behind a Scottish Nationalist shield, with the boy David holding her hand.' Foot said he was even more concerned about the fate of Steel than he was about her; she, he added, could 'look after herself'. 'But the leader of the

Liberal Party – and I say this with the utmost affection – has passed from *rising hope to elder statesman* without any intervening period whatsoever.'

Foot, as he had been careful to point out, meant the jibe affectionately but, like all political satire, it had included a grain of truth. Nearly twenty-five years Steel's senior, Foot had watched the thirty-something Liberal leader progress from shepherding just thirteen MPs to negotiating with, and ultimately sustaining in office, the government of which he was a member. Steel, for his part, had been genuinely tickled by what he later remembered as a 'very good crack'. 'I thought it was a wonderful remark,' he recalled in 1994, 'quite wicked, but very funny.'

At 10 p.m. the House divided and Callaghan's government fell by just one vote. 'Now that the House of Commons has declared itself,' Callaghan told MPs, 'we shall take our case to the country.' The following day a 28-year-old Liberal activist called David Alton won the Liverpool Edge Hill by-election with a majority of more than 8,000, giving his party a much-needed boost in the process. Bumping into Foot at the House of Commons, Steel cheerfully asked: 'How's Goliath this morning?' A single day had neatly encompassed the ups and downs in Steel's life thus far, and indeed a prescient indication of what was to follow.

2

THE BOY DAVID

David Martin Scott Steel was born at around noon on 31 March 1938, at the Forth Maternity Hospital in Kirkcaldy. He was, therefore, technically a Fifer, although he confessed much later that he did not 'feel like one'. The infant David weighed six pounds eight ounces, the eldest child in what would become a family of five. His mother, Sheila, had wanted to call him Iain, the Gaelic for John, but instead he was named after his father.

David Steel junior was in Scots parlance a 'son of the manse', his father being a minister with the Church of Scotland (or 'Kirk') in Buckhaven. Jeremy Thorpe once commented that a study of his successor's upbringing unlocked 'many of the clues to his character. Sons of the manse are, after all, by reputation, sturdy, independent boys who knew right from wrong.' Steel's father, and indeed his profession, would certainly be a key influence.

The family's roots were in Lanarkshire, and they took pride in descent from a martyred seventeenth-century Covenanter, also called David Steel. David's father, however, had been raised in Peterhead before studying divinity at Aberdeen University. Ordained in 1936, he classified himself as a 'liberal evangelical' theologically and, politically, a small-'l' liberal. Although Steel senior had what one obituarist called 'a prickly streak and combative style', he also had 'gifts as a conciliator'. In both respects, father would be like son.

The Steels left their home in Buckhaven before David was three, and he spent what he remembered as a 'very happy childhood' in Dumbarton. 'We lived in this huge, rather cold house designed for the days when ministers of the Kirk had servants,' he recalled in his memoirs.

> There was very little luxury on my father's stipend and my mother devoted herself to bringing up a family growing in number and size, under the austerity and rationing of wartime. My parents kept hens, and an allotment for growing vegetables, the manse outbuildings were given over to keeping cages of rabbits, not as pets but to help feed and clothe the family.

Steel noted the importance of the 'thrift' drummed into him by his parents and indeed his political papers betray a diligent pursuit of payments, refunds and expenses. 'This early upbringing also colours my political attitudes,' he also observed. 'I am genuinely shocked at the credit explosion which has been allowed to take place in recent [late 1980s] years.'

From Dumbarton, the Steels also witnessed the Clydebank bombing of 1941. One German air raid even damaged the manse; Steel's earliest childhood memory was 'sitting on an orange box in the cellar dimly lit by candles, listening to the thunder of bombs above, and waiting for the all-clear to sound'. His first school was Dumbarton Academy (where his speech was described as 'nasal'), followed by a spell at James Gillespie's Boys School in Edinburgh. At both, his grades were average, although his English was judged uniformly excellent. Steel clearly did not lack intellectual capacity but then, and indeed throughout his life, his failure to shine academically owed more to what one biographer called 'his energetic pursuit of wider interests'.

The scope to broaden his horizons was about to get a lot wider. Steel himself has often referred to the four 'deeply impressionable years' he spent in Kenya as a teenager, calling his time in east Africa perhaps 'the most formative time in my thinking'. Steel's father had been called to the Presbyterian parish of Kenya and Uganda having spent four years as secretary of the Church of Scotland's colonial committee.

Having secured a scholarship to Edinburgh's George Watson's College, the eleven-year-old Steel was 'torn between the sheer drama of disappearing to Africa for four years, and doubts about leaving all my friends and hard-won scholarship behind'. The turbulent heart of the British Empire was beyond his comfort zone. 'We'd no idea where Kenya was, never heard of Nairobi ... we'd never been out of Scotland,' he later recalled. 'This was a completely new experience and the whole experience of a huge liner and going to Africa was just mind-boggling for us as kids.'

Arriving in Kenya's capital after a three-week voyage, the Steels took charge of a large house in the city centre, as well as the usual colonial trappings of a cook, a houseboy and a gardener. 'Landing here [Nairobi]', Steel remembered, 'was a complete culture shock', and a complete contrast to what would otherwise have been a conventional middle-class Edinburgh upbringing. 'We had exciting adventures with elephants, I had a pet monkey, the sun was always shining,' he said, 'and there was wonderful food to eat, especially all that amazing African fruit. It was just wonderful and totally different to what we had been used to at home.'

The Reverend David Steel quickly threw himself into what he later remembered as an 'exciting and demanding ministry'. The old church building was overflowing so he launched an appeal to build a new one, the foundation stone of which was laid on Steel's twelfth birthday by the Duke of Gloucester. Princess Elizabeth also visited (with Prince Philip) three days before she became Queen, signing the visitors' book while Steel recorded the moment for posterity on his camera.

After finishing primary school Steel was enrolled at Nairobi's Prince of Wales School, an all-white institution run as if it were an English public school. Although contemporaries remember Steel, or 'Stainless' as he became known, having few complaints at the time, he later remembered hating 'the sub-English public-school values and the mediocre education'. Steel, however, clearly was not a model student, several teachers noting his 'shockingly untidy' work during the 1950 term, although otherwise his housemaster judged his work to be 'up to standard'. Steel recalled this period as a 'fairly miserable and uninteresting time', his schoolwork suffering through a 'lack of interest'. At the end of 1951 one teacher cryptically concluded: 'Has improved this term. Or has he?'[1]

The racial dimension at the Prince of Wales School also bothered Steel. 'One of the remarkable features of colonial education was that it was completely segregated,' he later recalled. 'Most of my school colleagues had no experience of, and consequently no interest in, the Kenya that existed outwith the British colonial society and values which had been imposed upon that country. They existed within a social cocoon in which they tried to pretend that Kenya was just another England – except hotter.' And that, he added elsewhere, 'was one of the things that made me political'.

Steel and his brother Michael, however, had more contact than most, attending a mixed-race YMCA camp along with two other white boys. 'It was a fascinating glimpse into a way of life of which we were totally ignorant,' he recalled in his memoirs. Contemporaries of Steel were even recruited into the Kenya Police Reserve. 'I used to listen at school to tales from sixteen- and seventeen-year-olds telling what they had done to various "wogs" on their campaigns during their holidays,' he said. 'It was obvious that many of them treated other races as, by definition, inferior beings.'

It was not Steel's style, however, to challenge such attitudes, at least not at this stage in his life. As his father later told a profiler, David had always 'had a very even temperament', adding, 'I've never known him to get rattled.' Growing up in a manse undoubtedly shaped Steel's personality, meeting people from all walks of life – some important, many in need of help – many of whom treated the minister's son as an equal. Inevitably, the Reverend Steel was busy. As he later admitted in a privately published memoir, 'Sheila was a wonderful mother and I was a very poor father.'

What Harold Macmillan later called the 'wind of change' was already beginning to blow, although as a teenager Steel was only

---

1   David Steel Papers (private collection), Prince of Wales School reports.

vaguely aware of the political breeze. A secret, frequently violent, society called the Mau Mau was then emerging, and by 1952 the colonial government in Kenya had declared a state of emergency. The Steels travelled everywhere with a loaded revolver in their car. Although Steel's father abhorred their violence, he was equally infuriated by the British response.

Steel knew almost nothing of this until more than fifty years later, having returned to Scotland in 1953, remaining there after his father had a spell of leave. Apparently spontaneously, the Reverend and Mrs Steel decided that David, aged fourteen, and his brother should not return to Africa. During the next four years, Steel saw his mother once and his father not at all, spending his holidays mainly with his maternal grandparents in Aberdeen. 'It was very hard to leave them,' he later reflected, 'it was very sad after his three months' leave … it was terrible being left behind.'

When his father died in 2002, Steel discovered a briefcase containing what he called 'the Kenya Papers'. Investigating his father's political activity for the Channel 4 series *Empire's Children*, Steel learned that his father had become increasingly concerned about 'Operation Anvil', the colonial government's crackdown on Mau Mau forces, having been fed information from a police officer in his congregation. The Reverend Steel communicated his concerns to the governor, Sir Evelyn Baring, but ultimately decided to go public via a sermon broadcast every second Sunday.

In the sermon, the Reverend Steel criticised the Kenyan government's indiscriminate campaign, arguing that a raft of emergency legislation gave the 'appearance of legality to practices not only unjust in the eyes of God but illegal by the accepted law of man'. The authorities, unsurprisingly, were furious, and attempted to deport him from the colony (only saved by an intervention from the Kenyan finance minister, also a member of Steel's congregation), while a local English-language newspaper wondered who would rid Nairobi of 'this turbulent priest'.

The Reverend Steel was an unlikely iconoclast, and when his son tracked down Mau Mau rebels released from detention camps as a result of his father's intervention, he was clearly very moved. 'It makes me very humble that these people remember him,' he said when interviewed by Channel 4. When asked to read from an account of his father's farewell reception in 1957, Steel welled up again, quoting from a contemporary account that 'many of us [the congregation] felt like the little girl who fixing a determined smile on her face but I'm crying inside' [*sic*]. 'And that was it,' he added, holding up the journal. Later, Steel reflected:

> Looking back on it now I realise that I really owe everything to what my father was doing here because my political life really started thanks to my father, which I never really fully understood before … I now appreciate just how much he meant to a lot of people – I suppose the downtrodden, the captives. He certainly left his mark on the history of Kenya, no doubt about that.

Father, like son, never quite got Africa out of his system, and when he died half his ashes were taken to Nairobi by his family and buried alongside Scottish missionary pioneers at Kikuyu, a town in Kenya's Central Province. Just four years in Kenya, as well as his upbringing as a son of the manse, had given Steel a mind of his own and an instinctive morality that, although it took some time to manifest itself, fashioned his political views. These, reflected Steel in his memoirs, were 'formative years', providing him 'with the beginnings of political awareness and a deep-seated opposition to racism in all its manifestations'. Africa was a continent to which he would return – both professionally and personally – for the rest of his life.

On returning to Edinburgh in 1953 Steel took up his long-delayed scholarship at George Watson's College, a grant-aided school on the outskirts of the city. He obviously found this more congenial educational territory. 'My secondary education up till this time had been at a school in Nairobi which was not of any high standard,' he later wrote, 'and which considered sport as important as education; consequently I never really enjoyed school life.'

It was at Watson's, therefore, that the young David Steel came into his own, despite having to repeat a year due to the 'backward' effect of his time in Nairobi. 'Watson's was a breath of fresh air,' he recalls. 'By then I was a boarder at a day school, so I had to find things to do with my time.' One of these things was 'the Lit', the school's Literary Society, a select forum for debate and public speaking. His first meeting had a 'profound' effect. 'I sat in awe during the whole meeting and that night I did not sleep until very late,' he recalled in a valedictory speech as the Lit's junior president. 'I realised then that here was something I had been looking for for years. I realised then that Watson's wasn't just another school – and it was my fifth – but that it offered something deeper, something richer than an ordinary scholastic education.'[2] The Lit, recalled Steel in his memoirs, 'became my main interest, and I never missed a meeting in my four years at Watson's'.

Elevation to the society's inner circle as fourth-year member of its committee was, consequently, a moment Steel would 'never forget'. To him, 'the members of the committee were almost deities and the Junior President, Secretary and Treasurer were the chief gods'. Steel relished being on intimate terms with the club's ruling elite, while his involvement enabled him to meet the Lit's two most distinguished old boys: the then Lord Chancellor, Viscount Kilmuir, and the Commons Speaker, William Morrison. 'I owe the club a great debt of gratitude,' said Steel in his valedictory speech, 'and through my career, which I hope will be in politics, I shall never forget it.'[3]

Beyond the Lit, Steel clearly made the most of his four years at the school. As his old headmaster told a journalist in 1966, 'He *ran* Watson's!' This sketch from the school magazine, *Phoenix*, describes the extent of his activity:

As Junior President of the Literary Club he commands respect, as a School Prefect he instils discipline, as a house prefect he

---

2   David Steel Papers TD 3431/4, undated speech.
3   TD 3431/4.

rules, as Editor of *Ecce* he wields power and as Vice-President of
ESCA [Edinburgh Schools' Citizenship Association] he exudes
charm. A liberal at heart ... he is also something of a plutocrat,
being the owner of a motor vehicle. After a period of hibernation
this limousine again graces the boulevards of Edinburgh and it
is understood that the motoring organisations have warned their
members accordingly.

A love of vintage sports cars was another passion that emerged
during Steel's time at Watson's, his first being an 'unroadwor-
thy' 1932 Morris 8. He also acted (in Christopher Fry's *The
Boy with a Cart*) but, more importantly, debated. Returning
to Edinburgh in 1957, his parents remember hearing their son
make 'really quite a brilliant speech', clearly taken aback at this
hitherto unknown talent.[4] *Phoenix* also preserved the following
account of Steel's attendance at a 'Mound Meeting', Edinburgh's
version of Speakers' Corner:

> Steel clutched his copy of the *Daily Worker* even more nervously.
> He invited the heckler to come into the centre and state his views.
> He refused. Steel looked triumphant, but the heckler continued to
> heckle ... Steel tried to praise the Liberal Party and again Harcus
> [another pupil] took over, declaring that he was a Liberal. Then
> Steel tried to edge out of the crowd unobtrusively, but his departure
> was commented on by the mob.

Such was Steel's introduction to the brutal world of politics. When
William Douglas-Home contested Edinburgh South as the Liberal
candidate in a by-election, Steel penned a vigorous editorial for

---

4   After two years as associate minister at St Cuthbert's, Edinburgh, Steel's
    father moved to St Michael's, Linlithgow, in 1959. There, he presided
    over the controversial restoration of the historic church, which had lost
    its crown steeple in a nineteenth-century storm. Instead of recreating the
    original, Steel commissioned a modernist take on the 'crown of thorns',
    which remains a prominent sight on the Edinburgh–Glasgow railway line.

Ecce supporting the future Prime Minister's brother (he came third). The high point, meanwhile, of Steel's early political career was a speech, 'The Public Be Damned', as part of the Lit's public speaking competition in June 1957. This was a spirited, if slightly clunky, restatement of classic Liberalism, and clearly influenced by the arguments of Jo Grimond.

'In our present society, the state is fast becoming a kind of spoon-feeding idol,' declared Steel, and given that the public were 'for the most part content to accept the influence of the state on all major issues' it could hardly be surprised the attitude of the state had become that of 'the public be damned'. He cited ill treatment of Cypriot prisoners by the British army, phone tapping, failure of the government to consult the Commonwealth and opposition over Suez, and a 'mad suicidal race to explode bigger and better bombs, regardless of what public opinion in the country may be'. He continued:

> We see it [the attitude] everywhere. In the small trader in the country who holds a monopoly and therefore charges the public exorbitant prices for his goods. In the public official, bursting with his own importance. But worst of all we see it in the man who is determined to get on in life, regardless of those whom his life affects. And I would connect apathy with selfishness.[5]

This was not so different to some of the themes Steel would pursue, within the next two decades, as a Liberal MP and his party's leader.

If Kenya had planted a seed that Watson's had encouraged to grow, then it was the University of Edinburgh that nurtured David Steel into a young Liberal politician. As he later explained to the broadcaster Robert McKenzie, as a student he became 'increasingly antagonistic' to the colonial policies he remembered from his early teenage years and to 'the whole issue of how we treated our dependencies; how the races treated each other'. 'Not

5   TD 3431/10, undated essay entitled 'The Public Be Damned'.

at that age,' he was careful to add, 'but in retrospect.' Already liberally inclined, he found that 'many of the assumptions' of Harold
Macmillan's colonial policy – notably the creation and subsequent
collapse of a Central African Federation (CAF) – directed him 'well
away from any linkage with the Conservative Party' (although he
remained a committed federalist).

A decisive moment would be the Sharpeville Massacre of 21
March 1960 – in which the South African police killed sixty-
nine black protestors – radicalising a whole generation of British
students including Steel, who joined the Anti-Apartheid Movement
as a result. Combined with Steel's first-hand experience of Africa
and her politics, its effect must have been all the more acute. Steel
was also active in the Jambo Club, 'a most successful multi-racial
society for students from or interested in East Africa' (in 1961
it held a dinner to celebrate the independence of Tanganyika,
later Tanzania).[6]

This period coincided with the relatively enlightened – if not
strictly liberal – tenure of the Anglo-Scottish Colonial Secretary
Iain Macleod. Memorably derided by Lord Salisbury as 'too
clever by half', Macleod introduced a decolonisation programme
vehemently opposed by the Tory right. In Kenya, for example,
Macleod ended the state of emergency begun while Steel was at
school in Nairobi, and freed Jomo Kenyatta (a keen follower of the
Reverend Steel's sermons while in prison), who would become the
independent Kenya's first President in 1964. 'For all his small "l"
liberal credentials,' recalls Steel, 'Macleod was very much involved
in keeping CAF going as an anti-Soviet buffer and linking up with
South Africa. So it was just the whole tenor of the Tory administration that was, in my view, wrong.'

This critique found its way into Steel's contribution to at least
one Liberal Club meeting following a visit to the Soviet Union
with the future MPs Donald Dewar and George Reid. 'In Moscow

---

6   Julius Nyerere, the future President of Tanzania, graduated from Edinburgh
    University a few years before Steel.

I saw some of the propaganda pro-communist literature produced which was based entirely on the failings and backwardness of Tory imperial policies,' he said, 'which have provided the communists with the best footholds in Africa – the very thing the Tories were so anxious to avoid.'[7] Having caught the travel bug in Africa, Steel also visited Poland, later recalling the 'traumatic experience' of 'looking with disbelief at the gas chambers and ovens of the preserved Auschwitz concentration camp together with a Polish student whose parents had been killed there'.

Steel settled upon the Liberals, however, more through a process of elimination. 'I knew I wasn't Tory and I knew I wasn't Labour, and rather negatively joined the Liberals,' he later admitted. 'Through attending their meetings and hearing from those who were more committed than I was, and from visiting speakers, I became more positively committed.'[8] An 'inspiring' speech by Hugh Gaitskell had almost tipped him towards Labour. If 'that is the authentic voice of the Labour Party,' he told John P. Mackintosh, a politics professor Steel had first encountered 'patrolling for support' at Watson's, 'I will join,' adding elsewhere that 'if the Labour Party had been as Gaitskell was, the need for and relevance of the Liberal Party at that time would have been largely eclipsed.'

Steel, meanwhile, stood for his first election as a first-year representative on the Students Representative Council (SRC). With just seven candidates contesting three seats, he felt sure of success, but when two students from London fought a brilliant campaign Steel was forced into third place. He won a place on the SRC, but only just. As a biographer later observed, it taught him 'never to treat any election campaign complacently'. By this point, Steel was also deeply involved with Scottish Liberal politics. In 1958 he joined a Liberal canvassing party in East Aberdeenshire, and the following year not only helped organise

---

7   TD 3431/20, undated speech to Edinburgh University Liberal Club.
8   Elsewhere, Steel admitted joining the Liberals 'more out of curiosity than conviction'.

a by-election campaign in Galloway, but helped form the Association of Scottish University Liberals from four different campus associations. During that year's general election, meanwhile, Steel made his first public speech at South Morningside School.

By the autumn of 1959, Steel was even confident enough to venture criticism of Liberal strategy. 'It is a party emerging from years of dithering in the political wilderness,' he declared, 'and there are still a host of cobwebs to be swept away in the party organisation and policy.'[9] Liberal propaganda was 'pathetic', *Liberal News* (the party's weekly newspaper) had to rank 'as the worst piece of political journalism in the country', while the general standard of Liberal publications was 'shockingly low', 'too detailed' and thus full of 'vague trivialities'. Steel called for a pamphlet (presumably of higher quality) setting out 'Twelve Declarations', the party's principal aims, which he ambitiously speculated 'would do more to accelerate the party's progress than a hundred helicopter tours by Mr Grimond'.[10]

It is interesting that even Jo Grimond was not exempt from Steel's critique, for the then Liberal leader was a key influence, preceding any direct engagement with party policy. 'I became committed not just to the man as leader of the Liberal Party,' Steel said of Grimond, 'but especially to his ideas and his publicly proclaimed vision of a realignment of the left in British politics.' Steel's relationship with Grimond was to mark a turning point in his life.

Leader of the party since 1956 and MP for Orkney & Shetland, Jo Grimond had resolved to revive Liberalism by redefining its strategy; urging his troops to march 'towards the sound of gunfire', he recast the Liberals as a safe haven for social democrats fleeing from Labour. It was a radical shift in strategy, given that his predecessor, Clement Davies, had preferred to engage with Conservatives. But

9   At the 1959 general election the Liberals polled 6 per cent of the vote, enough to elect the same number of MPs.

10   TD 3431/17, undated speech entitled 'Which Way for Youth?'

as a man of considerable intelligence and personal charm, Grimond won many converts.

Steel had been captivated since watching Grimond's final broadcast during the 1959 general election. He recalls:

> The party had no money and it was the first time the parties had produced television broadcasts. This one was just Jo Grimond in front of a camera. The American journalist Ed Murrow later did a review of all the broadcasts and he said Jo's was the best, remarking that nothing could beat putting a man with something to say in front of a camera. I can't remember what he said but the power of it was there.

Indeed, one of Steel's university contemporaries, Russell Johnston, viewed his politics in personality terms. 'David was always a Grimond Liberal,' he told Steel's wife in 2008, 'but you and I, Judy, we are [John] Bannerman Liberals.'[11]

Steel, however, quickly learned the Liberal script, reciting the following prospectus at a mock election in 1960:

> Liberalism in Africa, an end to the British independent manufacture of the H-bomb, and adoption of collective security through a reformed NATO, economic integration with the European Common Market, parliamentary devolution for Scotland, Wales and England, co-ownership and co-partnership in industry, a rise in the old-age pension, abolition of Schedule A Income Tax: all these policies are gaining wider support.

On most of those points Steel would prove remarkably consistent while also imbibing Grimond's realignment gospel; in 1960 he said

---

11 John Bannerman (1901–69) was a farmer, rugby union international and Scottish Liberal politician. Having tried to win a parliamentary seat on a number of occasions, he was given a peerage in late 1967. His Liberalism included a strong emphasis on Scottish Home Rule.

that the 'emergence of a social democratic party may well come from a union of the Liberal Party and the Labour right'. Indeed, the SNP politician George Reid (in the late 1950s a Labour student) later remembered a 'clandestine' meeting with Steel, in which they discussed how they were 'going to get Lib–Labbery, a contemporary social democracy, going', together with a 'Scots Parliament'.

It was Steel who persuaded Grimond to stand as Rector of Edinburgh University in 1960, an historic position elected at Scotland's four ancient universities by the student body. The rectorial campaign ('Go Jo!' urged flyers) and installation ceremony would demonstrate Steel's energy, tenacity and, less attractively, a mildly patronising quality. In a pro-Grimond pamphlet, Steel argued that

> the big issue in this rectorial may prove to be not the election of a Rector for the next three years but the office of Rector itself. The right to elect a Rector is a traditional and intensely democratic one which must be jealously guarded if we are to retain it in full measure. We, the student body, must ensure in the coming campaign that nothing in our behaviour calls into disrepute the high office of Lord Rector nor antagonises university or civic authorities towards it.[12]

Indeed, anticipating student unrest (the Tory Chancellor 'Rab' Butler had been covered in flour at his rectorial installation in Glasgow), the Edinburgh University Court decided to install Grimond at a small private ceremony in the Upper Library rather than hold the traditional public ceremony in the McEwan Hall. This alarmed Steel, who (as president of the Students' Representative Council) called a mass meeting of students and rather pompously informed them that unless they behaved with dignity, not only would they be excluded from the ceremony, but the post of Rector might well be abolished. 'There is nothing particularly amusing', he said, 'in inviting a distinguished man to be Rector and then giving him dog's abuse when he comes.'

---

12   TD 3431/23, Jo Grimond rectorial campaign pamphlet.

Steel battled hard on this issue against Professor Sir Edward Appleton, the principal and Vice-Chancellor, prompting John P. Mackintosh to remark that the 'great thing about student politics is that it teaches you how to deal with rogues and villains'. The university authorities gave way but resolved to stay out of the installation ceremony, now to be held in the McEwan Hall. Steel's mission, however, did not end there, as he issued the following sartorial instructions to students wishing to attend:

> You are advised not to wear a coat if the weather permits ... Men should wear lounge suits with white shirt, collar, and tie. Dark blazer is a very suitable alternative. Stewards and servitors have strict instructions to refuse admission to anyone who is obviously unsuitably dressed (e.g. leather jacket, tartan shirt, and corduroy bags!) Women should wear appropriate dress, suit, or blazer and skirt. (Polo necked sweater and jeans are definitely out.)

Steel's aim was to 'rescue' rectorial ceremonies from the 'bad reputation' they had acquired following 'deplorable behaviour' at Edinburgh and the other ancient universities. Again, he succeeded, although it seems likely that a controversy-free ceremony also figured in Steel's mind as a useful way of bringing his political and organisational talents to the attention of Jo Grimond. And so it proved; the installation ceremony was a success, and notably restrained despite two thousand people cramming into the hall. 'I shall never forget the dry feeling in my throat as the tail end of the procession entered the McEwan Hall to the strains of "the Saints" played by a jazz band,' recalled Steel in a university journal. 'Having briefly introduced the Rector I invested him with his gown of office and then Mr Grimond stepped forward to deliver his address "In Praise of Politics".' Indeed, this proved a memorable peroration:

> I urge you all to become politicians, Liberals preferably, but if you can't manage that even Labour or Conservative politics are better

than none. I urge you because politics are important, because politics are rewarding, but, most of all, because politics are one of the greatest, most natural, and most enjoyable of human activities.

In the case of Steel, Grimond was preaching to the converted.

The Liberal leader also unwittingly played matchmaker between his new protégé and his future wife, sitting Steel next to Judith MacGregor at a private SRC dinner in 1961. It was an unlikely match, particularly as Judy was involved with the Scottish Nationalist club and had come to regard Steel 'as an establishment figure', while he considered her 'an unruly backbencher'. But when, a week later, George Reid (later an SNP MP and Steel's successor as Presiding Officer) invited David and Judy to a 'thrash' (actually organised by another Liberal student called Willis Pickard) during a Scottish Union of Students conference in St Andrews, 'a year's antipathy was blown away in a romantic walk by the North Sea.' 'With David,' recalled Judy Steel in her memoirs, 'I was finding, for the first time in a romantic relationship, a real meeting of minds and common interest.'

The Grimond rectorial contest gave Steel a taste of national press coverage, with pictures of him with the Liberal leader appearing in several London and Edinburgh newspapers. It also boosted his standing within the Scottish Liberal Party organisation, winning him election to its executive committee in 1960, while Steel was also approached to contest East Fife at the next general election (he declined). He also worked hard at cultivating the UK Liberal Party establishment, exchanging friendly notes with Violet Bonham-Carter and Laura Grimond. But the most important contact was Laura's husband, with whom Steel kept in frequent touch. He most likely remained a little in awe of Jo Grimond, as were many young Liberal activists at that time. 'We all worshipped Jo,' recalls William Wallace, who would later become one of Steel's advisers, 'partly because he was so tall, looking down on us and thinking to himself: "Why are these young men taking me so seriously?"'

While politics proved all-consuming, however, Steel clearly found some time for fun. Judy Steel's memoirs depict an almost carefree figure who partied as well as politicked. Michael Shea, another university contemporary and a future press secretary to the Queen, recalled Steel

> taking the drunken and rumbustious James Robertson Justice and Compton Mackenzie back from a debate in the Edinburgh University Union to the latter's house in Drummond Place, and us immature young chaps being quite astonished at the vulgarity of these two distinguished figures as they tried, in their whisky-befuddled state, to insert a key in the front door.

Steel also had a profile in his own right as one of the most prominent student politicians of his day (not unlike Gordon Brown a decade later). On becoming president of the SRC in May 1960 he hoped it would 'undergo a radical change according to the wishes of the majority of the students', chiefly direct student representation on the University Court.

Speaking as Rector himself twenty years later (he served from 1982 to 1985), Steel recalled being one of the last 'non-full-time, non-sabbatical senior presidents of the SRC', although he had opposed moves to professionalise the position. 'Indeed, to the dismay of professors and parents alike,' he joked, 'I had spent more time running student affairs than studying for my degree.' His degree was of the old 'ordinary' variety, including a course on the liberal philosophy of John Stuart Mill and Professor J. D. B. Mitchell's lectures on the British constitution, which, Steel recalled, 'remained genuinely useful in my parliamentary life'.

Despite his interest in most subjects, Steel gained only a 'pass' as an undergraduate. On 30 May 1961, shortly before his graduation ceremony at the McEwan Hall, Steel delivered his valedictory address as SRC president. 'I hope now to take a more active part in party politics outside the university from which I have had a kind of forced semi-retirement during the past twelve months,' he said.

'After the cut and thrust and intrigue of university politics I expect to find it a heavenly retreat!'[13]

Steel remained at Edinburgh for another year to complete his Bachelor of Laws (LLB), after which he ruled out becoming an advocate (devilling was then, as now, unpaid) or a cleric ('as I got older I began to feel that the Church ... was in a sense too narrow a canvas for the particular things that I wanted to interest myself in and to achieve'). Steel had long since settled on politics as a career, at that time an unusual thing for a new graduate to do. Nevertheless, his three years at the University of Edinburgh had been the making of him. 'Looking back', he reflected in 1983, 'I realise how much of my own life was shaped [t]here.'

Steel had been adopted as the Liberal candidate for Edinburgh Pentlands during his LLB and, having completed, as he put it, 'two mediocre degrees', he also took up his first job, the newly created post of assistant general secretary at Scottish Liberal HQ in Edinburgh. For Steel, it was a merciful escape from becoming a trainee manager at Shell or Plessey, and also good for the party, which had decided to beef up its personnel during what appeared to be a Liberal revival in the wake of the Orpington by-election.[14] Paid £890 a year, Steel was responsible for publicity, publications and local government affairs.

The timing was also good in that Steel had just become engaged to Judy, marrying her in October 1962. 'I remember feeling so happy,' he later recalled, 'it was the start of a new path, a new adventure.' Steel, meanwhile, worked hard on his Liberal candidacy, even attempting to induce his best man, Michael Shea, to contest another Edinburgh constituency.

At Liberal HQ Steel 'became a professional, in the mundane, nitty-gritty sense'. 'I learned party structure and the nuts and

---

13 TD 3431/16, undated speech from 1961.

14 Held on 15 March 1962, a swing of nearly 22 per cent from the Conservatives to the Liberals surprised most analysts. Eric Lubbock (later Lord Avebury) won with a 7,855 majority and held the seat until 1970.

bolts of party organisation,' he recalled. 'That was essential.' He got along well with the party's chief agent, the rather authoritarian Arthur Purdom. When Purdom fell ill during the Kinross & West Perthshire by-election in November 1963, Steel took over the Liberal campaign, later recalling a 'glorious shambles' which at least gave him his 'first chance to meet the political media'. Following a particularly disastrous by-election in December 1963 (Dumfriesshire), Steel also resolved that Liberals ought not to waste time fighting seats that might produce the dreaded sentence: 'The Liberal candidate lost his deposit.' 'These six words', wrote Steel in *Liberal News*, 'do the Liberal cause more damage than any six sentences uttered by Tory or Labour propagandists.'

Steel's experience in these two by-elections also prompted a rethink of his own constituency aspirations. 'I felt very much a city product and not up to the task of representing rural interests,' he recalled in his memoirs, but he now 'realised that what people needed was simply competent representation: the ability to listen, to assimilate and present a case'.

During the winter of 1963–4 a vacancy arose for a Liberal candidate in the potentially winnable seat of Roxburgh, Selkirk & Peebles, which had briefly been held by a Liberal in the early 1950s and whose Conservative incumbent, Commander Charles Donaldson, was elderly and ineffective. Having impressed at the association's AGM the previous autumn, Steel swiftly expressed an interest and was adopted at the beginning of 1964. Jo Grimond had also played a part. After concluding that none of the prospective candidates were suitable, he said to Steel with a grin: 'I suppose you'll have to do it then!'[15]

Since a general election was called just a few months later, there

---

15   This caused ructions within the Scottish Liberal Party (SLP) as well as unhappiness in Pentlands. The SLP executive passed a vote of censure on the whole organisation committee for assisting with Steel's transfer (the original plan had been for another rising star called Michael Starforth to fight the seat in 1964, having fought East Renfrewshire in 1959).

was little time to marshal a coherent campaign, with Steel later
admitting it had been a 'muddle' in which he had managed to
hold very few public meetings. Even then, Steel transformed what
had once been a safe Conservative seat into a marginal, taking
Donaldson's majority down to just 1,700, and thus boosting the
chances of a win next time round (Labour's slim Commons majority meant no one expected to wait long). 'We need a few more
mediocre firsts,' quipped Arthur Purdom, 'and a few less brilliant
seconds.' Few wanted Steel to gain a first, mediocre or otherwise, as
much as Grimond. Steel had acted as his Scottish bag carrier during
the election campaign and, as Grimond's biographer observed,
'had been the beneficiary of considerable sponsorship' from the
Liberal leader.

But in the interim Steel needed work; his contract at Scottish
Liberal HQ had expired on polling day. He soon secured a position
with BBC Scotland's current affairs department, having carefully
cultivated media contacts during the previous two years (and having
also appeared in a 1964 party broadcast). Steel became a part-time
interviewer for a programme called *Checkpoint*, an experience
he found invaluable in developing his own broadcast technique.
'[H]aving worked briefly in television,' he later explained, 'I am
relaxed amid the technology.'

> In my view very little can be taught in television technique. It is the
> most revealing and testing of all the media, outstripping platform
> speeches, Commons performances or press conferences in its ability to
> expose the good and bad in every politician and especially the phony.

'Whereas most politicians were nervous or found the whole TV
experience strange,' he recalls, 'I was used to it from the other side
– that was a tremendous advantage.'

But Steel's television career was shortlived (he managed only two
broadcasts). Just six weeks after the general election, Commander
Donaldson died during minor surgery at St Thomas' Hospital in
London. Steel was working in Glasgow when he heard the news,

initially thinking it a practical joke by colleagues. Although his six-month contract did not prohibit political activity, the BBC decided to put him on gardening leave until the end of March. 'In effect,' recalled Judy Steel, 'the BBC would be funding David to be a full-time candidate.'

Steel protested that Geoffrey Johnson Smith, the Conservative candidate in the recent East Grinstead by-election, had appeared on a panel game in the course of which a passing reference was made to his political activities. The BBC got round this by admitting it had been wrong about Johnson Smith but did not intend to repeat the mistake with Steel. It took a long time for Steel to forgive his soon-to-be former employer for so zealously removing him from a job he enjoyed, albeit fleetingly. He would restrict his television work to commercial broadcasters until 1970, when he patched things up with the BBC by presenting an edition of *Songs of Praise* from his father's church in Linlithgow.

Meanwhile, there was a by-election to prepare for, one of six pending in early 1965. *The Times* reckoned that the Borders fight gave the Liberals a chance to increase their representation in the Commons, noting that Steel, 'a young and vigorous campaigner', had obtained the third-highest Liberal vote among the fifty-four Liberals who had come second in contests at the previous year's general election.

Given the slim Tory majority, Steel reckoned the seat could be a 'test case' for Grimond's realignment strategy. 'Only in 1959 had the Tories an overall majority against Liberal and Labour added together,' he wrote in *A House Divided*. 'Now a realignment of those two forces would itself be sufficient to put them out.' Peter Preston of *The Guardian* would later observe that Steel and the able Labour candidate, Ronald King Murray, sang 'diverting variations on the same theme so that the Lib–Lab duet is quite harmonious'. That did not prevent King Murray challenging Steel to say whether he was a genuine radical or a crypto-Tory, however, while Edward Heath described the Liberals on a campaigning visit as 'a petty annexe to the Labour government'.

It was the first time professional, US-style politics had hit the normally sleepy and deferential Borders; Steel's campaign was energetic and meticulous, breaking new ground in how the game of politics was played in that part of the world. 'THIS TIME DAVID STEEL' was the legend on posters, tin badges and car stickers, as well as a glossy election address that still looks impressive nearly half a century later. It amounted to a mini manifesto, augmenting a pamphlet (co-authored by Steel) entitled *Boost for the Borders* which, as Peter Preston reported, was 'not a shatteringly original document', but did 'propound rational answers to the familiar Border ills'.

As if that was not enough, Steel's team produced a four-page free-sheet called *The Border News*, which looked like a newspaper rather than the party propaganda it actually was. Central to the campaign were busloads of student Liberal activists from England. 'We thought David was the man of the future,' recalls Tony (later Lord) Greaves, who was among them, 'a modern Grimond-style Liberal, not one of those ancient free-traders who had joined the party in the 1920s or '30s. Grimond had brought in a lot of younger people and David epitomised that new breed.'

Against this whirlwind of activity the Conservative candidate, Robert McEwen, faced a tough fight. A rather dated figure (and unusually, in the context of the mid-1960s, a Roman Catholic) who wore shooting gloves while campaigning, he got tetchy with hecklers and unwittingly exemplified the 'grouse moor' image the then Scottish Unionist Party was anxious to shed. Visiting Tory grandees did not help. When Sir Gerald Nabarro dismissed Steel's concerns about depopulation as 'ballyhoo', citing a local (and titled) friend who had recently increased his personal staff, Steel was scathing: 'Now we know the Tory answer to depopulation. Everyone should hire more servants.'

Judy Steel was impressed at 'the extent to which David never lost control of the campaign'. 'He was the candidate and he would run it,' she recalled in her memoirs. 'He would choose the political ground: only he would answer questions, and at meetings, he

would always be the final speaker.' At Scottish Liberal HQ the
party chairman, George Mackie, rebuffed attempts by London-
based figures to interfere, while on the ground Steel forged a strong
relationship with his 'political mentor', the local Liberal activist
Andrew Haddon (who recited Borders ballads to him as they drove
between election meetings), and the by-election agent, Arthur
Purdom (with whom he felt a 'deep trust').

Eric Lubbock headed north to spread a little Orpington magic
on the third anniversary of his own by-election win, as did Jeremy
Thorpe and Grimond (although the latter travelled south rather
than north), addressing large meetings in the major Borders towns,
Galashiels, Kelso and Jedburgh. Anthony J. C. Kerr, meanwhile,
entered the race at the last minute as, curiously, an Independent
Scottish Nationalist. Rumours (picked up by the press) implied
that McEwen had anonymously sent Kerr £100 to guarantee his
candidature, presumably hoping it would draw votes away from
Steel. If true, it was wishful thinking. As the by-election neared
its conclusion, the consensus at Westminster clearly pointed to a
Liberal victory.

Memorably, Llew Gardner of the *Scottish Daily Express* cast the
whole by-election in terms of David versus Goliath (McEwen being
the Conservative giant). Forty-five years later Judy Steel could still
recall her husband's eve-of-poll speech. 'To look at the trees around
here, you might think that the Tories have the election in the bag,'
he said. 'But the votes do not belong to the trees, nor are they in the
pockets of local newspaper proprietors. The votes are in the hearts
of the people, and the hearts of the people are with us!'

The historian Hugh Trevor-Roper and his wife even drove all
the way to the Borders (where they owned a home) in order to
vote, McEwen being a family friend. But Trevor-Roper ended up
concluding, according to his biographer, that Steel was 'the best
candidate by far'. Xandra, his wife, voted Conservative and was
horrified when she discovered Hugh had not done the same. Trevor-
Roper was not the only Conservative to jump ship for, when the
votes were counted on 24 March, there was a 7.3 per cent swing to

the Liberals, giving Steel a decisive majority of more than 4,600 votes. The full result was:

David M. S. Steel (Liberal) 21,549
Robert L. McEwen (Conservative) 16,942
Ronald K. Murray (Labour) 4,936
A. J. C. Kerr (Independent Scottish Nationalist) 411

Steel's maternal grandfather had died earlier that day so, amid 'the high spirits,' as Judy Steel recalled, 'David's were low'. Still, he recalled that night in Jedburgh being the 'most thrilling and memorable' of his career; 'it was the beginning of a wonderful adventure that is the political life.'

John Bannerman was at the count, as was Jeremy Thorpe, although the flamboyant MP for North Devon had to blag his way in. Later, his eloquence persuaded a local landlord to open his pub so that everyone could celebrate. 'It's a historical moment,' proclaimed Thorpe. 'We can't let the licensing laws get in the way on a night like this!' The new Member of Parliament was carried shoulder high down the street and 'hundreds of Liberals', recalled Tony Greaves twenty years later, 'many for the first time in their lives, knew what it was like to win'. The next day's *Scottish Daily Express* carried news of what it called a '2 a.m. sensation', a banner headline announcing: 'IT'S THE BOY DAVID!'

3

BABY OF THE HOUSE

'The Borders are a distinct region,' wrote Jo Grimond in his memoirs, 'peppered with Dukes and Fox Hunts but with a strong radical tradition.' Sprawling across three counties, the constituency of Roxburgh, Selkirk & Peebles looked deceptively agricultural, although economically the sheep farms took second place to the knitwear and tweed industries of its scattered burghs. Grimond continued:

> In the woollen towns the workers are Liberal rather than Socialist. So must be many of the farmers and farm servants. Since the fifties Roxburgh and Selkirk had returned a Tory. But the tinder was there. David ignited it. He was a charismatic candidate, young, good-looking, confident, articulate. What more could you want?

That Grimond chose to associate David Steel with his new seat was significant for, as the broadcaster Ludovic Kennedy later put it, he was one of a handful of MPs who soon became 'so identified with their constituency that it is hard to imagine them apart'. During the by-election and over the next five years, the Fife-born and Nairobi-raised Steel made the economic problems of the region his own. As Willis Pickard wrote of Steel in a pre-by-election profile for *Liberal News*, 'He has made himself an authority on the Borders and has become accepted as a Borderer.' Steel even endured a gruelling 25-mile ride to become a 'Moss-trooper', a highly-valued equestrian (and Hawick) honour.

Steel and his wife Judy already lived in Ettrick Bridge by the time of the by-election, a smart move avoiding the intense inter-town rivalry settling in Hawick, Kelso, Galashiels or Peebles might have created. But such a constituency also brought mixed blessings, being useful restoratively but difficult logistically. Judy reinforced her husband's local credentials by quickly making it known she would not be basing herself in London, as was the norm for many MPs' wives at that time. 'No one can fully understand my political life,' reflected Steel in his memoirs, 'without a proper comprehension of life in the Borders.'

Above all Roxburgh, Selkirk & Peebles gave Steel a voice in Parliament. 'Independent minded themselves,' he later reflected, 'my Borders constituents allowed me, in the words of Edmund Burke, to give them my judgement but not my obedience.' But while impressive, Steel's by-election win did not stimulate a Liberal revival akin to that in the wake of Orpington a few years before. Rather it masked a lost deposit in a concurrent by-election at Saffron Walden and thus represented a bright spot for the Liberals in an otherwise difficult – and indeed short – parliament. 'TOP GRADE STEEL' was the jubilant *Liberal News* headline on 2 April, while a few days later the National Liberal Club hosted a luncheon in Steel's honour.

Nevertheless, *The Times* was correct in observing that Steel's election would 'have a profound effect on the political situation'. Not only did it increase pressure on Harold Wilson to hold an early poll (the Labour candidate in Roxburgh, Selkirk & Peebles had lost his deposit), but it also hastened the demise of the Leader of the Opposition, who hailed from the Borders himself. Alan Watkins noted in *The Spectator*: 'How much longer can Sir Alec Douglas-Home continue as leader of the Conservative Party? After the loss of Roxburgh the question does not really have to be asked. It asks itself.'

Thus when Eric Lubbock and George Mackie introduced Steel to the House of Commons there was what one newspaper called a 'lusty roar of welcome' from the Labour benches, loud enough

to drown out eight cheering Liberal MPs (Baroness Asquith also
watched from the peers' gallery, while Steel's parents and Judy spec-
tated from the other side). Another observer even talked up the
prospect of a Lib–Lab pact. 'Whether or not Mr Steel is the first
Lib–Lab MP remains to be seen but he certainly received the Lib–
Lab treatment,' judged the journalist. 'If there were any lingering
doubts that a Liberal–Labour pact exists, they were surely quelled
by the entrance of Mr David Steel to the House of Commons
today.' The government's Chief Whip, Edward Short, had gleaned
the same impression, later reflecting that as the Liberals often voted
with Labour, Steel's election 'was something of a gain for us'.

Steel celebrated his twenty-seventh birthday on 31 March,
although he already enjoyed the 'somewhat dubious title of baby of
the House'. 'Babies are very easily upset,' he quipped in his maiden
speech. 'I may be heard in future to cry loudly for food, but it will
be food not for myself but for my constituents.' Steel then repeated
some of the themes raised during the by-election campaign:

> During the last ten-year census period, 1951–61, there was a drain of
> population in the Scottish Borders of about 6.5 per cent ... in the
> age group 20 to 45 ... the drop in population was not 6.5 per cent
> but 21 per cent. No part of the country can afford a continual drain
> of its young and skilled people of that order.

Steel's solution was a more robust regional policy and he urged the
Chancellor to examine the 'possibilities of more regional variations
in taxation', perhaps via the employers' share of National Insurance
contributions. 'I should like to see a passion for regionalism', said
Steel, 'pervading every part of the government.'

Steel's first frontbench post was shadowing Ray Gunter at
Employment, making some 'worthy speeches' on the Redundancy
Payments Bill but little else. Despite the excitement of recent
events, Steel appears to have kept his feet on the ground. Jim
Archer, a school friend from Nairobi, remembers seeing 'Stainless'
being interviewed on television after the by-election. 'I gave him

a couple of days then phoned him and said "This is a voice from the past",' recalls Archer. 'He didn't hesitate and invited me to the House of Commons for lunch. I was so impressed it hadn't gone to his head; he was so matter of fact about it all.'

Steel's unassuming precociousness, however, marked him out as something of a prototype for the modern career politician. Prior to becoming a Member of Parliament he had had just two full-time jobs – both of which had been connected with politics – in a graduate career lasting less than three years. Although in the context of the early twenty-first century this would have been considered unremarkable, in the mid-1960s it was novel to say the least. As Steel admitted in 1981, he had often 'regretted' having 'came into politics quite so young' (he would have preferred 'to have done a few more things outside politics first, in order to have more experience and a greater variety of life'). He was, however, no 'here today, gone tomorrow' politician. The press took notice and by September 1965 the *Financial Times* described Steel as 'perhaps the most radical of the Scots MPs'.

Realising that his majority was not impregnable, however, Steel worked hard in advance of an anticipated general election, keeping busy in the House and holding frequent public meetings in his constituency. He also built a national television profile, appearing in a Liberal party political broadcast just a month after his election. Profiling Steel in 1966, one journalist's first impression was of

a tall young man with the pleasant freshness of a senior prefect; well-groomed; whiter-than-white shirt; alert, blue-grey eyes; fine features; firm yet sensitive mouth; lithe movements. His name suits, giving the suggestion of resilient steel which will never rust from disuse or laziness.

In other words, as a young MP Steel cut an attractive figure. He was also active in the party nationally, enthusiastically backing Jo Grimond when he flew a coalition kite about co-operating with the Labour government. In a speech in Manchester, Steel attacked

Harold Wilson's 'ruthless arrogance' in being determined to govern 'as though he had a majority of 100' rather than just four. 'He has made no concession to the Liberals in the House,' he added, 'while welcoming their support whenever possible.' Even so, Steel commented elsewhere, it remained 'the best left-wing government we've got'. 'The immediate alternative', he added with an obvious note of distaste, 'would be a Conservative government.'

Grimond set out his thinking in an article for *The Guardian* in June, and when *The Observer* canvassed Steel's reaction he responded with alacrity:

> Liberals who oppose this suggestion argue that Labour would gain the benefits of popularity in the next election. I believe this to be false. Liberals could point to the favourable effect they have had on Labour policies and thus plead for greater representation.

Steel's intervention, however, had little impact and he reflected in his memoirs that Grimond's attempt 'to educate the party to the realities of power was not very successful'. 'The MPs themselves divided into three,' he added, 'supporters of a Lib–Lab deal (Jeremy Thorpe and I), outright opponents and a majority of unenthusiastic acquiescents.'

Steel's frustration with his party had deepened that summer, following the death of the Speaker, Sir Harry Hylton-Foster, and speculation – initiated by the Liberal MP Peter Bessell – that his successor might be a Liberal. 'At this suggestion the party first demonstrated to me an endearing but infuriating lack of discipline,' Steel later recalled. 'They behaved like a flock of flapping chickens in a hen run at the appearance of a fox.' In the event, the eminent position went to a Labour MP, Dr Horace King. 'The Liberals therefore suffered indignity,' observed Steel, 'and gained nothing out of the fracas.' Indeed, one of the lessons Steel took away from his first year in Parliament was the need to avoid the 'most telling jibe against them [Liberals]; that they were split all ways'.

King's election as Speaker, together with by-election losses, reduced Harold Wilson's majority to just one. Yet still the Labour government intended to soldier on. Steel gave his response during a speech in Hawick:

> If the Prime Minister is not willing to give this country a stable government with a four-year declared programme of reform by bringing the Liberals into full consultation and drafting an agreed programme for a government with a majority of over twenty; if he feels that he could not carry his party with him; if he cannot abandon parts of the socialist programme which neither the Liberals nor the country supports; then his only honourable course is to call a general election and call it now.

'The Liberals', added Steel, 'should not be expected to prolong the country's agony.' This speech coincided with an article for the *New Statesman*, in which Steel said Liberals could not be 'expected to stomach a mass of bad Toryism and some irrelevant pieces of socialist doctrine in order to gain a few morsels of good radical legislation'. Grimond, meanwhile, made a dramatic Assembly speech about Liberal 'teeth being in the red meat of power', although this struck Steel as an overstatement. 'The Liberal Party's teeth had turned out to be false,' he wrote in his memoirs, 'and liable to fall out when it came to chewing a particularly difficult piece.'

In this respect Steel had been, and indeed would be, remarkably consistent, continually urging Liberals to consider co-operative politics, and preferably a formal coalition, as the means by which the party might achieve a degree of influence. Since the early 1960s he had never believed there was any merit in Liberals pretending they could somehow take Labour and the Conservatives by surprise and form a majority government. Steel's stance obviously brought risks. Shortly after the 1966 general election he was forced to deny rumours that he was about to defect to the Labour Party (with Ludovic Kennedy succeeding him in the Borders).

Ian McIntyre, selected in late 1965 to fight Roxburgh, Selkirk & Peebles for the Conservatives, also accused Steel of 'continuing to take every opportunity of singing the praises of the Labour government'. McIntyre was a Tory version of Steel – a bright young political activist who had developed a reputation as a talented campaigner – chosen within seven weeks of the by-election defeat to robustly challenge Steel and perhaps regain the seat. As Judy Steel noted in her memoirs, McIntyre 'was the most formidable opponent [David] ever faced'.

Steel, of course, was not at all complacent. 'The Tories think that we won the last time because we used fluorescent posters,' he joked, referring to McIntyre's campaigning colours. 'Now they are doing the same thing. And they have picked a colour which is used by the Co-operative to advertise cut-price jam.' Steel also featured alongside Ludovic Kennedy and Jeremy Thorpe in the Liberals' election broadcast (a 'fairly young Liberal lion,' judged *The Times*, 'his eager nose quivering like an anteater's'). 'DAVID AGAIN' was the straightforward campaign message.

Polling day fell on Steel's twenty-eighth birthday, 31 March. Technically a Liberal gain, Steel's majority was a modest but respectable 2,211 votes:

David M. S. Steel (Liberal) 20,607
Ian J. McIntyre (Conservative) 18,396
C. Lindsay (Labour) 6,131

Within two years of graduating from university, he had fought a by-election and contested two general elections. The stage was now set for the boy David to make his mark.

Luck plays a large part in the career of any politician and on Thursday 12 May 1966, in Committee Room 15 of the House of Commons, luck was on Steel's side. His name was drawn third in the ballot for leave to introduce a Private Member's Bill, only six of which stood a chance of becoming law. Almost immediately, individuals and organisations began to lobby Steel with proposals. Lord Arran pressed Steel to take up his Bill on homosexual law reform (the Wolfenden proposals of 1957 had yet to be fully implemented), while Vera Houghton (wife of Douglas Houghton, Harold Wilson's Minister without Portfolio) got in touch asking him to tackle abortion.

Vera Houghton was president of the Abortion Law Reform Association (ALRA), which had been lobbying for the reform of the UK's abortion laws since 1936. Recent events, meanwhile, had increased public support for change. The thalidomide scandal had been a factor (the Ministry of Health argued, hypocritically, that the births of deformed children ought to be prevented), while between 1958 and 1960, eighty-two women had lost their lives undergoing what were known as 'back street' abortions. By 1965, polls suggested seven in ten Britons supported a change in the law. Also influential was Alice Jenkins's book, *Law for the Rich: A Plea for the Reform of the Abortion Law*, which highlighted the class inequalities surrounding abortion (middle-class women were generally able to arrange the procedure via medical contacts) and urged men and women of 'sufficient zeal and active consciences' to 'take part in the final struggle for this reform'.

The ALRA had contacted Steel shortly after his by-election win to ask that he introduce a Bill should he be successful in the ballot. Steel replied that although he supported the ALRA's aims, he could not 'undertake to introduce a Bill on the subject if I am successful in the next ballot for Private Members' Bills since there are many matters of priority constituency interest which I am already pledged to take up if I am given the opportunity'.[16] Steel, in truth, did not feel particularly strongly about abortion beyond supporting reform, although he had some background knowledge. 'David and I had both taken the class in Forensic Medicine as part of our law degrees,' recalled Judy Steel in her memoirs. 'Among other things we had learnt in theory about criminal abortion and

---

16   Abortion Law Reform Association Papers SA/ALR/A.15/10/1, David Steel to ALRA, 14 April 1965.

its dreadful effects.' Judy also 'knew some girls who had undergone the frightful experience'.

Now that Steel had been successful in the ballot, the ALRA tried again, lobbying him quite intensely. Lunch was arranged with Professor Glanville Williams, the ALRA's president, while Vera Houghton bombarded Steel with notes and briefings. Steel, however, initially kept his options open. He appealed via the press for suggestions, while Nationalists (and indeed Judy) pressed him to pursue Scottish self-government. 'It wouldn't get through,' Steel protested to his wife. 'This is my chance to actually make legislation, not just to make speeches.' Steel had also toyed with the idea of a Borders Development Board, emulating that in the Highlands and Islands, but Willie Ross, the rather austere Secretary of State for Scotland, had made it clear such a Bill would not be looked upon kindly by the Labour government.

Indeed, Steel's decision was predicated upon tacit ministerial support. As Home Secretary, Roy Jenkins was keen to support reformist Bills of the sort that cut across party lines, so he encouraged Steel to pursue social reform – particularly homosexual law reform – indicating that it would enjoy his personal support. At this stage, constituency opinion was also an important consideration; while Borders opinion was hostile to reforming laws governing homosexuality (as was the Church of Scotland), it was relaxed about abortion. 'You can do unpopular things, and people will respect your integrity,' reasoned Steel. 'But only a fool tries to do things which are totally opposed by his closest supporters.'

Steel wrote to Lord Arran on 24 May 1966, informing him that he would not, after all, be taking up his Bill on homosexual law reform.[17] 'I saw Dick Taverne [the responsible minister] at the Home Office yesterday and told him that I was prepared to go ahead with the Abortion Law Reform Bill,' he wrote, 'which, although still not favoured by my constituents, does not meet

---

17   A Private Member's Bill sponsored by the Welsh Labour MP Leo Abse decriminalised homosexuality in England and Wales the following year.

with the same rooted objections.'[18] When Steel's decision became public, Ian McIntyre – his defeated Tory rival – attacked him for reneging on a pledge he had made prior to the 1964 general election to introduce a Private Member's Bill (if able to do so) to amend the Import Duties Act. '[W]hen is a pledge not a pledge?' McIntyre asked rhetorically. 'The answer seems to be "When it is given by a young Liberal on the make".' Steel hit back in a Border Television interview, saying McIntyre's attack was 'motivated by sour grapes'.

Meanwhile, the All-party Abortion Group had swung into action, as had the ALRA, dusting down previous abortion Bills including, helpfully, those of Kenneth Robinson, by 1966 Minister of Health, and Lord Silkin. The Labour MP Alex Eadie (whose Midlothian seat bordered Steel's) and the Conservative Lord Lambton acted as the Bill's co-sponsors, adding an important cross-party dimension. 'In an upstairs committee room in the House of Commons,' reported *The Scotsman*, 'the group, chaired by David Steel and reinforced by two gynaecologists, a psychiatrist and Mrs Houghton, of ALRA, master-minded the introduction of the Bill at its First Reading on June 15.'

That day Steel tabled his Medical Termination of Pregnancy Bill (the title was Judy's idea) to amend and clarify the law relating to abortion by registered medical practitioners. A second reading was pencilled in for 22 July 1966. Two texts had made a particular impression on Steel: a Church of England report on the subject ('the best summary of the ethics of abortion yet published') and the World Health Organization (WHO), which, in 1946, had defined 'health' as 'complete mental, physical and social well-being'.

Steel, therefore, insisted that the principal criterion for a termination, whether the risks to a woman's health and that of her foetus would be greater if she continued with a pregnancy than if she ended it, form the basis of his Bill. In essence, if two medical practitioners agreed on that, then an abortion – paid for by the NHS

18 SA/ALR/A.15/11/1, David Steel to Lord Arran, 24 May 1966.

– was possible for any woman, regardless of her background. The government remained friendly but cautious. Writing to Steel on 7 July, Taverne stressed that despite having offered extensive advice, 'I must again emphasise that this in no way implies government support for the Bill or any particular parts of it.'[19]

On 22 July the House of Commons debated the Bill's second reading. Steel delivered what the *Daily Telegraph* called a 'strikingly cogent and well thought-out' speech as a selection of correspondence and reports more than a foot high sat on the green bench next to him. He cited a 'growing tide of public opinion' in favour of reform, before lucidly setting out the specific terms of the Bill. 'The difficulty in drafting a Bill of this kind is to decide how and where to draw the line,' he told the House. 'We want to stamp out the back-street abortions, but it is not the intention of the promoters of the Bill to leave a wide open door for abortion on request.'

Steel concluded his speech with this thought:

The Report of the Social and Moral Welfare Board of the Church of Scotland quotes a German theologian as stating that human life in every form is sacrosanct but that we have to ask ourselves what quantitative item of sacrosanctity may be attached to each form of life – the ovum fertilised, the moving embryo, the born child and the mother. He said: 'A paper thin wall separates us from sacrilege – all such decisions can be made only under saving grace – such dangers always go with freedom. Those who want to avoid the dangers do so only by setting up a rigid dogma ... So there is obviously no perfect solution. The decision has to be taken in the light of God's understanding of our human frailty.' It is in that spirit that I have approached the drafting of the Bill, and I hope that the House will give it a second reading.

At the end of an emotional and highly charged debate, and in what *The Times* called 'one of the most massive demonstrations of

19   SA/ALR/A.15/11/1, Dick Taverne to David Steel, 7 July 1966.

approval ever given to a Private Member's measure', 223 MPs to twenty-nine – a majority of 194 – voted to grant the Bill a second reading. Among those voting in favour were Margaret Thatcher, the former Colonial Secretary Iain Macleod and Dr David Owen, who believes Steel's stewardship of the process was 'the model of how to handle a Private Member's Bill'.

Thus began one of the defining medical, political and ethical debates of the 1960s. There were rallies, radio and television broadcasts, and co-ordinated campaigns by those for and against reform, which arguably gave birth to the modern lobbying industry (not least the pre-printed postcards familiar to most MPs half a century later). Joan Stamper, Steel's part-time secretary, was on constant overtime, dealing with around thirty letters a day, some polite, many hostile. One such letter was short and wounding:

Dear Mr. Steele [*sic*],
What a pity your mother didn't have an abortion when she conceived you.
An ill-wisher.

One particular difficulty for Steel was the presence of around 3,000 Roman Catholics in his constituency, who tended to be more vocal and, indeed, unhappy at what their MP was proposing. 'The members of the above address', wrote one anonymous constituent from Jedburgh, 'have always been strong Liberal voters but in the future we will no longer support you.'[20] There were even rumours that an anti-abortion candidate would be fielded at the next general election. 'David Steel never sees his London pied-à-terre until after midnight,' observed *The Scotsman*, a reference to the National Liberal Club; 'four other Liberal MPs stay there – and it is another irony that one of them, the austere Alasdair Mackenzie, the MP for

---

20 SA/ALR/A.15/2/1, unsigned and undated letter; SA/ALR/A.15/2/2, letter dated 9 November 1966.

Ross & Cromarty and a Free Church elder, is one of the implacable opponents of the Bill.'

Always cool under pressure, Steel did not take the abuse personally. 'At the centre of the storm he is learning the realities of political life,' noted *The Scotsman*. 'And he is realist[ic] enough to know that in this particular storm his own political reputation will be made, or marred.' Pro-abortionists, meanwhile, could hardly have hoped for a better poster boy. As a later book on the Bill put it, in Steel the ALRA

> could hardly have made a better choice on personal grounds for so controversial and so delicate a cause. He was twenty-eight, good-looking, and in the middle of the campaign his wife gave birth to a son. He was a practising Christian and his father was a minister of the Church of Scotland.

Indeed, the press and public made much of the juxtaposition between Judy Steel's pregnancy and her husband's legislative battle. 'Strange isn't it, that he should be working on this Bill just at the time when he's so looking forward to fatherhood,' Judy told the *Daily Express* somewhat indelicately. 'No vested interest, I assure you. It might be different if this was to be our seventh child.' Graeme Scott MacGregor Steel was their first, born on 31 August 1966 at Galashiels Hospital. 'I recall vividly the excitement of seeing his purple and lopsided face over the first couple of days of his life,' Steel later remembered, 'and driving him ever so gingerly home from the hospital.' A couple of months later David and Judy broke with tradition and had their son christened by Steel's father at Caddonfoot Church, rather than in the crypt of the House of Commons. (Judy was actually pregnant twice during the passage of the Abortion Act, Catriona Judith Steel following in December 1967.)

It was a happy but busy period for the Steels. They had bought Cherrydene, their Borders home for the next quarter-century, in May 1966, while in the autumn of that year David somehow found time to present a weekly religious programme, *This Is the Day*, for Scottish Television. Sensing that the Bill had taken over Steel's life, Vera Houghton wrote to him as 1966 drew to a close: 'I hope you did not have to spend the whole of Christmas visiting hospitals and that you were able to enjoy some time with your family.'[21]

The small vote against the Bill at its second reading, however, understated the extent of the opposition it faced. Steel, therefore, had to steer a fine line; many of his supporters wanted to go further, while he had to appease his critics in order to attract majority support in Parliament. The long gap between the Bill's second reading and its committee stage in January allowed extensive scope for lobbying. 'My problem as sponsor of the Bill was that most of these bodies produced detailed recommendations, most of them useful, only after my Bill had been drafted,' recalled Steel. 'Moreover, no two specialist reports agreed with each other and all expected their advice to be taken exclusively! In fact I adopted the tactic of selecting what I thought best from each report and unashamedly playing one body off against the other.'

In November 1966, Steel met the midwifery specialist Professor Sir Dugald Baird and mental health expert Dr Malcolm Millar over a long lunch in Aberdeen. 'This meeting marked a watershed in his handling of the Bill,' recorded the Bill's historians. 'He emerged from the meeting with a deeper insight into the issues surrounding the subject, and from then on dealt with supporters and opponents more confidently.' Initially, the ALRA had found Steel 'business-like if inexperienced' in dealing with other MPs and 'the grand eminences of the medical profession', while there was also inevitable tension between Steel's priorities and those of the ALRA. In their 1971 book, *Abortion Law Reformed*, Keith Hindell and Madeleine Simms recorded the following impression:

In the seventeen months of parliamentary struggle which now ensued he concentrated on his own key role in the drama – never

---

21   SA/ALR/A.15/10/1, Vera Houghton to David Steel, 29 December 1966.

involving himself in the organisation and activities which harnessed the wave of opinion and pressure to carry his Bill through. Sometimes he seemed a little elusive to his supporters, or at least too busy with other – to them, secondary – matters. Being one of only twelve Liberal MPs ... he seemed to ALRA to spend most of his day sprinting from one committee to another. ALRA often received messages or letters from him at the eleventh hour which they felt should have been sent earlier. For him the Abortion Bill was only one of many important pieces of business, while for ALRA it was their sole concern and they were anxious lest the first real chance of reform should be let slip.

Pressure from opponents was indeed vociferous and sustained. The former Scottish Secretary, Michael Noble, led an attempt to have Scotland excluded from the scope of the Bill (as it would be from Leo Abse's later Sexual Offences Bill). January 1967, meanwhile, saw the launch of the Society for the Protection of Unborn Children (SPUC), chaired by Lord Barrington. A letter setting out its aims was published by the *Daily Telegraph* on 11 January 1967.

By the end of that month Steel had received around 600 letters and had to enlist a Liberal student to keep on top of it all. He reckoned 150 were supportive, mainly from doctors, the rest being virtually identical and co-ordinated by the Roman Catholic Church. By this point, MPs were busy with twelve weekly sittings of the Bill's committee stage. In February, meanwhile, *The Times* declared its opposition, arguing that law 'should accord with the general moral sense of the public' and was 'far too important a matter, in medicine, in ethics, in social behaviour, and in human suffering, to be subjected to legislation by pot shot and verbal refinement in standing committee'.

In March 1967 Norman St John-Stevas – Steel's nemesis during the abortion battle – sponsored a motion declining to give the Bill (the *Daily Record* dubbed it the 'stop-baby Bill') a third reading, by which point, according to reports, it looked 'to be in danger'. The standing committee concluded its 'verbal refinement' on 5 April and, in a spirit of mutual goodwill, Steel and St John-Stevas agreed a compromise on the Bill's so-called 'conscience clause', which would allow medical practitioners to opt out of performing the procedure if it conflicted with their religious beliefs. Even so, David Wood of *The Times* reckoned the exercise was 'almost certainly doomed' when it came before the full House on 2 July. 'Put bluntly,' wrote Wood, 'Mr. Steel lacked parliamentary experience to choose a Bill for which public opinion had been properly prepared, and he lacked the tactical skill to pilot it through an extremely rigorous committee stage upstairs.'

A *Scotsman* editorial on 30 May was more upbeat:

> There is ... no reason whatsoever why MPs should look upon the Bill less favourably now than they did last year. Mr Steel has been criticised for introducing such a difficult and controversial reform so early in his parliamentary career. But it will be a sad day for Parliament when MPs lucky enough to win a high place in the members' ballot are restricted to peripheral measures. If the Abortion Bill is unsatisfactory in some of its details, the government are to blame. Liberal-minded Ministers ought to have had the courage of their convictions and introduced a government Bill.

'Best of luck with your abortion bill,' wrote one anonymous correspondent as MPs prepared to consider the Bill's fate, signing off as 'A fellow liberal'. Another note simply read: 'Bless you for helping womenkind.'[22]

There were fifty-seven amendments, and the Commons sat all night in a quixotic attempt to deal with them all. Steel had to beg Richard Crossman, the Leader of the House, for more time, which the Cabinet approved on 6 July. An additional sitting later that month lasted twenty-four hours and twenty-nine minutes, the longest since 1951. There were moments of humour, but also drama when Steel produced (in a test tube) a seven-week-old

---

22   SA/ALR/A.15/1/5, undated letters.

human embryo, half an inch long, to illustrate that it was misleading to talk of it crying or wriggling. (Steel had earlier witnessed an abortion procedure at the invitation of the Royal College of Obstetricians and Gynaecologists.) Roy Jenkins also paid the first of what would be a series of warm tributes to Steel. 'I think that as a young member of the House with a marginal constituency and without a great party machine behind him', said the Home Secretary, 'he has shown exceptional courage in carrying on with the Bill in these circumstances.' Making it clear he was prepared to keep the House sitting throughout Friday night and even Saturday to get the Bill through, Jenkins then thwarted a threatened filibuster. 'It was indeed', he recalled, 'the liberal hour.'

'Not with a bang but a whimper', reported *The Times* on 15 July, 'did the great debate on the Medical Termination of Pregnancy Bill fizzle out just before noon today.' MPs voted by 167 to 83 to let it pass, giving the Bill a healthy majority of 84. Notes of congratulation arrived in Steel's office, including one from John Silkin, son of an earlier abortion reformer:

> My dear David,
>   A very fine achievement of which you can be proud. I was pleased to be able to give you just a little assistance from time to time!
>   Yours ever,
>   John Silkin

Steel's university friend Norman Hackett (a nephew of the Labour minister George Brown) also wrote from Colombia to congratulate him on achieving 'something rather great'. 'Because of your Bill, society is marginally that much more civilised, which is an immense performance on your part,' wrote Hackett, 'and through that society there runs a new enriching thread of awareness of human suffering and social injustice.'[23]

---

23   SA/ALR/A.15/4, John Silkin to David Steel, 14 July 1967; Norman Hackett to David Steel, 18 July 1967.

But although endorsed by the Commons, Steel's Bill still had to clear the Upper House. When peers passed a wrecking amendment by one vote, Steel threatened to win Commons backing to invoke the Parliament Act. Their Lordships backed down, reversing two major amendments passed at committee stage, and endorsed the Bill in October. 'You must be feeling as relieved and delighted as we are with the outcome of yesterday,' wrote Vera Houghton. 'It is still not quite believable after the past few weeks of anxiety ... Surely, there is nothing that can stop the Bill tomorrow getting the Royal Assent. It really will be a great triumph for you and you more than deserve it.'[24] Royal Assent was granted when Steel was in mid-flight, travelling across the Atlantic to attend the United Nations with a parliamentary delegation.

In a foreword to *Abortion Law Reformed* in 1971, Steel modestly played down his 'small role' in making what he described paradoxically as a 'relatively minor but significant social reform in our country'. But the impact of the Bill was immediate. Private abortion clinics appeared across the country and the cost of having the procedure plummeted, while it was possible to secure one on the NHS after a six-week wait. The medical 'basis', however, turned out to be little more than a formality, and abortion on demand was effectively established. From 35,000 per annum in 1968, the number of abortions rose to 141,000 in 1975. 'In other words,' observed the sociologist Jeffrey Weeks, 'many women were seizing the opportunity provided by the 1967 Act to deliberately control their own fertility.'

Writing in 1971, Steel conceded that abortion was 'being used as a contraceptive'. 'The present level is too high,' he added, arguing that 'free contraception should be available on the National Health, otherwise people will accept free abortion instead, because they either cannot or will not pay for contraceptives. It worries me greatly.' His moral and political angst was clear:

---

24   SA/ALR/A.15/10/1, Vera Houghton to David Steel, 24 October 1967.

Abortion has undoubtedly brought a lot of happiness. One does not
expect women who have had one to go round saying so, but doctors
who deal with these patients tell me it has meant a great deal to
them. Free abortion and contraception may have a marginal effect
on moral laxity. But it is much more important to avoid unwanted
pregnancy, though I agree it is important to prevent any addition
to the decline in morals. Abortion on demand need not follow free
contraception. The decision to have an abortion is much more
fundamental than one to use a contraceptive and must remain in
the hands of the doctor. The Act says there must be a real need, and
I stick to that.

A point often missed was that Steel did not believe abortion to
be, in itself, a desirable or even justifiable act. His reasoning was
essentially utilitarian, believing that – in knowledge of the likely
alternatives (i.e. back street operations) – a formal termination
was 'the lesser of two evils'. 'Some people talk as though abortion was invented in 1967,' Steel reflected in 2004. 'It wasn't. And
it was far worse before.' But for opponents of Steel's Bill, abortion
was viewed as evil no matter what the context.

Between 1969 and 1980 there were eight attempts to limit the
scope of the Act. Steel also encountered internal opposition; a
group called Liberals against Abortion – which included Young
Liberals such as the future MP David Alton – was formed in April
1972 to campaign against what it considered the 'calamity' of the
Abortion Act. Steel himself helped review the Act's operation in
private clinics, while in 1975 he joined a select committee charged
with recommending possible changes, and three years later another
committee which wanted to replace the Act in its entirety. When
this 'became bogged down in fruitless wrangling' (according to
Betty Boothroyd), six members including Steel withdrew, thus
depriving the committee of a quorum.

Only in 1990 did Parliament significantly amend the 1967
Abortion Act, reducing the time limit for the procedure from
twenty-eight to twenty-four weeks to reflect advances in medical

science. Pragmatically, Steel supported the reduction, while retaining his concern about its general use, imploring people to 'be a bit more responsible in their activities, and in particular the use of contraception'. Finally, in 2004, he called for the legal limit (for 'social' abortions) to be cut to twelve weeks.

It was often said that Steel's Bill had 'legalised' abortion, when in fact it merely liberalised the existing laws, the procedure already being legal in certain circumstances (a contrast memorably captured in Mike Leigh's 2004 film, *Vera Drake*). Nevertheless, the Act was recognised as a major social reform and earned Steel a reputation for hard work, affability and a shrewd grasp of parliamentary tactics. 'As he had correctly calculated,' judged Alan Watkins in a study of political leadership, 'the Act did him little harm, and some good, both with the Liberal Party and with his Roxburgh constituency.'

It helped that it had been an impeccably Liberal measure, establishing Steel as a national figure, and not just within the relatively narrow confines of his party. 'Moreover, for the first time, he worked across political divisions with like-minded people in different parties for a common cause,' reflected Judy Steel in her memoirs. 'It was an approach that was to influence the rest of his political life.' The important thing, reflected Steel in 1984, 'was that something had been achieved by a Liberal'.

Conscious of becoming too closely associated with abortion, Steel also concentrated on other issues, both local and national. In the Borders he fought his abortion battle concurrently with another to save the Waverley railway line, which ran through his constituency, establishing a Railway Action Committee to co-ordinate an energetic – if unsuccessful – campaign for an upgrade rather than closure. When the line closed in January 1969, Steel rode the last train and appeased crowds of angry constituents who tried to stop it.[25] Steel had also served as president of the British Anti-Apartheid

---

25   When this book went to press, part of the line was due to reopen in 2014 as a result of Liberal Democrat pressure within the 2003–7 Scottish Executive.

Movement since 1966, although he joked in his memoirs that it
was because he was not likely to join the government any time
soon, his predecessor, Barbara Castle, having made that transition.

Steel later reflected that the period 1967–70 had been
'undramatic' and 'frustrating' in terms of Liberal progress. Since
the coalition kite had come crashing down in 1965, not to mention
Labour's large majority at the 1966 general election, the party had
drifted, and when Jo Grimond broke the news of his intended
resignation (in early 1967) to Steel at his home in Orkney, Steel
remembered it being 'fairly devastating'. 'I think I indicated that I
was horrified,' he later recalled, 'but he had by that time made up his
mind, and he was telling me, not consulting me.' He told reporters
that Grimond's leadership of the Liberals had transformed it 'into
a growing and influential political force – the beginnings of a new
party instead of the end of an old one'. In his memoirs, meanwhile,
Grimond recalled Steel's 'positively Asquithian calm' at hearing
the news.

The campaign to succeed Grimond was undignified and messy.
When Steel and his wife returned to Edinburgh airport the press
were waiting, convinced that Steel's visit to Orkney indicated that
he was Grimond's preferred successor. The Young Liberals fleetingly believed they could marshal support for the 28-year-old
Steel as the standard bearer of a new Liberal generation, but he
firmly rebutted all such speculation. Instead he supported Jeremy
Thorpe as the 'best communicator and campaigner and the man
most determined to pursue the Grimond strategy', acting as his
unofficial campaign manager while juggling it with the ongoing
Abortion Bill.

When Thorpe won (with six votes; Eric Lubbock and Emlyn
Hooson each got three), Steel was appointed the new leader's
personal assistant in the House of Commons, as well as Liberal
spokesman on Commonwealth Affairs, an important portfolio
given the crisis in Southern Rhodesia. 'The simple fact is that
majority rule must eventually come about in Rhodesia one way or
another,' Steel wrote in *The Times* in May 1967.

Britain's prime task should be to aim for this as soon as possible without repeating the mistake made in South Africa in allowing a privileged white minority to take into their hands the legal rights as well as the power to decide the future of the country.

Apartheid in South Africa, of course, was Steel's principal concern. He campaigned against a colour bar in sport, called on the Marylebone Cricket Club (MCC) to cancel its proposed South African tour in 1968–9 and, under the auspices of the Anti-Apartheid Movement, protested at the proposed visit of Royal Navy ships to Simon's Town. In late July 1967, Roy Jenkins announced an extension of the Race Relations Act, a move warmly welcomed by Steel, but when the Labour government also introduced a Bill to stem the flow of Asian immigrants from Kenya (where they were being persecuted by President Kenyatta's government), Steel was appalled. James Callaghan (Home Secretary following the devaluation crisis of late 1967) proposed entry controls on British passport holders with 'no substantial connection' with the UK. Wittily, Jeremy Thorpe observed that Callaghan, having devalued sterling at the Treasury, had now gone to the Home Office in order to devalue the passport.

In his memoirs, Steel modestly observed that on the Kenyan Asian issue, he 'was one of the few MPs who knew and understood the situation'. When details of the proposed controls emerged, they caused panic in Nairobi, where the 'beat-the-ban' rush to enter the UK generated hysterical scenes at the city's airport. Fully aware the Commonwealth Immigrants Bill would rouse passions on all sides of the House, Callaghan intended to steamroller the legislation through both Houses of Parliament in less than a week. As Commonwealth Affairs spokesman, Steel was summoned to move a resolution opposing the Bill at a Liberal Party Council meeting in London. He decided to go even further, and committed the party to voting against the Bill's second reading, thus providing, as Steel put it in his speech, 'an opportunity for members of the other parties to defy their whips and join us in the lobby'.

That weekend there was an 'impressive multi-racial demonstration' against the Bill, a march from Hyde Park to Downing Street, where one protestor burned her passport in protest. Briefed by an adviser called Praful Patel – who had lived in both Kenya and India – Steel did the rounds amid a welter of public and media opposition. 'Progressive people,' recalled Steel, 'in the social, political and religious field, were opposed to the Bill in the country. The same was to be true in the parliamentary struggle.' The Liberals managed to divide the House six times during the Bill's committee stage, but it still moved directly to a third reading and passed by 145 votes to thirty-one. When, passing through the House of Lords, Steel overheard a Labour whip tell a colleague that the government could 'rely on the Tories' to get the Bill through, he recalled feeling 'physically sick'.

Back in the Commons (peers having not passed any amendments), Steel watched as the Speaker announced Royal Assent. 'At this there were cries of "shame" from all parts of the House,' he recalled. 'The Speaker adjourned the sitting at one minute past ten, and Members, physically and mentally exhausted, trooped quietly out at the end of a unique and discreditable chapter of our parliamentary history.' Steel went further in his memoirs, calling it 'a major concession to racism'.

In August 1968 Steel flew to Nairobi to see for himself the consequences of the legislation:

> One family I visited consisted of an expectant mother aged twenty-five (she looked forty) with two boys aged five and three and a girl aged two. The family home had been given up after the sudden departure of the husband, a railway clerk, on a charter flight. When I visited them they were lying on two beds in almost pitch darkness in a squalid rented basement room. The children were pale, dark-eyed and hollow-cheeked. The mother was quietly courageous and spoke optimistically of the time when her husband would send for them. The single electric light bulb was turned out again as I left, to save the electricity bill. This was only one tiny part of the trail of misery we had created.

Steel included this grim anecdote in his first book, *No Entry: The Background and Implications of the Commonwealth Immigrants Act 1968* (ghostwritten by Peter Bartram, who later produced the first biography of Steel), which concluded that the time had come to 'establish a fundamental Bill of Rights'. 'Yesterday it was the Kenya Asians who had the fundamental rights that they have taken for granted trampled upon,' argued Steel, 'but who will it be tomorrow? ... A Bill of Rights would build a second outer wall of defence around the liberty of the subject.'

Less than two months after the Act became law Enoch Powell, 'like the Roman', saw the River Tiber foaming with much blood (the Liberal MP Emlyn Hooson upset Steel by saying he could see nothing wrong with assisting immigrants who sought repatriation), prompting Praful Patel to suggest the creation of an organisation to deal with problems arising from the Act (this became the Committee on UK Citizenship).

More than any other political issue, racial prejudice and inequality fired Steel up. As he put it at the 1981 Liberal Assembly, 'The fight against racialism is one of the most important concerns of my political life.' Yet crucially Steel espoused Liberal radicalism while looking like a Young Conservative. On the basis of the Abortion Act and the fight to protect the rights of Kenyan Asians, Steel became established in the public mind as a conservative radical, more likely to pursue his ideals via conventional means. 'These events left a profound impression on me,' he wrote in his memoirs. 'Once again I was in the thick of parliamentary debate, joining with like-minded people of other parties.'

Steel had always supported Jo Grimond's policy of 'radical realignment'; indeed he and Jeremy Thorpe had been his only convinced supporters among Liberal MPs. Thorpe's leadership, however, failed to rejuvenate the strategy and when, in early 1968, *The Guardian* carried a gloomy editorial ('They are about to miss their chance again') along these lines, a former Liberal candidate called Richard Holme – later to become one of Steel's closest advisers

– approached Steel with an idea for a Radical Action Movement (RAM) to co-ordinate like-minded figures from other parties.

Formed in April 1968 by Steel, the Liberal MP for North Cornwall, John Pardoe, and the Labour MP Peter Jackson, the only 'movement' turned out to be rhetorical. Steel was clearly enthusiastic, persuading another Labour MP (Ben Whitaker) to join, as well as Des Wilson of Shelter (Steel was chairman of the housing charity in Scotland, a position from which he enjoyed 'refreshing, down-to-earth, practical work with visible results'). 'Now the opportunity for political realignment is even greater outside Parliament than within,' declared Steel. 'If the Liberal Party can grasp the initiative in bringing this about, it deserves success.' Regarded with suspicion by most Liberals, and as a Liberal front by the Labour Party, the RAM never really took off, becoming, in Steel's words, 'no more than a minor talking shop'. When an RAM-backed Liberal candidate polled only 15 per cent in a Swindon by-election, it slipped quietly into political obscurity.

Developments in Scotland also provided Steel with a pretext for experiments in co-operative politics. Winnie Ewing's victory in the Hamilton by-election of November 1967 permanently altered the dynamic of Scottish politics, introducing a fourth party – the Scottish National Party (SNP) – and a new, overtly constitutional, dimension to what had hitherto been regular two-party, left/right British politics. The rise of the SNP also raised strategic questions for the Scottish Liberal Party (which was, after all, federalist in both structure and political aim): should it fight the Nationalists or negotiate an electoral deal?

The broadcaster Ludovic Kennedy and a young Liberal candidate called Michael Starforth had been pushing a pact with the SNP for some time, stepping up their efforts following a near Nationalist win at a by-election in Glasgow Pollok. In 1966 Kennedy proposed a motion to the Scottish Liberal conference that Home Rule was 'the principal aim and object of our policy', which to his 'great astonishment' was 'carried unanimously, and thereafter, equally unanimously ignored'. The prospect, however, split the Scottish

Liberal Party (SLP), with most MPs (including Steel) being in favour, while Russell Johnston and George Mackie were against. It was, recalled Steel in his memoirs, a 'running sore' in the 1966–70 parliament.

At the 1967 SLP conference in Perth, all these tensions came out into the open. Kennedy and Starforth again called for an electoral pact with the SNP, 'to avoid splitting the self-government vote and to join in achieving a Scottish parliament before Britain's entry into the Common Market'. But in a stormy session, with a number of close votes, the Assembly narrowly accepted a compromise amendment drafted by the Liberal MP for West Aberdeenshire, James Davidson, and Steel, which rejected a Liberal approach while inviting the SNP to take the initiative 'if they recognised the need ... to place the national interests of Scotland before short-term party interests'.

The SNP, however, was also reluctant to make the first move. Frustrated, Kennedy resigned from the Liberals so that he could speak on Winnie Ewing's behalf during her by-election campaign (although he never formally joined the SNP), thus destroying any hopes of a joint campaign (which Steel and Grimond had attempted to broker). 'It was a great boost to the SNP,' reflected Steel some years later, 'and an unnecessary blow to us.' Following Kennedy's lead, Starforth also resigned from the party and actually joined the SNP. On the brink of resignation, George Mackie demanded that MPs (who favoured a pact) ought to listen to their constituency parties (who were generally against).

Ahead of an important meeting of the Scottish Liberal Party Council in early December, Steel, Davidson, Grimond and Alasdair Mackenzie wrote to Mackie setting out their thinking:

1. We have failed to maintain our position as the effective advocates of self-government...

2. We should cease passing resolutions or making statements hostile to the Nationalists since it is impossible to do this without giving the impression that like the Labour and Tory parties we are hostile to self-government itself and unwilling to co-operate. Of course

where SNP and SLP candidates conflict the SNP will have to be treated as opponents, but our objective should be to prevent this happening in too many constituencies.

3. We should say that although we disagree with some of the SNP proposals we are ready to co-operate on the aim of self-government and argue about the extent of its powers when this point is established. If it proves impossible to co-operate with the SNP we must pin the responsibility for this on to them and make it clear that we tried.

4. We should cease discussing our own disagreements and our position vis-à-vis the Nationalists and concentrate on making publicity for Liberal policies.

5. No resolutions or statements on this topic should emanate publicly from the Council on Saturday.[26]

Russell Johnston, naturally, did not agree, while, in the event, Mackie managed to persuade the party to state unanimously that 'the gulf between the separatist policy of the SNP and the federalist system of self-government proposed by the SLP shows no prospect of being bridged'.

At the 1968 SLP conference Johnston even rebuked Grimond, which as Steel observed in his memoirs 'was the Liberal equivalent of swearing aloud in church'. By this point Steel was acting as the Liberals' Scottish whip (this earned him a better office in the House, which he shared with Eric Lubbock), and occasionally fielded letters from Michael Starforth, who still held out hope for an electoral arrangement between the two parties. 'The SNP have not so far been prepared to come together with us', replied Steel to one Starforth initiative in October 1969, 'on the simple proposition of the right of the Scots to decide their own future.' Starforth responded on 2 November, relaying a message from Grimond that he was confident Steel could 'carry' the SLP in order to work 'for a "sovereign" electorate situation'. He continued:

---

26   Letter courtesy of Devin Scobie (private collection).

You know that I only dare 'interfere' because I think we are working for the same end. I would dearly like to see the SNP refrain from fighting four out of five Liberal seats (and have frequently said so) … As I said in my letter of application to the SNP fifteen months ago, I want to see a *Liberal* Scotland as soon as possible and that won't be achieved via London![27]

Again, no progress was made, most Liberals – including Jeremy Thorpe – remaining reluctant to suppress other policies in favour of self-government. Steel, however, recognised that it was theoretically possible. 'The two Home-Rule parties in Scotland – the Liberals and the Nationalists – could effectively campaign together', he wrote in his contribution to Neil MacCormick's 1970 book, *The Scottish Debate*, 'on this theme of the Scots having the right to decide the future for themselves (including the right to total sovereignty and separation if so desired). This possibility has so far been rejected by the SNP, who insist that all should adopt their own doctrines.'

Steel's analysis of the situation was tactical, rather than being based on any affinity with Scottish Nationalists (whom Johnston, for example, loathed). 'David's attitude seemed naïve,' recalled Willis Pickard, another member of the SLP executive; 'he did not appreciate the need to assert the party's fragile identity, which in a Home Rule alliance with a party that simply banged the Scottish drum [the SNP] would be lost to the electorate.' Rather Steel advocated federalism, which he defined as 'the maximum amount of Home Rule consistent with common sense'.

Otherwise Steel took a rather conventional view of Scottish 'Home Rule', proposing a series of modest administrative reforms in a 1968 pamphlet called *Out of Control: A Critical Examination of the Government of Scotland*. This offered a cogent critique of a Scottish Office 'remarkably out of touch with the feelings of the people whom it exists to serve', before setting out plans for a select

---

27 David Steel Papers STEEL/B/9/2, David Steel to Michael Starforth, October 1969; Michael Starforth to David Steel, 2 November 1969.

committee on Scotland (soon established by Harold Wilson's government), regular questioning of Scottish ministers by the Scottish Grand Committee, which he argued should also meet more often, in Edinburgh (which happened in the early 1980s) and around Scotland (in the 1990s), as well as under the glare of Scottish television cameras.

If nothing else, Steel believed his proposals would act 'as the thin end of a most effective wedge in securing a Scottish Parliament'. *The Times* was relatively impressed, pointing out that, if only to fend off rising Home Rule sentiment, Steel's 'interim proposals are well worth bearing in mind'. Careful not to neglect his constituency, in early 1969 Steel had also prepared a ten-minute-rule Bill to establish a Highlands and Islands-style development board for the Borders, where Steel feared 'slow but steady decline' in the absence of affirmative action.

As one eventful decade gave way to another, Steel's various activities – party, anti-apartheid, abortion and Scotland – were conflated as MPs awaited the dissolution of Parliament. As he noted in his memoirs, his first five years in Parliament had been a 'formative period in [his] political outlook', the main tenor being 'inter-party co-operation to achieve common objectives'. 'My activity', reflected Steel, 'was more as a Liberal working with others outside the Liberal Party than within it to advance Liberal causes.'

Jeremy Thorpe's leadership of the Liberals coincided with a period of drift in which the party appeared to lack any clear purpose, launching a 'Great Crusade' with considerable flourish but little follow-through. 'For Jeremy as leader, little had gone right in the three years since he took over from Jo Grimond in 1967,' recalled Steel in his memoirs. 'A year later there was much muttering and plotting against his leadership. The party's finances were in an appalling state, and the headquarters moved from the prestige of Smith Square to more reduced circumstances up a squalid litter-strewn lane off the Strand.'

Worse, in twelve out of the twenty-eight by-elections held during the 1966–70 parliament the Liberals lost their deposit.

Attendance at the party's annual Assembly fell as the years went by, as did the party's tally of candidates and councillors. Steel also had problems to face, particularly when the anti-apartheid campaign led to a clash between his local and national interests. Rugby in the Borders enjoyed a semi-religious status, so when the South African team, known as the Springboks, proposed a tour, Steel realised he would have to oppose a match scheduled to take place in his own constituency.

'There is no more feeble argument than "I disapprove of apartheid but...",' Steel later reflected. 'There can be no "buts" in the eyes of the majority of the people in South Africa or in the rest of the world. Sporting contacts have done nothing to alleviate apartheid. They have merely depressed those struggling against it.' Cannily, however, Steel distanced himself from the more extreme elements likely to protest, organising a (thinly attended) meeting at which the former Scottish Olympic athlete Menzies Campbell spoke in his support.

Steel lost sleep before the match, held in the Borders on 17 January 1970, at which he encountered what an earlier biographer called the 'first ... real hatred he has ever had from his own constituents'. As he and a few other demonstrators distributed 5,000 leaflets about the realities of apartheid to rugby fans, Steel was even spat at. He had persuaded the Anti-Apartheid Movement not to send its shock troops to Netherdale, instead handling the protest himself while managing to convince a banner-waving mob of protestors from Glasgow to leave as soon as the match started. Prominent among these was the nineteen-year-old Peter Hain, who had spearheaded the 'Stop the Seventy Tour' campaign. Indeed, the Young Liberals (of which Hain was a prominent member) caused the party (and therefore Steel) repeated problems during this period.

Fallout from the incident lingered for several months, so much so that Steel later admitted that had a general election followed immediately after the rugby tour, the electoral consequences 'would have been pretty fatal'. Local Conservatives, naturally, took full advantage of Steel's predicament. Russell Fairgrieve, the new Tory

candidate, was another talented campaigner, claiming that Steel
wanted to halt British exports to South Africa while circulating a
leaflet showing a ball sailing between a couple of rugby goal posts
and the slogan 'Convert to Conservatism'.

Many of Steel's constituents did just as Fairgrieve requested,
reducing the Liberal majority to three figures (an anti-abortion
candidate also stood). When the Conservative candidate arrived
at the count, he initially believed he had won but, after two 'nail-
biting' recounts at Jedburgh town hall, Steel's majority settled at
550. 'The Abortion Bill was not exactly a help,' Steel later recalled,
'and my opposition to the South African rugby tour a positive
hindrance.' But, as with the abortion legislation, Steel had taken a
calculated – and arguably extremely brave – risk in boycotting the
Springboks tour, and he had won. But only just.

4

A BUMPY ROAD

The general election result was a shattering blow to the Liberal Party, not least because it made all Jo Grimond had worked for appear to have been in vain. Although it polled more than two million votes, only six MPs survived, three of whom retained their constituencies with uncomfortably small majorities. As David Steel, one of the trio, later recalled: 'The party came very much closer to being wiped out than most people think.' Part of the problem had been the party's strategy, or rather the absence of one. 'We had no very clear message except the assumption of innate virtue and superiority in a host of Liberal policies.' Thus Steel and five other Liberal MPs returned to Parliament 'a depleted and dispirited band'.

Never one to tell the party what it wanted to hear, Steel swiftly rejected the option of plodding on 'as before, spending the next ten years building back up to a dozen or fifteen MPs only to face near annihilation again on a sudden small swing of the pendulum'. Rather, constituency organisations ought to 'promote Liberal policies and principles whenever they are to be found', although his suggestion to include supporting certain Tory or Labour candidates was later dismissed as 'nonsense' by Russell Johnston. The Liberal grassroots response, meanwhile, was 'almost uniformly hostile'.

At this stage Steel was a young man in a hurry, no doubt exploring how far he could push mainstream Liberal opinion. On 30 July 1970, he initiated a 'useful and amicable' meeting with William Wolfe, the leader of the Scottish National Party. Beyond agreeing on the 'right to self-determination' for Scotland, however, the prospect of a pact was not pursued. And on the eve of the September Liberal Assembly, a gloomy and thinly attended affair, Steel further antagonised his colleagues by writing in the *New Statesman* that it was still 'worth having another attempt at creating a relevant Liberal party'. 'Those unwilling to risk the discomfort of the journey', he continued, 'would do better to get off the train now rather than spend their time pulling the communication cord once it is under way.' Transport analogies were to be a feature of the next six years.

One important legacy of an otherwise forgettable Assembly was a Young Liberal motion advocating something called 'community politics', the leading advocates of which were Trevor 'The Vote' Jones and Tony Greaves. Steel, however, showed little interest, with Greaves later doubting whether he had 'any understanding of community politics at all'. As Steel later explained, his issue with some 'theoreticians on community politics' was their postulation of a society where 'everybody is going to damn well participate whether they like it or not', something he regarded as 'Utopian'. Nevertheless, the energy, campaigning methods and analysis of the community politics movement helped galvanise the Liberals, later producing a string of by-election victories. In the long term, meanwhile, this philosophical gulf between Steel and many Liberal disciples of community politics would explain much of the tension between the two in the latter stages of Steel's leadership of the party.

By this point Steel had replaced Eric Lubbock (defeated in Orpington) as Liberal Chief Whip and spent what he called two 'consistently depressing' years picking up the pieces of the 1970 general election. The Scarborough Assembly in 1971 was, as he later recalled, a 'disaster'. 'The shock of the 1970 election setback had numbed us through that year's conference,' he explained, 'but developed into disillusion and bitterness in 1971.'

Instead, Steel continued to concentrate on extra-parliamentary activity, notably African affairs. When Idi Amin expelled Asians from Uganda in 1972, he saw for himself how it had brought Kampala's commercial life to a standstill. And on a fact-finding trip to Rhodesia in October 1972, Steel was detained at Salisbury airport and banned from re-entering the country by Ian Smith's regime, his passport having not disclosed his real identity (it listed his occupation as 'company director'). Smith later claimed the decision was based on Steel's 'known support for terrorist movements'. For the next forty years Steel kept a framed copy of the 'Prohibited Immigrant' certificate (he had been compelled to sign in Salisbury) in his Parliament office.

As Chief Whip, meanwhile, Steel was – according to *The Times*'s Geoffrey Smith – 'no more than a partial success', neither consulting widely enough nor particularly good at maintaining relations with the wider party. Similarly, an early biographer noted that Steel was criticised 'for his non-attendance at party committee meetings', making 'little effort to conceal his impatience with the more impractical comments and proposals which emerge from party committees'. Steel conceded as much in his memoirs, noting that while Thorpe delegated much of the party liaison role to him as Chief Whip, the 'same accusations that the leader was remote from the party machine came up again in my time'.

With only five MPs to shepherd, it was not in any case a particularly demanding job, and one whose status meant little to the general public. When, shortly after his appointment, Jo Grimond invited Steel to meet his constituents on a walkabout in Kirkwall, he introduced 'our Chief Whip, David Steel, who has come all this way to speak tonight. You will all, of course, be coming?' 'Oh no, Mr Grimond,' one responded, 'the [Liberal] branch have organised a whist drive.' That evening Steel addressed an audience of twenty, while 150 attended the whist drive. The *Daily Mail* was kinder, judging Steel as Chief Whip to be a great 'oil-on-troubled-waters man ... Quiet. Unflappable. Modest.'

Despite ongoing financial difficulties, during this period the Liberal Party gradually become more professional, the community politics movement having helped cultivate fertile ground for a string of by-election gains. This began in October 1972 with Rochdale, where Steel had persuaded the larger-than-life Cyril Smith to stand, and thereafter in Sutton & Cheam (Graham Tope), Ripon (David Austick), Isle of Ely (Clement Freud) and Berwick-upon-Tweed (Alan Beith). In March 1973, Dick Taverne resigned his Lincoln seat as a Labour MP and won a by-election under the 'Democratic Labour' banner following factional infighting. Steel helped ensure the absence of a Liberal candidate, while Jo Grimond spoke in his support. 'He won,' recalled Steel, 'and was the precursor of the bigger realignment to occur ten years later.'

In January that year, Steel had told Tyne Tees's *Challenge* programme that he would welcome the formation of a new centre-left party comprising Liberals and social democrats from the Labour Party, arguing that little divided Liberals from figures like Taverne or Roy Jenkins. The country, said Steel, was disillusioned with the two main parties:

> The question it poses for us is whether we can turn this rather nega-
> tive feeling of reaction against the two parties into positive support
> for us. We have begun to do it. I think if one tried to pinpoint one
> main reason for this disillusion, it is perhaps that the two main
> parties are seen to be very much alike. They shift their policies and
> then often end up with the same policies.

Steel, therefore, interpreted Taverne's by-election win as evidence of a popular desire for a third force in British politics. Bill Rodgers (the Labour MP for Stockton-on-Tees), however, took a different view, saying that 'the quicker we reject the chimera of a centre party the sooner we shall learn the lessons of the by-elections'. Whatever the explanation, by July 1973 *The Times* was hailing 'much the greatest Liberal revival since the war', while praising Steel as 'an outstanding member of Parliament, perhaps the most impressive member in his middle thirties of the present house'. (The previous month had seen the birth of Steel's third child, Rory, who emerged, as his father recalled, 'looking like a skinned rabbit'.)

As stock in Steel rose, the political market took an increasingly dim view of the incumbent leader, Jeremy Thorpe. The North Devon MP had never really shed his pre-leadership image as more of a comedian than an MP, while the then Liberal adviser William Wallace judged that Thorpe, for all his strengths 'as an organiser, a money-raiser and a public personality', was 'largely uninterested in policy, and not much concerned with strategy'. As speculation grew that the resurgent Liberals might coalesce with Labour, strategy was more important than ever. Harold Wilson even felt the need to assure his 1973 party conference there would be 'no arrangement, no fix' with the Liberals, to which Steel retorted that if Wilson intended 'to lead a possible minority Labour government into its new left-wing programme ... then he would indeed lead Labour to disaster'. Presciently, Steel also warned his party to prepare for two general elections rather than one.

By the beginning of 1974, all the UK's political parties were preparing for a snap general election, and although the Parliamentary Liberal Party had almost doubled its numbers to eleven, the party was polling the same figure in percentage points. Furthermore, it had only around 250 candidates in place. Talk of coalition was still in the air and, in *The Times* Steel set out his party's demands should that become a reality: a prices and incomes policy which included a 'major redistribution of wealth and privileges'; overhauling industrial relations (although the Liberals were silent on this during the campaign); pursuing industrial democracy; devolving power to Scotland and Wales 'without further procrastination'; and finally direct elections to the European Assembly.

For once, talk of a hung Parliament was not idle speculation, for that is precisely what the general election of 28 February produced: Labour the largest party with 301 seats and the Conservatives on 297 (though with a larger share of the vote). The Liberal vote surged to more than six million votes, an increase of 11.8 per cent on 1970 and the largest third-party vote for almost fifty years. In Roxburgh, Selkirk & Peebles, Steel – defending a narrow majority – secured more than 50 per cent of his constituency poll and almost 26,000 votes.[28] The situation, however, was complicated. With Labour seventeen seats short of an overall majority and the Conservatives twenty-one, the Liberals' fourteen MPs were not enough to give either party the chance of forming a government.

But when Edward Heath, who had gone to the country on the basis of 'who governs Britain', summoned Jeremy Thorpe for talks at Downing Street, the Liberal leader – who had fought an ebullient campaign – neither hesitated nor consulted his colleagues. The first Steel (still Chief Whip) heard of it was on his car radio, something he sardonically classified as 'somewhat unusual'. Although he had talked up the prospects of coalition before polling day, Steel realised the Liberals had done well on the basis of getting Heath out of Downing Street, not keeping him in. When a 'confused and irritated' Steel finally got hold of Thorpe by telephone, he had already seen Heath.

Arriving in London, Steel urged Thorpe to go back to Downing Street to clarify that the Liberals might consider a coalition should there be a 'cast-iron commitment' to changing the electoral system. 'So late that Saturday night I drove his car round to the side entrance in Downing Street,' recalled Steel in his memoirs, 'and sat waiting in the dark while he went in for a second – this time secret – meeting.' The following day, Steel, Lord Byers (leader of the Liberal peers) and Jo Grimond had Sunday lunch at Thorpe's Orme Square home, where the mood remained firmly against any deal, Heath having offered the Liberal leader a Cabinet seat and no more than a Speaker's conference on electoral reform. Steel also contacted Roy Jenkins to discuss a possible Lib–Lab arrangement, only to be told that Harold Wilson's instinct was to govern as a minority before seeking a larger mandate in a second election.

Thorpe's dalliance with Heath arguably weakened his standing as

---

28 The defeated Conservative candidate, Stuart Thom, later wrote a rather graceless letter to *The Times* arguing that Steel had enjoyed an unfair advantage because of his higher media profile. He had been at school and university with Steel.

party leader, but when the fourteen Liberal MPs convened for their first meeting, Steel was concerned at the adverse reaction to even considering a deal with Heath, feeling strongly that 'it was one thing to say this was not the right thing to do, but quite another to advance the general argument, which a lot of people in the party did, that under no circumstances should anything like this be contemplated'. To Steel, these were 'two entirely different propositions', but confirmed his belief that 'so long as we kept dodging such questions and simply pretending to be an alternative government in exile we would continue to fail.'

Between March and another general election in October, Liberals did little to appease Steel's concerns, so he resolved to persuade his colleagues that the 'way forward was to secure a firmer grip on the next parliament and achieve electoral reform inside a coalition government'. In June he used a party political broadcast to push the coalition argument in the most ostentatious way possible. Anticipating the likely reaction, Steel consulted nobody about his script, only giving Thorpe – who asked for some minor amendments – sight of it at the last minute. In the broadcast, Steel argued that the fight against inflation was too big for any one party:

> In our crisis we surely need a much more broadly based government backed by a real majority of public opinion, and that means that all parties must be willing to come together on an agreed programme in the national interest ...We are ready and willing to participate in such a government if at the next election you give us the power to do so. Naturally, like the other parties, we would prefer you to give us an overall majority of seats, but if you don't, we remain ready to contribute towards the kind of fair government based on partnership which you, the electorate, might be seeking.

Although Thorpe supported Steel by arguing that a government of national unity reflected 'the views of millions of people', other Liberals were less than keen. The Liberal activist Michael Steed considered the broadcast 'ill-judged', and indeed even Steel agreed with David Butler and Dennis Kavanagh's view that it had been 'sprung on an unprepared party'. Four days later the party's National Executive Committee repudiated Steel's broadcast, passing a resolution to the effect that 'the Liberal Party will not join a coalition with the Conservative or Labour parties separately and will make this clear at the next election.' Steel bluntly told them such a resolution was worthless. 'Possibly it was rash at the time to make that broadcast and it did lead to criticism,' Steel later acknowledged. 'But it did have its effect. It got a lot of attention.'

Indeed it did, finally prompting the Labour MP Christopher Mayhew to cross the floor and join the Liberals. The coalition strategy also came up during a dinner at the French embassy, Steel 'obviously planting a warning' with Harold Wilson's policy adviser Bernard Donoughue. 'He prefers to ally with Labour but was trying to say that there could be a coalition without Labour,' noted Donoughue in his diary. 'I have put this to HW, but he discounts it, saying that if you look at the seats, the Liberals cannot benefit unless some Tory MPs stand down – and the Tories won't have that. Steel is a wise and decent man. I wish he was in our party.'

Steel might have agreed as Liberals convened for their September Assembly. Peter Hain, at that time a leading figure in the Young Liberals, led the charge against any talk of coalition with the Conservatives. 'The Tories have sheltered in the palaces of inequality and injustice throughout their political lives,' he argued. 'Liberals have been storming those palaces all our lives ... The Liberal Party is the radical alternative or it is nothing.' Although Thorpe managed to persuade the party not to close its mind to a deal with the Conservatives, the result was a fudge: the Assembly passed two motions, one opposing any kind of coalition and another allowing Liberal MPs to decide after the October election. Total breakthrough was the aim, argued Thorpe, with coalition merely a last resort. 'I disagreed at the time with that strategy,' Steel said later, 'and thought the party had really flunked the issue of participation in government as a means of getting more Liberals into Parliament.'

In another Liberal broadcast after the Assembly, Steel tried again, describing 'a growing revulsion against the present see-saw of the class-based two-party system'. A government with a strong Liberal representation, he added, would not be a government of the 'soggy centre' but 'way out in front'. But with the less than inspiring slogan 'One More Heave', the October Liberal campaign was, in Steel's words, 'a slightly less successful re-run of February'. Compared with the previous election, the party lost one seat and 1 per cent of its support.

Subsequent analysis generated mixed messages: on the one hand there was an ongoing process of de-alignment in British politics, with increasing number of voters moving away from the two main parties, but on the other the Liberals' core vote – i.e. the proportion of voters who consistently voted for them – remained relatively small. So would Steel's preferred strategy have made any difference to the result? In his memoirs, he claims Liberal poll ratings 'jumped' following his June broadcast 'because we were again both relevant and in tune with public feeling', but that the moment had been squandered by the September Assembly. This seems unlikely; the Liberals would have found it difficult to campaign *for* a hung Parliament or a coalition, although they could certainly have taken advantage of the former had it occurred. But then nor was total breakthrough – a Liberal majority – even remotely possible. Strategy in the context of 1974's two elections was probably less important than Steel believed. After all, the elections of 1970 and February 1974 had both been fought without grand political strategies, and both had delivered very different outcomes.

An anti-climactic pall hung over the Liberal Party as the dust settled on the events of 1974. Now equipped with a tiny majority of just four seats, Harold Wilson neither asked for nor expected co-operation from the Liberals. All the talk of 'national' governments and 'one more heave' had come to nothing. Such was the mood, Steel was the only Liberal MP to attend a post-mortem meeting of the Liberal Party Council, at which he set out the priorities for the new parliament. 'On the surface our problems are economic. But essentially I believe the solutions are political,' he said, adding optimistically: 'We are poised for breakthrough, but with our crazy election system no one can tell just how many seats we might win.'

Even after the February 1974 general election Steel had grown tired of the Chief Whip's job and had attempted to resign. Thorpe convinced him to stay, but after October, noted Cyril Smith in his memoirs, Steel was 'determined to step down'. 'The decision of his replacement could only be made by Jeremy Thorpe,' recalled Smith, 'who seemed very reluctant to make it.' Jo Grimond advised Steel to broaden his horizons, so he held firm and Thorpe eventually acquiesced, appointing him spokesman on foreign affairs, Steel having stood down as Chief Whip in June 1975.

At around this time, the North Cornwall MP, John Pardoe, began to emerge as a Liberal evangelist in the Grimond mould. 'Unless we regain faith in ourselves, our mission and our message,' he said in April 1975, 'who can blame others for losing faith in us?' With doubt surrounding Thorpe's future even before scandal broke, it was an obvious bid for the leadership. An opportunity to boost Steel's profile, meanwhile, conveniently presented itself with a June referendum on the UK's continued membership of the European Economic Community (EEC), otherwise known as the 'Common Market'.

The 'yes' campaign brought together politicians from all parties, the issue having rumbled on since the Commons vote to join the EEC in late 1971 (which, significantly, initiated Jenkins's move away from the formally anti-EEC Labour Party). The Liberals, meanwhile, were keen to capitalise on their pro-EEC united front, even though, ironically, polling evidence showed most Liberal Party members were likely to vote 'no' (the Liberal activist Roy Douglas also launched a 'Liberals Say "No"' movement in April, although this 'refrained from embarrassing the party').

Having supported a referendum on EEC entry for some years, Steel was co-opted into early morning breakfast meetings of the European League for Economic Co-operation at the Dorchester Hotel. Thus he became one of the 'Britain in Europe' (BIE) campaign's 'principals', a position he naturally exploited to maximise Liberal exposure. This led to over-zealousness on the part of Liberal HQ, which issued pro-European propaganda that was also conspicuously pro-Liberal, while distributing BIE grants to constituency organisations rather than spending them centrally. 'The Liberals tended to play it dirty and to see their campaign as a purely pro-Liberal exercise,' one Conservative remarked in an academic study of the referendum, although he also noted that 'David Steel did a good deal to put this right' and personally 'played it straight'.

Steel's media talents were also exploited in print and on television, forming part of the pro-Market side (along with Ted Heath and Roy Jenkins) in a quasi-parliamentary debate staged by Granada's *State of the Nation* team. Beyond the profile-boosting element of campaigning, to Steel the 'expertise and contact network of the two big party machines was a real eye-opener to someone used to the poverty-stricken organisation of the Liberal Party'. 'The basic materials which Liberals scratched hard to find or finance simply appeared at the flick of fingers,' he later recalled: 'cars, aeroplanes, helicopters, film units, stage equipment, photocopiers, typewriters.' The experience also consolidated Steel's realism when it came to what the Liberals might achieve. 'It was an exciting and effective campaign,' he wrote in his memoirs, 'but it gave me an insight into what we as a party were up against.'

More to the point, 'trailing around the country in this cause enabled me to get on closer terms with senior figures in the other parties.' Significantly, it brought Steel into close contact with Roy Jenkins for the first time since they had co-operated on the Abortion Act. As Judy Steel put it in her memoirs, 'David loved the European campaign,' not least because 'it gave him the chance to share platforms with senior politicians, those almost of another generation, such as Edward Heath, Willie Whitelaw and Roy Jenkins.' At the time, the Home Secretary praised Steel as a 'most admirable Liberal', recalling in his memoirs that of 'all the people I dealt with during the campaign he was one of the best'. Other future Social Democrats were also heavily involved, including Bill Rodgers, Shirley Williams and Dick Mabon. The referendum, observed the historian Matt Cole,

> had thrown the potential benefits of inter-party co-operation in terms of publicity and leadership recruitment into sharp relief for some Liberals; but for others it had highlighted dangers for the clarity of the Liberal message and the independence of the party.

The result of the referendum was decisive, with 67 per cent of voters expressing support for continued membership of the EEC on a 65 per cent turnout. In Scotland, an exceptionally high 'yes' vote in the Borders (72 per cent) was attributed to Steel's performance. On 6 June all the movement's leading lights – including Steel – were given a reception fit for heroes, while Roy Jenkins hosted a celebratory dinner at Brooks's. Indeed, the whole campaign had been a personal triumph for Steel, and significant in terms of his future leadership of – and strategy for – the Liberal Party.

Following the referendum, Steel later wrote, 'there was much loose talk of keeping the politicians of the centre together', and in that spirit Steel spent a 'fascinating' week at the 1975 Labour Party conference on behalf of the BBC's *Tonight* current affairs programme. He also appeared to have been converted to the political usefulness of referendums, advocating another on Scottish independence so that the inevitable 'no' vote would allow everyone to concentrate on 'effective devolution, which is what the great majority of Scots ... actually want'. As Wilson's government got on with tackling inflation, Steel pledged qualified Liberal support while also accusing Labour ministers of presiding over a 'new illiberalism' in relation to homosexuality and prosecution policy.

Perhaps conscious of a perceived weakness when it came to policy matters, as well as the need to set out his leadership stall, Steel published a pamphlet called *Strategy 2000: The Liberal Way Forward* ahead of the 1975 Liberal Assembly. Certain proposals were far sighted, such as that to convert local authority tenancies into mortgages, subsidised according to need. 'This would at once provide greater freedom of choice for the individual who would be free to buy or sell his house at will,' explained Steel, 'and would in due course end the social distinctions between owner-occupiers and council tenants.' The Young Liberals did not approve of this apparent nod to Conservative thinking, or Steel's suggestion – to discourage irresponsible industrial disputes – that social security payments to strikers' families should be limited to stoppages supported by at least half of those entitled to vote. *The Times*, not surprisingly, thought Steel's pamphlet was 'excellent', although it was arguably ideologically muddled, apparently at odds with Steel's warning that the 'motivation of greed [was] year by year taking a greater grip of our society'. Never really comfortable with political philosophy, in his memoirs Steel made an improbable claim to having read E. F. Schumacher while preparing *The Liberal Way Forward*, which, he later immodestly claimed, was a 'much neglected publication'.

Much quoted several years later were Steel's concluding thoughts, that he and his liberally minded friends in other parties sat 'around discussing avidly the prospects of political realignment in Britain and the creation of a truly radical and adventurous government'. This, he said, was 'an exciting prospect – given impetus by the experience of working together in the referendum campaign – but one which is fairly dim unless they are prepared to do something about it.' He continued:

> I hasten to make it clear that I am not thinking in terms of the cosy centre government advocated by some leader writers. For a start there [are] no more than a couple of dozen Tory MPs who could be accommodated within any genuinely liberal movement. On the Labour side though, the internal splits in both policy and philosophy are more fundamental and substantial. Many of the self-styled social democrats would be happier company in combination with Liberals than Socialists. Should such an opportunity for an effective regrouping of the left come about it is important that the

Liberal Party should not behave like a more rigid sect of the exclusive brethren, but be ready to join with others in the more effective promotion of liberalism.

Again, this anticipated much of what Steel would tell delegates at the 1976 Liberal Assembly. At the 1975 gathering, however, all the talk was of leadership, both the means by which the party ought to choose one in future and, indeed, who it might be. Writing in *The Times*, Robin Young reckoned Steel was the three-to-one favourite as Jeremy Thorpe's successor:

> He has more support than any other candidate among Liberal MPs, but only narrowly. Against him is the party political broadcast he made between the two 1974 elections, reviving coalition talk, now seen as having sent party strategy on a misjudged course at a crucial time. Detractors say he has a 'head prefect' image, is arrogant, untrustworthy politically and has aged prematurely in his political attitudes.

Thorpe, of course, was soon to resign as Liberal leader, although no one at this juncture – beyond a few on the inside track – could have predicted why. 'The glorious summer [of] 1975 was a period of celebration and the autumn one of fulfilment,' recalled Steel in his memoirs. 'Yet the storm clouds were gathering. Down in the West Country, a man shot a dog.'

By the beginning of 1976, Jeremy Thorpe's leadership of the Liberal Party was running out of steam. Increasingly accused of possessing a surplus of style over substance, he had also become increasingly autocratic, while his survival – particularly after the electoral disappointments of 1974 – led to public questions as to whether he was the man to take the Liberals forward. His speeches in the Commons were 'now couched in a curiously heavy, almost pompous style'. 'He felt he had to move away from the image of the sharp, witty debater to being grave,' observed Steel. 'It was disastrous.' Watching Thorpe make one such 'strange rambling speech' in March 1976, Bernard Donoughue detected that an 'internal Liberal battle' was at play, with 'some of them wanting to defeat Thorpe'. 'He has behaved honourably in the recent Thorpe affair,' Donoughue said of Steel, 'but seems very depressed about their future.'

Steel's depression was justified, not least because he knew more than most about the 'Thorpe affair'. An often-absurd saga of alleged homosexual affairs, hired assassins and dodgy financial deals began in May 1971 when a Liberal activist called Mrs Parry-Jones contacted the Liberal MP Emlyn Hooson on behalf of a young model called Norman Scott. Hooson showed her letter to Steel and when Parry-Jones turned up at the House of Commons with Scott, it was Steel who greeted them, Hooson having been called away on legal business. Both Steel and Hooson assumed the complaint related to Peter Bessell, a shady associate of Thorpe's who had retired as the Liberal MP for Bodmin in 1970. While Steel was 'immediately impressed' by Parry-Jones, he was 'sceptical' about Scott, who he remembered having a 'limp, clammy handshake, seemed to perspire profusely and spoke softly and hesitatingly, giving the clear impression of having had some kind of nervous breakdown'.

When Scott made his central allegation about Thorpe – that they had had a four-year affair in the early 1960s – Steel was shocked. As Judy Steel observed, her husband 'always, always, wants to believe the best of people', so he 'hoped, and persuaded himself to believe' that Scott was lying or fantasising. Steel had, of course, been aware of rumours about Thorpe's private life but had dismissed them as insubstantial. 'What made this story alarming', recalled Steel in his memoirs, 'was the fact that he [Scott] produced out of a bag a whole series of letters signed by Peter Bessell ... referring to sums of money enclosed.' Scott further alleged he had been promised £5,000 by Bessell to resettle in Wales, which is how he had come to know Mrs Parry-Jones.

A shaken Steel spoke to Hooson the following day ('Jeremy will have to go,' they agreed. 'We'll have to meet him at the airport when he comes back from Africa') and together they confronted

Thorpe with the allegations. Calmly, the Liberal leader conceded that Bessell had handled a problem with Scott's National Insurance card (Scott's main concern) 'clumsily', but denied everything else. When Hooson asked if he would resign as leader if everything was shown to be true, Thorpe replied: 'Of course, but it isn't and I won't.' Reluctantly, Thorpe also agreed to an internal Liberal inquiry to be chaired by Lord Byers.

Interrogated again by Steel, Hooson and Byers around a 'large oval oak table', Scott initially held up well (although certain aspects of his story were fantastical). When Hooson asked if he was after money, however, 'Scott broke down and declared that he still loved Jeremy and felt he had been rejected and badly treated.' 'At this point Frank Byers, who was notoriously short on suffering fools,' recalled Steel in his memoirs, 'exploded and told Scott he was nothing but a dirty little blackmailer or words to that effect.' Scott then burst into tears and fled from the room. 'I felt the exchange', observed Steel with characteristic understatement, 'had been less than useful.' Byers then asked Thorpe to set out his dealings with Scott in a letter, a copy of which was passed to the Home Secretary, Reginald Maudling, who replied saying neither he nor the Metropolitan Police commissioner could 'see any reason to disagree' with Thorpe's description of Scott as a 'nutcase'.

'That', believed Steel, 'seemed to be that,' and indeed nothing further emerged for another five years. Left to choose between 'the word of a neurotic stranger and the explanation of our parliamentary colleague', Steel and others 'unanimously agreed that the matter was closed'. But it remained a difficult situation. Only Steel, Hooson and Byers were privy to potentially explosive allegations about Thorpe, thus their involvement had to be carefully managed lest any of them appear disloyal. That said, Steel was only human and, more to the point, a politician impatient to climb the greasy pole. With the possibility of Thorpe's resignation hanging in the air, Steel must naturally have considered the implications for his own career, although at this point he believed Hooson would have been the 'main contender' to replace Thorpe.

There is, however, a question mark hanging over Steel's conduct during this period. He was certainly loyal, seeking to protect his leader's reputation and career beyond what could have been expected of most young and ambitious MPs, but therein lies the point: given the nature of the allegations, Thorpe's petulant response and the likelihood that it would all – at some point – blow up and damage the party, had Steel done the right thing by keeping it quiet along with two others? It was undoubtedly a difficult decision. Steel says himself he was inclined to give Thorpe the benefit of the doubt, that the evidence – though compelling – was incomplete. Only when the allegations against Thorpe became public did Steel act, and even then relatively late in the day.

On 29 January 1976, the diminutive figure of Norman Scott finally entered the public consciousness. Coded stories had been appearing in *Private Eye* about the shooting of Scott's Great Dane, Rinka, and, indeed, the apparent threat to Scott himself in the middle of Exmoor. Charged with defrauding the Post Office of £58, Scott used the privilege of Barnstaple Magistrates Court to repeat all his old allegations against Thorpe, as well as the apparent attempt on his life. Finally, the press was free to publish without being damned, although Scott's outburst – initially at least – generated more sympathy than condemnation for the Liberal leader.

But as more and more details, often bizarre (Harold Wilson muddied the waters by suggesting South African agents were behind the attempt to smear Thorpe), emerged, Steel despaired at the 'devastating effect' it was having 'on party morale'. 'No one could go canvassing because no satisfactory explanation could be given of anything which kept appearing in the newspapers,' he recalled in his memoirs. 'The Liberals in general and Jeremy in particular were the subject of jokes in every pub and club in the land.' When a Tory MP embarrassed Steel's assistant Andrew Gifford with such a joke, Steel demonstrated his consideration for staff by demanding an immediate apology. It also impacted on his family, both Graeme and, later, his foster child Billy being taunted in the playground about their father's association with Thorpe.

When the Liberal candidate lost his deposit at a March
by-election in Coventry, support for Thorpe among his colleagues,
including Steel, began to ebb away. The Liberal leader tried to stall
by offering to submit himself for re-election following the 1976
Assembly (under a new electoral system then being developed),
but it was too late. Steel privately told Thorpe to quit, reasoning
that 'the lifeblood was ebbing from the entire party because of this
increasing mess. I told him that in the interests of both the party
and himself he ought now to resign the leadership.' But Thorpe
'simply refused, saying he was not going to be brought down
by a lot of panicky colleagues'. Meanwhile Pardoe and Steel – by
this point Thorpe's two most likely successors – agreed to avoid
a divisive leadership election by inviting Jo Grimond back as
interim guardian of the Liberal flame. Grimond was not exactly
keen, memorably protesting to Steel that he could not even 'read
a teleprompter, which is what gives my broadcasts that air of
unmistakeable sincerity'.

Thorpe, however, limped on for another couple of months
until two newspaper stories made his position untenable. First,
Peter Bessell spilled the beans to the *Daily Mail* ('I TOLD LIES TO
PROTECT THORPE'), and second, the *Sunday Times* published letters
from Thorpe to Scott (one of which included the memorable sign-
off 'Bunnies can (and will) go to France'). A meeting of Liberal
MPs endorsed Grimond as interim leader, and Steel arranged to
see Thorpe on the morning of Monday 10 May at the House of
Commons. That weekend Thorpe stayed with Clement Freud, one
of the last Liberal MPs to remain loyal, and Steel (acting Chief
Whip in Alan Beith's absence) joined them after catching the
sleeper south. In 'a tired and dejected atmosphere' they discussed
a draft resignation letter, which was later issued to the press. In it,
Thorpe petulantly reminded the party it had passed a unanimous
vote of confidence in him as leader with a view to holding an election in the autumn. There was also a swipe at the press ('a sustained
witch hunt') and a parliamentary colleague (who had 'taken to the
air publicly to challenge my credibility'), but despite the letter's

general tenor, it ended 'Yours affectionately, Jeremy'. Steel's generous reply ended with the same, undoubtedly forced, salutation.

The resignation, as Matt Cole has written, split the Liberal Party
at every level:

> many MPs, candidates and activists regarded Thorpe's departure as
> a coup in which disloyal colleagues had fallen for a homophobic
> conspiracy promoted by the Tory press; others believed that Thorpe
> himself had betrayed the party and that his resignation was vital to
> its survival.

In public, Steel had at first been loyal, then measured and regret-
ful, although in private he was apparently 'incandescent', telling
the philanthropist Jack Hayward, a friend of Thorpe's, that he had
'known this man a long time and it's only just become apparent
that there are two characters'.[29]

But in spite of the opportunity a swift Thorpe resignation would
have offered Steel's own career, he had kept quiet for almost five
years. As the revelations continued, however, particularly those
relating to inappropriate use of Liberal Party funds, his opinion
understandably hardened. And, having understood that Thorpe
would resign if the allegations became public, Steel was genuinely
appalled when he tried to hang on. The stress must also have been
acute. 'When he [Steel] came into my room I thought he was going
to burst into tears,' recalled George Thomas on being informed
that Thorpe had resigned. 'He was clearly upset and … said that as
Speaker I had the right to know, but he asked me to keep it secret
because as yet not all Liberal Members of Parliament had been
told.' Thomas concurred, and 'indiscreetly' added his hope that
Steel would become Thorpe's successor. 'A dedicated Christian,' he
noted approvingly, 'his radicalism had revealed itself over the years.'

---

29 As this book went to press, writer Michael Bloch's authorised biography of
    Jeremy Thorpe remained unpublished, as did Emlyn Hooson's account of
    the affair.

Conveniently, a new system for electing the Liberal leader was almost in place, subject to approval by a Special Assembly on 12 June. Under new rules devised by Cyril Smith, a specified number of Liberal MPs were required to nominate candidates, who would then be put to the whole party membership, with votes cast by constituency associations based on the strength of Liberal support at the most recent general election. Thorpe had hoped this appeal to the grassroots would save his leadership; now it presented Steel with an opportunity, although ironically he and Emlyn Hooson had been opposed to giving ordinary party members a say. 'The extension of the franchise beyond the MPs', Steel later admitted, 'meant that I could not assume that I was heir-apparent.'

The Liberals, noted *The Times* the day after Thorpe's resignation, now required a 'long haul'.

> That is a young man's task. There are two who are the natural front-runners: Mr Steel and Mr Pardoe. Both have strong qualities. Mr Pardoe has the drive and zest specially needed to lead a smaller party. He would probably be better equipped to rouse the enthusiasm of his followers. But the Liberals need more than that. At a time of great uncertainty in British affairs they need a leader who can provide a sense of purpose and a reason why those who are not Liberals should look to that party.

'Mr Steel', concluded an editorial, 'is the better qualified for that task.' In the event, Liberal MPs did indeed nominate Pardoe and Steel, while Pardoe tried to bounce Steel into nominating Russell Johnston so that he could join the contest. Steel, however, refused to play ball, understandably reluctant to widen the field unnecessarily. 'Russell and many of my fellow-Scots were less than pleased,' he recalled in his memoirs, 'but it was not to be the last time I would have to be hard-hearted in taking a political decision.' Offered the chairmanship of the Race Relations Board that same month, Steel's thinking in turning it down (though it must have been tempting given his record in that area) was clear.

Steel launched his candidacy in Hampstead on 18 May, concluding his speech with Harry S. Truman's famous aphorism, 'if you can't
stand the heat, get out of the kitchen'. 'In these days it has been put to
me bluntly that if you find yourself in the kitchen anyway,' he added,
'you might as well take charge of the menu.' But it was style rather
than substance that set Steel apart from the other chef, John Pardoe.
Their respective manifestos revealed few policy differences, although
both were ambitious in campaign terms: Steel promised eight million
votes at the next election through a 'narrow front' strategy of only
fighting winnable seats, while Pardoe urged a 'broad front', fighting every seat while setting up 'commando' teams in areas hitherto
devoid of Liberal support. As Steel's former press aide Stuart Mole
has observed, Liberals generally liked Pardoe's 'aggressive and abrasive
style, his intellectual dynamism and his clear analysis of the party's
future'. 'If Pardoe appealed to the heart, excited by his rumbustious
claim to be "an effective bastard",' explained Mole, 'Steel's appeal was
to the head: his solid record, his clear ability as a publicist, his shrewd
toughness, his calm pragmatism and his obvious electoral appeal,
through television in particular, to a wider electorate.'

Steel's campaign team consisted of the MPs Clement Freud and
Stephen Ross, and aides Archy Kirkwood and Andrew Gifford.
Their implicit aim was to win over the 'silent majority' of Liberal
Party members. Early support also came from the influential *Times*
columnist Bernard Levin, who reckoned Steel had the 'smack of
political originality about him'. The contest, noted *The Economist*,
'at least brings it [the Liberal Party] useful publicity – not something
it gets much of between general elections'. Hustings around the
country were often well attended, with a few hundred enthusiasts
genuinely interested in what Messrs Steel and Pardoe had to say.
The latter's manifesto was the more utopian of the two ('Without
a realistic hope of power, the Liberal Party will become a political
eunuch'), while Steel's cautioned that the

role of the Liberal party should not be that of a shadow government
with a detailed policy on every single issue of the day, ready and

waiting in the wings for a shift in electoral opinion to sweep us into power. That is the role of Her Majesty's opposition and we are nowhere near that position yet. Our task is a very different one. It is to spell out a clear vision of the society we want to achieve – to provide long-term goals to a people weary of the politics of pragmatism, expediency and compromise.

This emphasis on style rather than substance inevitably made the contest highly personal. Pardoe played on Steel's ecumenical political contacts and love of the high life, telling Liberals 'he's too fond of breakfast with Roy Jenkins' (who hoped Steel would win, 'not only out of friendship and respect', but because he believed it was 'very much in the interests of the country'), or 'he's never out of a dinner jacket', while Steel gave as good as he got, implying to journalists that his rival wore a toupee. This remark was deliberately chosen to provoke Pardoe into going 'over the top', thus demonstrating his unsuitability for a leadership role.

Pardoe duly obliged, provoking a 'blazing row' with Steel in the Liberal whips' office and telling journalists the campaign was 'descending into the sewer'. Cyril Smith, meanwhile, denigrated Steel as a feeble politician who 'couldn't make a bang with a firework in both hands'. Memorably, Judy Steel hit upon the idea of quoting from A. A. Milne's *The House at Pooh Corner*. Alluding to Pardoe, Steel described the scene in which Tigger gets muddled up in a fight with a tablecloth before poking out his head and asking, 'Have I won?' While all of this made good copy for the newspapers, the contest was, as Chris Cook has observed, 'not terribly dignified'.

Pardoe admits 'it was a dreadful experience.' He recalls:

I certainly wished *after* it had happened that it hadn't. It caused me – as much as any other factor – to eventually lose my seat in North Cornwall [in 1979]. I didn't come out of it at all well. Having discovered that David had a much higher profile than me (largely because of the Abortion Bill) early on in the campaign, I'd had to

work harder and that was dangerous because I got caught saying
things I shouldn't have been saying.

Steel was clearly the establishment choice, talked up by the press
and considered by the party's rank and file as the safer pair of
hands, particularly in light of Pardoe's more pugnacious statements. Despite finding him 'rather remote' and 'somewhat
arrogant', even the *Radical Bulletin* backed Steel, as (it was generally understood) did Jo Grimond, who thought the contest might
become 'a competition as to who is the bigger bastard'.[30] Thus
the declaration on 7 July, following what Steel called a 'tedious'
count at Poplar Civic Hall, was not much of a surprise. Steel won
the constituency association votes by 12,541 to Pardoe's 7,032, a
decisive margin of victory and a personal triumph for Steel, who
was still only thirty-eight. Among MPs, Steel was supported by
Geraint Howells, Emlyn Hooson, Stephen Ross, Clement Freud
and Alan Beith; Pardoe by Richard Wainwright, David Penhaligon,
Cyril Smith and Russell Johnston (it is not known how Thorpe and
Grimond voted, although it seems likely at least the latter backed
Steel). Significantly, Steel was the first leader of a UK political party
to enjoy such a mandate from his party membership. 'Now that
the election is over,' said Jeremy Thorpe in a post-election message,
'I ask every Liberal to give David their loyalty and enthusiasm.' 'I
know', he added bitterly, 'he will need both.'

After the declaration Steel and his wife Judy retired to Emlyn
Hooson's chambers for celebratory champagne. 'My life was changing,' she later reflected, 'and would do so in more ways than that
of being a party leader's wife.' Indeed, a few days later a 'troubled
teenager' called Billy turned up at Cherrydene. Judy agreed to
foster him for the summer of 1976 and when he asked to stay on

---

30 Grimond's full quote (carried in the *Scotsman*) was: 'In a competition to
    see who is the bigger bastard, I should be hard put to give a ruling. I won't
    damage their reputations by saying they are nice … but it is said that both
    are reasonable husbands, passable fathers and kind to animals.'

permanently, she 'thought of the uncertainties of his life so far, of how blessed my own life had been, and those of my children, and felt that there should be room in my family for another child'.

But when she put the idea to Steel he was 'unhappy', understandably worried about the effect on his biological son Graeme, who would be displaced as the eldest child. Social workers doubted Judy's ability to cope on her own during her husband's absences, which, with him now party leader, were about to increase – doubts shared by Steel. 'On the other hand,' he reflected in his memoirs, 'surely we, whose lives had been so lucky, should be prepared to share?' 'As a family, we were moving into uncharted waters,' remembered Judy, 'with David's higher public profile and the greater demands of the party.'

In the end, Steel gave in, perhaps conscious of the need to allow Judy autonomy over this aspect of their lives. Billy remained fostered between the ages of thirteen and sixteen, at which point he was released from compulsory care and took the family name (although he remained close to his real mother), staying with his now adoptive parents for another seven years. But, as Judy frankly admitted in her book, 'everyone was right who foresaw the effect it would have on Graeme.' 'It is something for which I cannot forgive myself,' she added, 'my insensitivity to the needs of my firstborn son, and it was to cause much estrangement between us over the years before the wounds were healed.'

The Times, meanwhile, judged Steel to be 'the best leader that the Liberal Party could have chosen because of all those who ran or sought to run he is the one with the broadest appeal in the country', while presciently predicting that Liberals could only 'break out of their present confined position' via the 'creation of a coalition' or a 'split in the Labour Party'. 'Neither eventuality could be brought about by the Liberals alone,' continued *The Times*. 'They would have to take what opportunity was presented to them, which would depend on both instances on their capacity to cooperate with others. Mr Steel is undoubtedly the best qualified in that respect.'

Geoffrey Smith, the newspaper's political editor, also contrib-
uted a perceptive sketch of the new Liberal leader:

> The public impression of David Steel is of a cool, detached and
> eminently sensible politician. The private impression of David
> Steel is of a cool, detached and eminently sensible politician. But
> the public and private personalities of a politician never coincide
> exactly. As a man David Steel has both a greater sense of fun and
> a greater strength of feeling than one might suppose from those
> controlled features on television. As a politician he is harder and
> more calculating than the popular image might suggest. He is a
> political animal through and through. He would not be the new
> leader of the Liberal Party if he were not, because this is not an office
> which has simply been thrust upon him by admiring colleagues. It
> is a post for which he has fought with more deliberation and judge-
> ment than his rivals.

All of that was true, while Smith had touched upon intriguing
aspects of Steel's character. Untypically for a politician, as David
Penhaligon's widow Annette later observed, Steel was 'reserved,
even shy, by nature', someone for whom exuberance did not come
naturally. His clean-cut, son-of-the-manse image did, at least, put
to rest the Thorpe affair, for there was not even a whiff of scandal
in the Steel closet. The leadership campaign had also highlighted a
ruthless side to Steel's character and, for the first time, revealed him
to be a clever infighter. But while the election 'brought to an end
the unhappy final saga of the Thorpe era', as Chris Cook has said,
'it did not change the fundamental problems facing the party.' Steel
reckoned the three-week leadership campaign had done much to
're-establish the party's self-respect after the earlier imbroglio', but
had also opened up some sores. Cyril Smith, for example, initially
refused to serve under the new leader, explaining in his memoirs
that while he found Steel 'an exceptionally agreeable man' he
felt that, like Thorpe, he was essentially a 'drawing room politician,
a smoother-down of ruffled feathers' who lacked the 'killer instinct'

necessary for the Liberal Party to 'drag itself out of its gentle minority status to become a full-blooded and effective political force in this country'. After some persuasion, however, Smith agreed to become Social Security spokesman. Indeed, Steel's ability to win over sceptical parliamentary colleagues would be a consistent strength of his leadership.

The bruised Pardoe ego also needed some soothing balm. As Judy Steel put it, 'To lose any such election is bad enough, but to lose to a man who could hold down the job for twenty-five years must be awful.' 'He had been his own worst enemy,' Steel later mused, 'but I had been less than kind to him.' Pardoe, though, was a bigger man than many assumed, and his subsequent loyalty to not only Steel as leader but also his controversial strategy was often under-appreciated. It also took Steel a while to establish a working relationship with Hugh (later Sir Hugh) Jones at Liberal Party HQ, not least because Steel was wary of the party's justifiable reputation for mismanagement. But Steel, as Jones noted in his memoirs, shared a predilection for 'method and agendas' and the pair soon struck up a rapport.

Jo Grimond, meanwhile, had grown increasingly detached from the party he had once led ('Whenever you try to use it [the Liberal Party],' he told Steel at around this time, 'it breaks in your hands'), toying – as was Mrs Thatcher – with classical economic liberalism, and indeed from his young protégé, to whom he gave 'cautionary advice' about dealing with Labour shortly after his election; Grimond had even cooled on his once forcefully held views on realignment. '[The Liberal Party] must become the radical opposition, like the Scottish National Party in Scotland,' explained Grimond. 'The Labour right has depleted and is not likely to join up with the Liberals as I once hoped.' Nevertheless, he told Hugh Jones the Liberal Party was 'lucky to have David Steel'.

No such doubts appeared to have entered Steel's mind. He told *The Guardian* within weeks of becoming leader that Liberals had to 'start by getting a toe-hold on power which *must* mean some form of coalition', while also using BBC Radio 4's *The World This*

Weekend to warn the party to prepare 'psychologically' for coalition. That Steel continued to use the 'c' word after the events of 1974 was a calculated risk, but then, as Stuart Mole has observed, he had long 'exhibited what for some Liberals was a distressing character defect – he was interested in power'. And given that – according to the journalist Simon Hoggart – the new Liberal leader was 'slightly off-balance within the party' and did not 'entirely share its obsessions and its political style', Steel chose to exercise his authority at once.

When Steel showed the text of his first Assembly speech to one or two intimates they 'paled visibly', although importantly John Pardoe cleared it in advance. Steel thought the speech 'a good one, but far too long', and later confessed to being 'appallingly nervous' before he delivered it. Having spent the summer writing and rewriting the speech at his home in Ettrick Bridge, Steel had rejected moves to tone down the text, arguing that if the coalition issue was not dealt with immediately then it would simply rumble on for years, as it had under Grimond and Thorpe. Clement Freud and Steel's advisers Richard Holme,[31] Archy Kirkwood and William Wallace all urged caution on the eve of the speech, but after initiating a late-night sea-front walk with his aides, Steel decided the crucial passage ought to stay in. Contributing to his nerves would have been reports that the Young Liberals were planning a demonstration from the Assembly floor should the word 'coalition' emanate from Steel's lips. (The heckling duly occurred, with a young David Alton among those holding up signs saying 'NO'.)

The speech began conventionally enough, Steel's clear, resonant tones owing more than a little to hundreds of Kirk sermons imbibed as a child in Africa and Scotland. Although he professed not to

---

31   It was at this point, according to Des Wilson, that Richard Holme 'became an indispensable unpaid aide to David Steel, writing speeches, helping with day to day responses to political events, and undertaking a lot of the "fixing" behind the scenes.' Holme, added Wilson, 'was an enthusiast to the point of fanaticism about politics'.

enjoy platform oratory, the speech demonstrated for the first time an aptitude for precisely that. The argument for a new strategy only built towards the end, with Steel making three central points. First, Liberals had to 'stop behaving like one of the purer sects of the exclusive brethren' and welcome others into their midst; second, the party had to improve its messaging and the 'tortuous nature' of its constitution; third, Steel said the party had to be prepared to 'follow through the logical consequences of our own policies and utterances' as he had no desire to lead little more than a 'nice debating society'. He continued:

> I want the Liberal Party to be the fulcrum and centre of the next election argument – not something peripheral to it. If that is to happen we must not give the impression of being afraid to soil our hands with the responsibilities of sharing power. We must be bold enough to deploy the coalition case positively. We must go all out to attack the other parties for wanting power exclusively to themselves no matter how small a percentage of public support. If people want a more broadly based government they must vote Liberal to get it. And if they vote Liberal we must be ready to help provide it.

'The road I intend to travel may be a bumpy one,' concluded Steel, 'and I recognise therefore the risk that in the course of it we may lose some of the passengers, but I don't mind so long as we arrive at the end of it reasonably intact and ready to achieve our goals.'

When Steel came off the platform and returned to his hotel, he was physically and mentally exhausted. 'The strain and tension of the previous days,' he later recalled, 'and the lengthy delivery of the speech itself had made my back go rigid.' The press was generally enthusiastic, particularly Geoffrey Smith at *The Times*, who gushed that Steel had 'emerged at Llandudno as a leader of the kind that the Liberal Party has not possessed since the war … in stating his position on coalition so firmly he showed that he has the mettle to meet a revolt directly and without compromise – and to win.'

Paddy Ashdown recalled being 'electrified' by the speech, in his view one of Steel's very best, 'courageous, cogent, passionate'. But others, such as Jo Grimond, 'listened in vain for [a] radical voice' rather than statements of strategic intent. 'What Steel has to do now is to forge a new libertarian radicalism,' he urged, 'and get it past the party to the public at large.' Thus Steel's maiden speech as Liberal leader neatly encapsulated both his strengths and his weaknesses. Facing the choice between what Ashdown called 'purity and power', Steel was courageous enough to tell his party precisely which he intended to choose, while the absence of any cogent restatement of Liberal philosophy betrayed his essential lack of interest in such abstract concerns.

It can be seen as a fairly accurate statement of Steel's political beliefs, a personal manifesto which he would constantly reference, particularly under pressure at subsequent Assemblies, in the years ahead. When Steel finally sat down, a four-minute ovation greeted his maiden speech as Liberal leader. But several observers noted that this was misleading. Far from indicating that Steel had won the party over to his strategy, rather it demonstrated they liked their new leader and, more to the point, they badly wanted him to succeed.

5

PERMANENTLY ON THE
BRINK OF DISASTER

The Liberal–Labour Pact of 1977–8 was the defining period of David Steel's first two years as party leader. History, however, has not been kind to what he has called 'a parliamentary but not government coalition – a unique experiment'. Writing in 1996, Don MacIver said it was 'seen by some as a missed opportunity, by others as simply a misjudgement, but by few as a triumph'. Similarly the Liberal Party's most perceptive historian, David Dutton, concluded that its 'achievements were limited and its impact upon the Liberal Party of questionable value'.

The Lib–Lab Pact, as it became known, was a product of the Labour's slender parliamentary majority. In November 1976, the government of James Callaghan (who had succeeded Harold Wilson in April) lost by-elections in Workington and Walsall North and, therefore, its majority. It was living on borrowed time. 'Has Callaghan talked to you yet?' Edward Heath asked Steel following a remembrance ceremony at the Cenotaph. 'No,' replied Steel, 'why should he?' 'He will,' was Heath's terse response.

Spotting an opportunity, Steel put forward an eight-point 'programme of national recovery'. 'What Mr Steel would like is a public change of attitude by the government on the principle of co-operation with other parties,' reported *The Economist*. Proportional representation (PR) for direct elections to the European Parliament, industrial democracy, progress on devolution and a halt to nationalisation were floated, all of which later formed the basis of the Lib–Lab Pact.

Devolution was, however, a running sore, and one that severely tested Labour's strength in the House. When MPs debated a guillotine motion on the Scotland and Wales Bill – which proposed the creation of devolved assemblies in Edinburgh and Cardiff – Steel argued that the government's use of the guillotine was 'an attempt to restrict discussion of individual parts of the Bill'. As 'an opposition party whose objective is to support, amend and improve the Bill', he added, Liberals could not 'be expected to go into the Lobby to support an enforced timetable, and we will not'.

When it came to a vote, the government lost and thus the Scotland and Wales Bill fell. Although Steel had not anticipated the political consequences, the government had little choice but to initiate cross-party talks in order to find a way forward. The Conservatives (having recently become anti-devolution) refused to take part, leaving the Liberals with an opportunity to begin formal talks alone, something Steel came to regard 'as the embryonic stages of the Lib/Lab pact'. 'To put it crudely,' as he later wrote in the *Sunday Times*, 'it proved necessary to kick them [Labour] in the teeth before extending the hand of friendship.'

During one of these meetings on devolution, the Prime Minister told Steel he needed at least eighteen months to sort out the economy, a 'crucial length of time [which] stuck firmly in Steel's mind'. In March, with Labour left-wingers threatening to abstain and force the defeat of a white paper on public expenditure, the government tried to dodge the revolt by withdrawing the resolution at the end of the debate. Mrs Thatcher responded by tabling a motion of no confidence in the government and, with the SNP riding high in the polls and the Liberals still reeling from the Thorpe affair, Callaghan and Steel – in short – needed each other. 'We weren't in a strong position to fight an election,' recalls Steel. 'I was very new as leader and we had the whole Thorpe business hanging over us; we simply weren't in the condition to fight an election. It would have been torture.'

Following an initial approach from the Liberal MP for Rochdale, Cyril Smith, to the Prime Minister in February 1977, Steel wrote to the Labour whip Cledwyn Hughes about 'the wider scene' on an 'informal and friendly basis'. Hughes then relayed the Liberal leader's thoughts to the Prime Minister:

As a new leader and a young man he felt it would be impertinent for him to approach you and he was glad, therefore, to have the opportunity of giving me these views ... he said that the postponement of an election would not help the Liberals. They might just as well have an election now. This is the view of the Parliamentary Liberal Party. They will vote against us tonight and should there be a Motion of Confidence on Monday, they will vote against us then, in the absence of a broad understanding of our forward policies. They would like to be in a position to say publicly that they had, as a party, been able to influence government policy; this would enable them to defend themselves against Tory attacks in the country.

Personally he does not relish the idea of a Tory victory. He much prefers your leadership and does not think Mrs Thatcher could cope with our current difficulties. He thinks we [Labour] would have a chance of winning an election in late 1978 or 1979.

But the short point, as he puts it, is that the government cannot expect to 'drag the Liberals along' without any consultation. He said, however, that he fully appreciates your difficulties in the sense of appearing to make any concessions.

I contented myself with saying that if there were to be an election now, the Liberals would be dealt a savage blow and that there could be a Tory government with an overall majority. He did not disagree.

Hughes concluded with the impression that the government could rely on the Liberals 'for a good deal of support if they were consulted on broad policy issues and on legislation'. 'I think this must mean that you would have to see him [Steel] from time to time,' Hughes told Callaghan. 'You would not be creating a precedent, because

Harold Wilson saw Jeremy Thorpe frequently. You will obviously need to consider the implications of this, as they would want some "quid pro quo".'[32]

In another conversation, Steel tried to convince Hughes that the Liberals were ready for an election. Given that opinion polls suggested the Liberals would, as Tony Benn wrote in his diary, 'be massacred in an election', this was clearly a bluff. Steel later admitted to the journalist Hugo Young that his party would have lost 'some seats', although this had not been the main consideration. Rather it was the Conservatives emerging as the largest party and the SNP increasing their support in Scotland, thus making the Liberals 'generally more irrelevant'.[33]

When the press began to ask Steel what the Liberals planned to do in the no-confidence vote, he issued a statement saying that

> either the government now proceeds on the basis of agreed measures in the national interest for the next two years, in which case we would be willing to consider supporting such a programme, or else we have a general election … the one thing we cannot do is stagger on like last night with a lame-duck Labour programme which has neither public nor parliamentary support. The political decision as to which course to take, therefore, rests squarely with the Prime Minister and the Labour Party.

To prove he was serious, Steel later issued another statement, saying that if Labour did not 'respond [to] and acknowledge' this new political reality then thirteen Liberal votes would be cast against the government on Wednesday evening. This firmer wording had the desired effect, leading Saturday's lunchtime news bulletins and receiving widespread coverage in the Sunday papers.

At this stage, judged the authors of an early book on these events,

---

32   James Callaghan Papers Box 113, Cledwyn Hughes to James Callaghan, 17 March 1977.
33   Hugo Young Papers HJSY/2/4, notes dated 25 March 1977.

Steel had decided that he wanted a pact with Callaghan, that he wanted consultations between his party and the government about all the details of the legislative programme, and he was going to get it. The other twelve Liberal MPs would have to be jollied, pushed along and almost forced if necessary to provide the votes which would make the Pact possible. So over the weekend he spent a long time phoning his colleagues and consulting them.

Jo Grimond, whom Steel spoke to that weekend, had the opposite impression, recalling in his memoirs that at this point his leader was 'inclined to vote against the government and so was I'. Grimond did not share his colleagues' gloomy prognosis about an early election, reckoning that Steel would come across well on television and fight a good campaign.

On Sunday Steel was interviewed by the Prime Minister's son-in-law, Peter Jay, for ITV's *Weekend World*, although he did not give much away. Indeed, when Jay suggested that 'having got the government into a position where it would have to pay heed to Liberal demands, there were very few worthwhile demands for them to make,' Steel's reply was thin and unconvincing. He cited legislation like the Local Authorities (Works) Bill and a forthcoming measure on water industrial reorganisation, which stood little chance of getting through in any case. As Alistair Michie and Simon Hoggart later wrote, this exchange was 'the firmest, clear sign that the Pact was going to bring the Liberals some awfully dreary political gains'.

An important upshot of Steel's television appearance, however, was a phone call from the Transport Secretary, Bill Rodgers, who had worked with Steel during the 1975 referendum on EEC membership. 'He seemed to want an overall agreement that could be sustained until the autumn of 1978,' recalled Rodgers in his memoirs, 'and a formal liaison committee between the two parties.' Rodgers thought Steel's conditions specific but reasonable, and relayed them in a phone call to Callaghan (who was at Chequers) at 9 p.m. Again Steel, who felt he could speak 'freely and frankly' with

Rodgers, had played the election card, reasoning that he did not 'want an election but his honour was at stake and he could not be seen to duck one'. He also indicated there were various points on which the government had to move, asking for (at the very least) a 'pay roll' vote (i.e. every Labour MP with a government position) in favour of elections to the European Parliament on the basis of PR, as well as progress on similar electoral reform for the devolved assemblies in Scotland and Wales.

Steel was also clear minded on the duration of any deal: 'He did not wish just to save the government on Wednesday but to stabilise the position for eighteen months, the time needed to put the country right,' recounted Rodgers. 'There had to be a liaison committee on a regular basis to underlie that commitment.' Rodgers and Callaghan discussed this but concluded it was 'unacceptable', fearing that 'a formal liaison committee would look too [much] like a coalition'. And there the future of the government rested, with the Prime Minister due to meet Steel at 6 p.m. the following day.

'This is a decisive week,' wrote Bernard Donoughue, the head of Downing Street's Policy Unit, in his diary entry for 21 March. 'We have no majority in the Commons. *All* the opposition parties say that they will vote against us. So we will lose unless we get some kind of coalition/arrangement.' That evening Callaghan saw Steel alone following his regular haircut at Simpson's on the Strand. 'The meeting was friendly,' judged his biographer Kenneth Morgan. 'Callaghan, much the older man, was warm, almost paternal, towards the boyish Liberal leader.'

Steel told the avuncular Callaghan there was no point 'discussing immediate policy issues' as his party was not interested in a 'one-night stand'. Callaghan agreed, adding that he would 'prefer to go to the country rather than proceed on that basis'. On specific legislation, he warned Steel that his government 'could not undertake to remove from every Bill everything that the Liberals did not like and if that was not accepted their relationship would break down straight away'.

Callaghan said 'he was not ruling out an arrangement' but asked frankly: 'Can you deliver?' Steel joked that 'his colleagues were all behaving very well at the moment' and that they 'would rather see themselves supporting the present government than precipitating a Tory landslide'. Steel expressed his desire for 'two pieces of machinery, (a) publicly acknowledged policy meetings between ministers and Liberal spokesmen ... and (b) regular meetings between party managers about House of Commons business'. Concluding the conversation, Steel stressed once again the need for 'firmer guarantees' on PR for direct elections and the devolved assemblies. 'The Prime Minister said that he certainly could not deliver these before Wednesday ... And if the goal was PR for direct elections, then a lot of work was needed on his party.'

The meeting lasted an hour and a quarter. Bernard Donoughue, who had been sitting in the anteroom with Tom McCaffrey and Roger Scott from Callaghan's private office, spoke to Steel when he emerged at 7.15 p.m. 'He seemed bewildered,' he recalled. 'He took me by the arm and told me to come and see him tomorrow. He obviously was not satisfied with the talks. He wanted another go.' Callaghan was similarly gloomy, telling Donoughue that while the Liberal leader had been 'rational and realistic', he had found the meeting 'very unpromising', having failed to 'get hold of anything'.

The following morning Tom McNally, Callaghan's political secretary, and Donoughue pushed the case for co-operation with the Liberals while Steel consulted his colleagues. Usefully, Liberal HQ had compiled a summary of party opinion that was generally supportive. Although Liberals in the country were 'not anxious for a general election', there was 'almost unanimous and very strong support for the way in which David has handled the situation so far'.[34]

Steel then drafted a letter saying that the 'Liberal Party will be prepared to consider sustaining the government in its pursuit of

---

34   Liberal Party Papers LIBERAL/19/2, undated minute.

national recovery',[35] but only if a series of demands relating to PR, devolution and other matters were agreed in advance. 'To anyone reading them cold, they must have appeared a thin and gruel-like list,' judged Michie and Hoggart, 'considering they were supposed to save the life of the government and possibly rescue the Labour Party from years of defeat.' In short, they added, 'it reflected the fact that Steel was far more concerned with the general idea of a pact and the idea of consultations than he was in any policies which it might bring about.' Indeed, this was the general thrust of Steel's approach, during both the Lib–Lab Pact and the later Alliance between the Liberals and the Social Democratic Party.

But what looked weak to some was still too strong for the Prime Minister. When Ken Stowe, the Prime Minister's private secretary, showed Steel's letter to Callaghan, he threw it on a coffee table and said, 'Well, I cannot take that.' 'The rest of us agreed it was not a good negotiating letter,' recalled Donoughue. 'The PM was behaving as if that meant the end of it.' McNally and Stowe then redrafted the letter to make it more acceptable to the government, with which the Liberals concurred, 'except for PR on direct elections to Europe and on elections to the Scottish Assembly'.

For the young leader of a small third party, Steel acquitted himself well. Seeing Callaghan again that evening, he stressed that 'a proportional system for direct elections was really the *only* sticking point'. A formal minute recorded his argument thus:

> The problem was that he must sell this arrangement to his Party in the country, and he could not do so without something on this ... If an agreement was reached, however, then there had to be something specific in the verbiage, and direct elections was where he was looking for it. He pointed out, however, that he was only asking the government to 'commend' a proportional system for direct

---

35   National Archives PREM 16/1399, David Steel to James Callaghan, 21 March 1977.

elections, and on a free vote there was no guarantee that their recommendation would secure the legislation in the House on this.

Steel's exasperation was justified; it was not much, in the circumstances, to ask of a government without a majority, although it also demonstrated that he was not negotiating particularly hard. From his initial demand for a whipped 'pay roll' vote on PR for direct elections, now all Steel required was a commendation from the government.[36]

On this point, however, the talks reached an impasse. 'We are in danger of coming unstuck on one point, direct elections,' an anxious Steel told Bill Rodgers. 'Everything else is negotiable but not this.' When Steel met Callaghan for a third time (this time accompanied by John Pardoe), however, a deal with four main elements gradually took shape: a consultative committee (to be chaired by Michael Foot) to which any major departmental Bill would be referred; regular meetings between the Chancellor, Denis Healey, and Pardoe; rapid progress on the Scotland and Wales Bill; and, of course, PR for direct elections to the European Parliament. On the last point, the government finally came round to Steel's suggestion that it commit to a 'free vote' on regional list PR. Callaghan emphasised that he could not promise what he could not deliver, and although Steel understood that, he also 'accepted an important addition – his [Callaghan's] private assurances that when the time came he would back PR himself'.

Importantly, Pardoe had to leave this meeting early to take part in a television broadcast in which he cast doubt on the likelihood of an agreement. At that point things were going badly, so Pardoe's gloomy prognosis had been sincere, but on returning to the meeting and learning what Steel had agreed to, he recalls being 'absolutely aghast'. As he later told the writer and former Labour MP Phillip Whitehead:

---

36   PREM 16/1399, minute dated 22 March 1977.

Steel was in his room and I said, 'What happened?' He said, 'Oh, we signed.' I said, 'You what? You mean he conceded on PR?' – 'Well, not exactly, John, but he's done the best he can and really you mustn't expect people to do more than they can deliver.' David was determined to do a deal at all costs.

Pardoe still maintains, as do others, that Steel had made a 'terrible mistake'.

Labour would have given more, I'm absolutely certain Labour would have given more. We had to get an absolute commitment from them [the government] and that they'd whip it. The idea that ministers would do their best, give a lead and so on, that was guff; it wasn't going to happen. We lost out on that. Even if it hadn't worked it would have taken Labour down the right road.

The Liberal historian David Dutton has argued that it 'could not be claimed that Steel had driven a hard bargain'. Indeed, some Liberals doubted their leader's ability to push Callaghan hard enough, a view shared by some Labour figures. David Owen, for example, thought the free vote element of the Pact had been 'incredibly weak', writing in his memoirs that he was 'astonished' the Liberals – or rather Steel – had agreed to it so willingly. He was certain the Cabinet would have fallen into line on PR, a view shared by Tom McNally. 'By leaving it to a free vote everyone knew it would be lost,' recalls McNally. 'If there was a thing he [Steel] could have planned better or played more hardball on that was probably it.'

Indeed, the government had already conceded PR for elections to the European Parliament in Northern Ireland, treating the province as a single constituency using the Single Transferable Vote method as a quid pro quo for agreeing to review Northern Irish representation at Westminster.[37] Owen believes it is possible Callaghan convinced Steel that a free vote would be more likely

---

37   Callaghan Papers Box 113, Roy Mason to James Callaghan, 23 March 1977.

to deliver the correct outcome than a three-line whip. 'Jim might have implied it was easier to get it through that way,' he recalls. 'Callaghan could have told David: "Tie me down and you actually reduce my strength."' As Owen wrote in his memoirs, Steel 'allowed himself to be persuaded that Jim could not deliver a firm commitment to proportional representation and he signed up for the watered-down version that was presented to us in Cabinet'. Steel's aide Archy Kirkwood, however, reckons his boss worked 'tirelessly' to secure PR for direct elections. 'No one could say that it wasn't pushed as far as it could have been within the context of that time,' he says. 'David couldn't have done more.'

On the day of the no-confidence motion, however, no one dwelled on this point for long. Cabinet, meeting in emergency session, backed the plan by twenty votes to four. Michael Foot, according to Tony Benn's diary, looked pale and drawn, but Callaghan acquitted himself well, arguing that there was no alternative to an agreement with the Liberals. Denis Healey agreed, remarking that a deal with 'Nats and nutters' was the only other option. Another source remembered the terms being met with 'some incredulity by the Cabinet', the Labour Party having 'simply undertaken to do what it had anyway intended to do and desist from what it could not do'.

In the House, the speeches of Steel and Callaghan 'were punctuated by Tory jeers', but, as the Prime Minister recalled, 'they were cries of rage and frustration which we could easily withstand, and I could not help recalling the old saying that the best rejoinder is a majority.' Bernard Donoughue reckoned Steel had been 'quite good in the circumstances', arguing that the Pact would usher in 'a period of stability' and had therefore been forged in 'the national interest'. When it came to a division, the government survived by 322–298. The political crisis, unlike the economic one, was over.

Mrs Thatcher, however, was furious. Judy Steel believed she 'never forgave David for denying her an election in 1977', an election she believed her party could have won. 'Instead of having a government with steel in its backbone,' she said of the agreement, 'we have one with Steel in its pocket.' The Tory-leaning press was also outraged. The *Daily Telegraph* denounced a 'Liberal act of appeasement', while *The Sun* depicted the Prime Minister as a cat who had swallowed the Liberal mouse whole. But Steel had good reason to be content, with even the otherwise cynical Michie and Hoggart conceding that 'Steel had got what he really wanted.'

He had got the consultative committee, his own meetings with Callaghan, and the Liberal Party locked into the whole process of government. It was the first stage towards his dream of a Liberal Party first in coalition, then in power. Labour MPs might scoff at the deal, Liberals might fret and nag about the terms, but Steel had placed himself right on the spot he had aimed for.

On 24 March Steel wrote to Liberal Party candidates in obvious high spirits:

Admire the photos of the Liberal MPs in the *Daily Mail!* When did photographs of all the MPs last appear on the front page of a popular daily? ... You will have a difficult time. You will have resignations in your constituency ... Don't be defensive. Be aggressive. Go all out to detail the bridling of socialism. Forget the textual analysis of the Agreement. It's what we make of it that matters...[38]

Steel echoed some of these sentiments at a press conference the same day, telling reporters it mattered 'what we actually make of it rather than the wording itself'. He continued:

Mrs Thatcher has been talking about socialism being sustained by Liberal MPs and of course the Conservative propaganda machine will be going into full blast ... But the truth is that socialism is the one thing this country is not now going to get as long as this

---

38 LIBERAL/2/32, David Steel to Liberal candidates, 24 March 1977.

agreement lasts, and this is the significance – I believe – to the wider public of the agreement to which we have come.[39]

Steel was correct, but only up to a point. The real check on 'socialism' had been the International Monetary Fund loan of 1976 (which compelled the UK to cut spending), but it was true that the bogeyman of the left, Tony Benn, had been neutered by the agreement.

As if in the first flush of a new political romance, at first the Pact went swimmingly. On 28 March Steel unveiled his 'Shadow Administration', and the first consultative committee meeting took place two days later 'in a small drab conference room just below the Commons chamber'. Speaking privately to the journalist Hugo Young, Steel agreed the meeting had gone 'very well indeed', being both 'cordial' and 'helpful', although he also confessed that some 'perils' were 'already showing themselves'. When the draft of a Liberal campaign letter for the Birmingham Stechford by-election – in which the Liberal leader boasted of being 'in control' of the government – ended up in the *Daily Mail*, a frantic Steel had to call Downing Street in order to assure them the offending phrase had been removed from the final document.

'The most difficult part will be the first few weeks,' Steel told Young. 'The early tests and evidences of the collaboration must be good ones from [the] Lib[eral]s' viewpoint. The longer it goes on, the easier it becomes to disagree with Labour or be seen to have had some Lib[eral] plans rejected.' More widely, Steel realised the Pact's success depended upon the economy.

> If it goes well, Lib[eral]s can claim some unmerited responsibility. Moreover, Labour will find it hard to disengage from the Lib[eral]s at an election: [it will be] hard to attack the alliance if it has delivered some of the goods. Economic failure will mean that the plot has not worked. But it will not leave the Lib[eral]s any worse off than they

39   STV Archive BL28359.

are always likely to have been. They live permanently on the brink of disaster. They lost half their seats in 1970 without hav[ing] had any collaboration, and with clean hands.

For a party 'permanently on the brink of disaster', this clearly demonstrated that Steel had a limited – as he saw it realistic – expectation of what the Pact could achieve for his party. He also had in mind the long-cherished aim of realignment, hoping that moderate Labour voters might see voting Liberal 'as the newly respectable way of getting the Tory out', while leftish Tories would 'be similarly attracted: deeming Thatcherism to be dangerous and unpalatable'. In short, as Steel told Hugo Young, 'the famous social democratic alliance is now appearing before our very eyes.'[40]

Trouble, however, was not long in coming. The Birmingham Stechford by-election had been played out against the backdrop of the Pact negotiations and for most of the campaign the Liberal candidate, Graham Gopsill, had argued *against* Labour and *for* a general election. But when the Pact was agreed a week before polling day, he was forced into an abrupt U-turn, suddenly becoming pro-Labour and anti-general election. On 31 March, Gopsill polled 8 per cent of the vote, less than the far-right National Front.

Steel met the Prime Minister on polling day to discuss Budget resolutions, which, crucially, had not formed part of the agreement. Pardoe had informed the Chancellor (who sometimes felt Pardoe was 'simply Denis Healey with no redeeming features') that Liberals would not support a 5.5 per cent increase in petrol tax. Steel suggested ditching that specific resolution but the Prime Minister was unwilling to forgo £300 million of revenue. In turn, Callaghan suggested the Liberals abstain, something Steel rejected as it 'would amount to a double somersault'.[41] The Prime Minister was unflinching, basically telling Steel to, in Bernard Donoughue's words, 'go away and do something about it'. A few days later

---

40 HJSY/2/4, notes dated 25 March 1976.
41 PREM 16/1399, minute dated 31 March 1977.

Callaghan warned Steel that if Liberals voted against it would amount to a vote of no confidence.

The Liberals backed down and abstained, although after a 'great deal of haggling' the increase was dropped at the Bill's committee stage on 9 May. 'The reduction took place on 5 August', Steel later noted, 'and was the first fruit of the Lib–Lab agreement to benefit the pocket of the man in the street.' A frustrated Donoughue, however, reckoned the Liberals were 'flashing' their 'new-found virility'. 'Having power at last after so many years,' he wrote in his diary, 'they want to unzip and show it off every other day.'

Devolution was another sticking point, even more so given its prominence in the text of the agreement. When the Liberals raised PR for the devolved assemblies, the future Labour leader John Smith, who had responsibility for devolution policy, bluntly said there '[i]s no point in discussing the intellectual or political merits of the case: the Scottish Executive of the Labour Party w[ill] not have it', and that was that.

Steel obviously could not hope to conduct all policy discussions personally, and when he detected 'rumblings' that his colleagues were 'not always very effective or well briefed in these discussions' ('My dear,' the Liberal Lady Seear used to tell Bob Maclennan in meetings at the Department of Prices and Consumer Protection, 'I think everything you're doing is simply wonderful') the Liberal leader's caustic wit revealed itself:

> While I have encouraged the inclusion of our own outside experts, there should not be too many at any meeting, and they should be expert … it is no use taking along garrulous and vague Liberals on the humanitarian principle that you wish them to feel 'involved'. These are not group therapy sessions, but hard political negotiations.

Direct elections to the European Parliament quickly emerged as the hardest point to negotiate, what Steel called 'a slow fuse which would smoulder through to the autumn threatening to blow up the agreement'. At a meeting on 21 April the Prime Minister said he 'regarded himself as having a personal commitment to Mr Steel to use his best endeavours to persuade the Cabinet to propose a proportional representation system: if that then proved to be unacceptable to the House, then so be it'. Steel said he 'wholly agreed with the Prime Minister's understanding of the position', while both men agreed their respective mailbags 'showed quite clearly that their supporters in the country at large were in favour of the agreement'. Local government elections in May told a different story, however, with the Liberals losing three quarters of their county councillors.

Direct elections came up again on 3 May, with Callaghan warning Steel that his government 'was divided about the date, the method and the principle. He had put the Liberal position very strongly but saw little chance of securing Cabinet support for it.' In turn, Steel warned that his party's 'attachment to a proportional system for direct elections was so strong that, if they did not get it, they could not go on with the agreement with the government in the next session'. Although Steel disagreed with his colleagues on this point, 'he could not go on without party backing.'[42]

Liberal colleagues, however, were not alone in detecting a certain lack of resolve on this point. Lunching with Steel a few days later, Roy Jenkins, by now in Brussels as President of the European Commission, attempted 'to stiffen [him] in his pressure on the government about direct elections'. Although Jenkins found Steel agreeable, he 'certainly needed this stiffening'.

At a Liberal Shadow Administration meeting on 15 June there were calls to take a 'firm line' on PR for direct elections,[43] while Steel also used a television interview to fire a warning shot across Labour's bow. He was clearly nervous; Bernard Donoughue wrote that Steel was 'very unhappy with the way things are going and he wanted me to tell the PM that this time he was serious that the alliance was in peril'. Despite being Callaghan's main policy adviser,

42   PREM 16/1400, minute dated 3 May 1977.
43   STEEL/A/3/1, minute dated 15 June 1977.

Donoughue was sympathetic. 'I think Steel was honest – he has received nothing back so far for his support.' Meeting the Prime Minister later that month, Steel complained that the Liberals 'had suffered electoral damage from the pact because they had got no credit for some of the changes that had been brought about'.[44]

In late June, however, the Parliamentary Liberal Party decided in 'favour of renegotiation, not instant renewal', with Steel agreeing to present ten out of nearly fifty policy ideas to the government. These 'Ten Commandments', as the *Daily Express* dubbed them, included the central planks of the original agreement (devolution and direct elections), as well as a package for 'industrial democracy' (profit-sharing and workers' councils) and tax reform (including a wealth tax).

Despite the unresolved issue of PR for direct elections, Steel was determined to renew the agreement, although the troika of Jo Grimond, Cyril Smith and David Penhaligon voiced reservations. The Prime Minister also found the ten demands 'pretty unacceptable', complaining to Steel that Liberals 'seemed to think there was no limit on the legislative time available: they had proposed enough for three years!'[45] All the Prime Minister was prepared to concede was an 'understanding' that Labour would take full account of the Liberals' point of view. On 26 July, however, Steel informed Callaghan that his colleagues 'were happy to accept the general outline of the proposed agreement' even though there remained 'trouble on the "shopping list"'.

Steel would later be criticised for not having driven a harder bargain at this stage when, arguably, his leverage was relatively strong. Could he have insisted upon a three-line whip rather than a government recommendation in favour of PR for direct elections? Many Liberal (and indeed Labour) MPs believed so, although Steel stuck to his line that there was no point asking Callaghan for something he could not deliver. While Steel thinks criticism on this

44   PREM 16/1400, minute dated 27 June 1977.
45   PREM 16/1401, minute dated 18 July 1977.

point is fair, he maintains he could not have secured 'a cast-iron guarantee'. He recalls:

> I assumed that around 100 Tory MPs, who had backed PR for the devolved assemblies, would also back PR for direct elections when it came before the House, and maybe that's the reason I accepted it [Callaghan's offer of a free vote] so readily. This was stupid, for by that point the Conservatives weren't going to do anything to help sustain the Lib–Lab Pact.

To Callaghan's biographer Kenneth Morgan, the renewal of the Lib–Lab Pact was 'an event of considerable political significance'. By giving the government a realistic prospect of surviving a full term, the Pact 'had created a moment of opportunity' in which the economy could be stabilised. From the Liberals' point of view, the Pact still enjoyed broad support in the party, with party HQ noting confidently that 'initial reactions ... with relatively few exceptions' were 'favourable', and that 'the party will stand solidly with the Parliamentary Party and the leader'. Senior Liberals in the Lords even wrote to Steel calling for 'a more stable and longer term agreement'.[46]

Meeting with Michael Foot shortly before the summer recess, Steel remained fixated on the Brighton Liberal Assembly, saying he was 'most anxious to make as much play as possible ... on the advantages and achievements which had stemmed from the agreement'.[47] The party continued to be punished in by-elections, the Liberals coming a poor fourth in Birmingham Ladywood, once again behind the National Front. Even in such difficult circumstances, some MPs retained a sense of humour. David Penhaligon turned up at one meeting with a copy of the *Evening Standard*. A headline read 'Steel loses one million a day' (a reference to British Steel rather than the Liberal leader) and to 'shouts of laughter from

---

46 LIBERAL/19/3, Lords Byers *et al* to David Steel, 21 July 1977.
47 PREM 16/1401, minute dated 29 July 1977.

everyone, especially David S[teel]. David [Penhaligon] slapped it down on the table with the wry comment, "Is that pounds or votes, David?"'

When Parliament reconvened in September 1977, Steel arranged to see Callaghan on the sixteenth ('If he comes early in the morning,' noted the Prime Minister, 'there probably won't be any photographers').[48] '[Steel] was quite confident about getting through his conference OK and seemed very relaxed about the Lib–Lab alliance,' observed Bernard Donoughue following a long talk with Steel. 'It was quite clear that he ought to be in the same party as us. He knows it. So does his colleague John Pardoe.'

The Liberal leader was certainly on increasingly friendly terms with Michael Foot, whom he had admired (primarily as a Commons performer) since entering the House in 1965. Steel even offered Foot early sight of his Assembly speech while complaining that his party had not been forewarned that Harold Lever (the Chancellor of the Duchy of Lancaster) had been appointed to examine the challenges facing small businesses, one of Steel's 'ten commandments'. If 'the Liberals were to claim any credit in an area of special concern', argued Steel, 'they would need to be in a position to issue an almost simultaneous press notice'.[49]

As Stuart Mole said of Steel's 1977 Assembly speech, it 'was a time for explanation, reassurance and a steady nerve'. Thus he deliberately played down the Pact, stressing that it was purely an 'agreement' between the Parliamentary Liberal Party and the Labour government, 'freely' admitting he had 'underestimated' the reaction to the agreement, not least 'how frightened we have become in this country of innovation, of trying to do things in a better way'. Steel also reminded delegates of his 'bumpy road' speech and his prediction that the party might lose some of its 'passengers' along the way. 'Some of them must have had a pretty tenuous hold on the vehicle,' he quipped, 'for they fell off at the first pot-hole.' For good

48   PREM 16/1402, minute dated 2 November 1977.
49   PREM 16/1402, minute dated 26 September 1977.

measure, Steel paraphrased Henry V: 'He that hath no stomach for this fight, let him depart.' If the Liberals were to depart from the Pact over a loss of nerve, they would 'acquire and deserve a reputation as purposeless incompetents'.

Cyril Smith was not won over and told the *Daily Telegraph* that 'Liberal MPs were not elected [to] be lobby fodder for the Labour Party.' And when a Smith-inspired amendment called for the Pact to be terminated was defeated by almost two to one Smith and Jo Grimond quit as frontbench spokesmen. Even so, when Steel next saw the Prime Minister (who was also in Brighton), he claimed to be 'pleased with the outcome' as 'he had got it to do all he wanted'.[50]

In October 1977 the Liberal Party's National Executive Committee (NEC) met to discuss strategy. This included consideration of a paper by the Liberal activists Bernard Greaves and Gordon Lishman, which presciently identified a breakdown in the post-war consensus and the likelihood that British politics would polarise between right and left after the next election. They concluded:

> We believe that it is important to re-establish the distinct nature of Liberalism and to communicate it as an 'image', by which we mean the simple presentation of basic attitudes and beliefs. We do not believe that there is room in this country for a Liberal Party which defines itself weakly as being midway between Conservative and Labour. Nor is there room for another conventional, centralist, social democratic party. We are opposed to the 'Party of the Centre' argument because it is neither true nor useful.

Steel was curtly dismissive. While Lishman had 'some good ideas', they had been 'smothered in a mass of verbiage'. Instead he focused on tactics, contrasting previous spells of Conservative and Labour rule with the Lib–Lab agreement:

---

50   PREM 16/1402, minute dated 30 September 1977.

> While in the past I have steered clear of the 'party of the centre'
> image because of the 'soppiness' risk, I now think that it could have
> great appeal against the potential extremism of a Labour majority
> or a Thatcher … majority. It is simple and relevant. Into that setting
> can be dropped many of the Lishman themes … We should go
> unashamedly for the balance of power as never before.

Steel's caustic wit also revealed itself. 'There may be something in
[Lishman's] approach to special minorities,' he concluded, agreeing
that it be developed further. However, he also saw difficulties. 'I
know what to say to homosexuals, but I'm damned if I know what
his line would be to ornithologists.'

At this point election planning was predicated upon an October
1978 poll, Steel believing that a spring 1979 contest was only likely
if 'the government panicked or we pulled out of the Agreement'.
And far from considering it a handicap, Steel urged his party to
'sell [the Pact] hard'. 'We were changing the political system,' he
enthused. 'The longer the Agreement ran successfully, the better.'[51]
Steel's thinking on this point had changed, writing to Lord Wade
that he was not now convinced 'a pre-election period free of the
pact is actually necessary'.[52] *The Guardian's* Simon Hoggart characterised this as the 'David Steel view', while the 'Cyril Smith view'
was to make a clean break with Labour as soon as possible. 'Not
surprisingly,' judged Hoggart, 'it is the people like Mr Steel himself,
Mr John Pardoe and the Chief Whip, Mr Beith, who have most to
do who seem to get most fun out of it.'

Events, however, continued to militate against Steel's fun. On 19
October the London *Evening News* carried the story of an alleged
plot by Jeremy Thorpe to assassinate Norman Scott, the fallout
from which was to distract Steel for the next two days. Bernard
Donoughue feared the press would use the revelations to bring

---

51   STEEL/A/2/7, minute dated 18 October 1977.
52   STEEL/A/3/1, David Steel to Lord Wade, 26 October 1977.

down the Pact, while Ken Stowe told the Prime Minister that Steel's plan was to try and 'keep his distance from it all'.[53]

On 2 November Steel and Callaghan discussed the significance of the mounting press campaign against Thorpe as well as possible election dates (the two issues were not unrelated). The election date also came up when Steel and Archy Kirkwood (who had just taken charge of the Liberal leader's private office) met Bernard Donoughue. 'He [Steel] stayed for a couple of hours, drinking tea by the fire,' Donoughue later wrote.

> [Steel] is very nice. He is clearly planning for the next election, and said his main problem – and interest in the polls – was how to win the Labour vote in the marginals where Labour came third. He agreed with me that there was [nothing] in the Liberals continuing in the future as they had in the past, winning a few by-elections but never getting near power.

Indeed, Steel was acutely aware that electoral support had been declining in the Liberals' most winnable seats. Election planning therefore focused on a second-vote strategy, with HQ preparing guidance on 'Putting over the Pact', as well as leaflets asking: 'Who Knocked Sense into Labour?'[54]

Knocking sense into Steel's own party was, however, another matter. PR for direct elections to the European Parliament continued to preoccupy grassroots Liberals, which Steel (correctly) considered 'a point of arcane unimportance to the general public'. But Steel had not counted on, as he saw it, the 'destructive capacity of the Liberal Party Council', which in November decided that a Special Assembly should reconsider the Pact should Labour MPs fail to back PR in sufficient numbers. Although this was, on the face of it, a reasonable proposition, Steel considered it 'a direct threat to the authority not just of the leader but of the Parliamentary Party';

---

53   PREM 16/1402, Kenneth Stowe to James Callaghan, 20 October 1977.
54   LIBERAL/19/1, undated flyers.

indeed *The Observer* went further and reported that he would resign
if a Special Assembly was even held.

When they next met on 28 November, Callaghan finally
'disclosed that he would himself be supporting the regional list
system', while strongly advising Steel 'not to commit his personal
position as leader of the party on the issue of direct elections'.[55]

This was a clear indication that both men anticipated a Commons
defeat, which is exactly what transpired on the evening of Tuesday
13 December 1977. Although direct elections to the European
Parliament were approved by MPs, the PR element was rejected by
319 votes to 222. That a significant number of Labour MPs, including sixteen Cabinet ministers (Michael Foot, surprisingly, was
one of them), provided scant comfort for Steel, who had wrongly
assumed around 100 pro-PR Tories would vote accordingly.

Steel saw the Prime Minister at 11 p.m. and left 'disconsolate',
deciding to give his colleagues a fright by pretending Callaghan
was about to call an election. 'You kept your face deadpan,' Cyril
Smith later told him. 'It shook us and finished the meeting [of the
Parliamentary Party].' Steel, however, realised all he had done was
'buy time' until the now inevitable Special Assembly, having found
his colleagues 'much angrier and [more] upset' than he had expected.

After a sleepless night, Steel was not on 'peak form' when he
chaired a meeting of the Parliamentary Party the following day.
His mood had not been helped by a bad-tempered interview Cyril
Smith had given to *The World at One* that, as one official remarked
to the Prime Minister, 'rather gives the impression that Mr. Steel
is coming to tell you that the Pact is in effect over'. Steel, however,
told Callaghan the mood among his parliamentary colleagues
was that they 'would be defeated on the issue of the Pact with the
government at a special conference, and that therefore it would be

---

55   PREM 16/1794, minute dated 28 November 1977. Perhaps as a sweetener,
     Callaghan later offered to appoint John Pardoe to the Privy Council while
     telling Steel he saw 'no difficulty in principle about appointing a Liberal'
     (Lord Winstanley) as chairman of the Countryside Commission.

better to bring the Pact to an end'. Steel dissented from this view but realised he was in a minority of one. He suggested reviving the issue of PR for direct elections at the Bill's report stage, but Callaghan was not enthusiastic, telling Steel that

> if the agreement was to be ended, the Liberals would be responsible and would be seen publicly to be responsible. The Tories would be delighted. It would give the Prime Minister an excuse for an election at any time. The Liberals would now have to decide if they wanted to end the Pact and face realities rather than acting as though they were living in an Oxford college. If the Liberals wished to end the Pact they must formally tell the Prime Minister so.

Having re-examined the texts of the March and July agreements, Callaghan correctly informed Steel that 'the government had done what it had promised to do,'[56] delivering a majority of Labour votes in favour, just not enough. But that uncomfortable truth still left the Liberal leader in a precarious position. As Bernard Donoughue wrote that night, Callaghan had taken 'a very tough line with Steel', offering nothing and 'simply saying that it is a problem for the Liberals', who 'must grow up'. The Prime Minister's avuncular instincts, however, surfaced as the meeting drew to a close, saying he 'deeply regretted what had happened and was sure that this would not affect his personal relationship with Mr Steel'.

Steel then had to face his MPs empty handed. 'He made it clear that an end to the Pact would put him in an intolerable position,' recorded Michie and Hoggart. 'He did not threaten to resign, but then he did not need to, since none of the other MPs thought that he would last if they voted the Pact down.' Steel's tactic worked, and his MPs voted by six to four to keep the Pact going. Significantly, there were two abstentions; one was John Pardoe, who at this point began to disassociate himself from the Pact, and the other was Jo Grimond, who despite continued scepticism of the Pact loyally supported Steel, telling his

---

56   PREM 16/1794, minute dated 14 December 1977.

colleagues Callaghan had behaved honourably and that PR had little resonance with voters. 'The pact continued, and we announced that without revealing the vote,' recalled Steel in his memoirs, 'but I now presided over a hopelessly split Parliamentary Party and had a potentially hostile Assembly to face. It was a bleak moment.'

Steel admitted as much to the Prime Minister when he saw him again that evening. Again, Callaghan slipped into avuncular mode, telling Steel 'that if his future as leader of the Liberal Party was in doubt, he should come to see the Prime Minister to discuss the possibilities for other posts'.[57] According to Steel, Callaghan told him 'that if the worst came to the worst and I did have to resign, he would like me to join the Cabinet'. 'I thanked him warmly but said that was quite out of the question,' recalled Steel in his memoirs. 'Infuriating though I sometimes found them, I simply could not desert my fellow Liberals and I would stay loyal to whatever the party decided.' Revealing the conversation to no one except Judy, Steel also added the rather defensive qualification: 'I believe that my interpretation was correct.' Indeed, Tom McNally (Callaghan's political secretary) thinks it highly unlikely that any such offer was actually made.

The only strong card in Steel's hand at this stage was in fact the threat of resignation. Choosing a fourth leader (including Grimond's caretaker period) in less than two years was not a welcome prospect, even to his critics. Steel was initially inclined to include this threat in a letter to Liberal candidates, but in the event he made it implicit rather than explicit:

> No one can say that they did not know where I stood, and I am not going to change course now. I think the party would be crazy to change course but you are entitled to do so if you wish at the special assembly … A small group of thirteen [MPs], especially if divided among themselves, cannot go against the decision of our Assembly or its entire strategy and keep the Liberal Party intact. Therefore if you decide to break off the agreement it will be broken

---

57   PREM 16/1794, minute dated 14 December 1977.

... I could not be party to breaking the agreement delivered over my signature to the Prime Minister. You did not conclude it: I did, and therefore you may not have the same inhibition. Nor could I lead the party into an election arguing a case in which I do not believe. No party can put its leader in that position.

In mid-January 1978 Steel was persuaded to attend a meeting of his party's NEC, never a gathering he relished. This one quickly ran out of control, with representatives of the Association of Liberal Councillors and the *Radical Bulletin* group accusing their leader of 'destroying the party by his autocratic pursuit of the pact'. 'It was a vicious attack, descending at times into bedlam as members sought to shout each other down,' recalled the Liberal Party secretary-general, Hugh Jones. 'Fortunately we were able to keep it within closed doors, with no serious leak to the press. David Steel kept his cool throughout, to his credit, but was naturally appalled by the onslaught.' In his memoirs, Steel recalled listening to claims the party was 'disintegrating' and 'worthy verbal essays about "participating democracy"'.

Jo Grimond helped shore up Steel's position in advance of the Special Assembly, writing that although he had always opposed the Pact, 'since it was struck, things have undoubtedly got better as far as the country is concerned.' Steel, he added, had 'attracted more attention and put the party nearer the centre of power than did his immediate predecessors ... So it would be crazy, having entered into the pact, to tear it up at this moment.' Even the increasingly semi-detached John Pardoe pre-empted leadership speculation by stating: 'No one should assume that if David Steel resigns I shall pick up the pieces; my aim is to ensure that David will not resign.'

Gathering in Blackpool on 21 January, delegates had three options:

1. An immediate end to the Lib–Lab Pact.
2. Giving notice to end it in July 1978, after the passage of the Finance Bill.

3. Setting no firm date, but leaving it to the judgement of the thirteen Liberal MPs.

Number three was the 'official' Assembly motion and the preferred
outcome of Steel, who had of course hinted at resignation should
delegates opt for options one or two. The leader's speech was
occasionally raucous. When Steel insisted the Prime Minister
had 'delivered exactly what he undertook to deliver on PR', some
delegates shouted 'Rubbish!' Otherwise, tempers had cooled since
mid-December, and by the time Steel finished speaking, 'gleaming
in the lights with an air of confident self-vindication, the issue was
a foregone conclusion'.

By meeting his critics head on Steel triumphed, with delegates
backing option three by 1,727 votes to 520. In retrospect, he admitted having been 'wrong to be so hostile to the holding of a special
assembly', as it had actually served to boost his authority and
strengthen the unity of the Liberal MP group. But although the
Pact had been reprieved for the remainder of the parliamentary
session, 'most delegates regarded this as allowing the pact a dignified demise in preference to administering a lethal injection; it was
not an encouragement to attempt to revive it.'

On 7 February Steel told the Prime Minister he had been 'careful
at Blackpool to keep every door open', but that he believed 'they
should [by Easter] have some idea about how long they could go on
supporting the government with the agreement.'[58] By the following
month, Callaghan agreed 'the Liberals should disengage from the
pact with the government in July.' This would leave him 'free to
go to the country in October', although, in certain conditions, he
might 'think it sensible to carry on'.[59]

Although the Lib–Lab Pact was clearly winding down, Steel
continued to work on 'selling the Pact' in seats where tactical voting
might result in Liberal gains.

---

58   PREM 16/1794, minute dated 7 February 1978.
59   PREM 16/1794, minute dated 7 March 1978.

The Liberals planned a threefold election pitch: the party had stabilised the economy via the Pact and had therefore helped the country, while it had also curbed the left and at least 'opened the door to Liberal ideas'.[60] The sticking point remained the lack of any tangible achievements to justify the third claim. The Inverness MP, Russell Johnston, wrote to Steel summarising the problem thus, that although everyone agreed the Pact might continue the Prime Minister 'didn't know what to offer you (us) and we didn't know what to ask him for'.[61]

When Steel met Callaghan on 20 March there was an implicit threat that Liberals might end up supporting Tory amendments to the Finance Bill if no concessions were forthcoming. By 10 April, however, Steel assured the Prime Minister that while they might disagree on detail, 'he was quite clear that it would be foolish to tear up the agreement with the government over these issues and force an early election.' Steel added that some of his MPs 'wanted an early election partly because they were still unhappy about the pact with the government, partly because of their fears of the impact of the ... [Norman] Scott affair'. The Prime Minister, meanwhile, thought 'these fears were exaggerated'.[62]

In April's Budget there at last appeared an identifiably Liberal policy amid ongoing efforts to tackle inflation. The profit-sharing measures may have been modest, but they represented an important victory for John Pardoe, as did a new lower tax rate of 25 per cent. As the *Financial Times* observed, Steel and Pardoe were 'entitled to claim that this is a Budget with a Liberal imprint'. Steel dwelled at length on this in his memoirs, arguing that successive Tory Chancellors expanded the Liberals' basic profit-sharing scheme (devised by Pardoe and a Liberal candidate/solicitor called Philip Goldenberg). 'Although there were lots of minor achievements recorded elsewhere,' judged Steel, 'this was the biggest positive

---

60 STEEL/A/2/7, paper dated March 1978.
61 STEEL/A/3/1, Russell Johnston to David Steel, 16 March 1978.
62 PREM 16/1794, minute dated 10 April 1978.

impact we made into legislation; but it was not the one on which the party at large had set its heart.'

By the end of that month, however, Liberal support for the Finance Bill was still not guaranteed, and Pardoe was becoming increasingly erratic. The Prime Minister thought he 'seemed to be adopting kamikaze tactics and looking for a breakdown in the agreement', while Steel confirmed that Pardoe was 'very depressed about the situation'. They then discussed how the Pact might be brought to an end 'and agreed that it was far better to have a clean break at the end of this session, which would enable the Liberals in any general election to refer creditably to their agreement and would not require the government to attack the Liberals'.

But by 9 May Steel was becoming impatient and bluntly informed Callaghan he planned to use his party's next Party Council meeting to terminate the Pact. The Prime Minister found this 'very disconcerting' and asked ('begged' according to Steel) that nothing be said until July for fear of upsetting the markets. After the meeting, Callaghan told his private secretary that Steel 'seemed to be in a very insecure position, being driven along by his colleagues'. Although he 'was playing it straight personally', he added, 'his colleagues were undermining his position.'

Callaghan's impression was vindicated the following afternoon when Steel, this time accompanied by Pardoe, attempted to extend the pact until 1979 in return either for PR elections to the devolved assemblies (Steel's idea) or 'a referendum in the whole of the UK on electoral reform' (Pardoe's). The Prime Minister was not convinced. 'He did not see that it would help the Liberals who had to get out and fight for the Liberal Party,' recorded the official minute, while Callaghan also doubted he would be unable to carry his own party. Rather, he 'remained of the view that they should shake hands and part in July at the end of the session', adding that as an election drew closer, the 'Labour Party itself would not want the pact to continue'.[63]

---

63   PREM 16/1794, minute dated 10 May 1978.

Callaghan reported this exchange to Tony Benn, telling him that 'David Steel would actually like to go on into the next session … but he will demand a referendum on proportional representation.' Benn agreed the Labour Party would 'not risk never holding office again for the sake of an extra six months now'. The Prime Minister, meanwhile, was clearly agitated about a premature announcement of the Pact's termination. 'That could create tremendous anxiety about an impending election,' he told Benn, 'it might affect the markets, and the whole thing might fall apart at the seams.'

Steel, however, stuck to his guns, telling the Prime Minister at a decisive meeting on 24 May that the Liberals were becoming 'increasingly restless' and needed some indication of where Callaghan stood. He also expressed doubts about the government's ability to control inflation due to difficulties over the 1977/78 pay round. It would only have been possible to sustain the Pact into 1979, Steel told the Prime Minister, if Labour 'had been able to offer something substantial'.[64] Callaghan tried playing for time, repeating his concern about the market reaction, but finally gave in, although he insisted the Liberals ought to initiate the end of the agreement rather than the other way round. They agreed to do so the following day, on 25 May. 'This suits us both,' noted Bernard Donoughue in his diary.

It leaves us free to call an autumn election, because we must have a majority. And the Liberals can fight an independent campaign from now on. It has been a fruitful and civilised relationship. A great credit to Steel, though sadly he has not got any political benefits from it – yet. He is hoping that in an election campaign he can sell the Liberals as the party which will tame the extremists of either side. And if we get another 'hung Parliament', he will be able to negotiate tough terms – possibly proportional representation, or a coalition with seats in a Cabinet.

---

64   PREM 16/2201, minute dated 24 May 1978.

On 25 May, Steel took a call 'in the middle of Cabinet ... [from Callaghan] pleading for an extra couple of hours' delay – until the Stock Exchange closed', but at 4.30 p.m. it was announced the Lib–Lab Pact would come to an end in July. Understandably relieved, Steel 'gave endless television interviews and flew to Edinburgh for dinner at Holyrood Palace'.

Liberal support for the Finance Bill, however, remained unresolved. On 14 June Steel gloomily told Callaghan that 'we were in a mess', the Prime Minister agreeing 'it was trouble either way'.[65] At an emergency Cabinet meeting that day, Michael Foot joked that he had tried everything with the Liberals, 'including having them psychoanalysed. He thought David Steel was an honourable man, doing his best with what was effectively a rabble.' The sticking point was the employers' insurance premium. 'The Liberals insisted on a 1.5 per cent increase instead of 2.5 per cent and we gave way,' recorded Donoughue in his diary. 'This was no problem for us ... Also the PM is keen to give the Liberals a victory. The worse they do in an election, the better for the Tories. Labour needs the Liberals to do well.'

Indeed, recent opinion polls had put the Liberals on just 7 per cent compared with the 18.3 per cent they had secured in October 1974. Translated into seats this did not bode well, with recent by-elections adding to the gloom. In April the Liberals had not even bothered to fight the Glasgow Garscadden by-election, while at the end of May Steel compelled his party's candidate in Hamilton to withdraw, arguing that another poor result would simply generate unnecessarily negative publicity. (In the ten by-elections between the initiation of the Pact and its demise, the Liberal share of the vote dropped by an average of 9.5 per cent.) Personally, Steel was also not on form. Archy Kirkwood told Bernard Donoughue he was 'very low in morale, and exhausted from carrying the whole burden of the Lib–Lab agreement', while at the Scottish Liberal

---

65   PREM 16/2201, minute dated 14 June 1978.

Party conference in June, Steel wearily admitted it had 'been an appallingly difficult time for Liberals'.

Finally, on 19 July 1978, the burden was lifted. Blandly, an official minute recorded the Prime Minister and Steel having 'a personal talk at which no one else was present'.[66] As agreed, there was an exchange of letters. 'The stability provided by your support in Parliament', Callaghan told Steel, 'had enabled the government and the country to make progress towards the economic recovery on which the future prosperity of our people depends,' while in an unpublished note, the Prime Minister spoke in more informal terms: 'It has been a pleasure to work with you, and I hope it won't do you any harm!'

In a television broadcast shortly after, Steel argued that the UK had just had 'a taste of government by common sense, free of the strident spitefulness of the major party organisations, and it works'. 'We've had a rest from the idiocies of the left, from the divisiveness of the Tories,' he continued, 'and what we've had is the sort of government many other successful countries in Europe have enjoyed for years. Government of common sense, not class warfare.'

So was the Lib–Lab Pact a success? The contemporary judgement was mixed, the *Daily Mail* summing it up as 'a squalid little affair', while *The Times* considered it 'a brave attempt to establish the conditions in which minority government can be made to work'. For many Liberals, in Parliament and in the country, it had been a bruising eighteen months, but for Steel 'the Pact brought almost exactly what he wanted: a taste of power for the Liberal Party and the invaluable experience of being locked into the mechanism of government, something denied to Liberals since the end of the last war.' Similarly, Steel later told a biographer that however unpopular it had made the party, it 'had at least brought it political relevance',

66   PREM 16/2201, minute dated 19 July 1978.

encouraging political commentators and voters to treat the Liberals as a serious political force at the forthcoming election.

In *A House Divided* (also the title of a 1973 book on Northern Ireland by Callaghan), Steel's excessively detailed account of the Pact, he listed four achievements: fulfilling the 'main short-term objective of controlling inflation', providing 'much-needed parliamentary stability', demonstrating 'that bi-party government' could keep the 'extreme dogmas of the larger party ... under control' and, finally, presenting 'the country with the first taste of a distinctive Liberal policy'.

And in a television interview recorded during the Pact's final phase, Steel expanded upon these themes:

> I don't see what the future could [have been] for the Liberal Party in the long run unless we were at some stage prepared to take a risk and accept some degree of responsibility ... [otherwise] where would our argument have been for people? It would be falling back either on 'vote for us because you don't like the others', we're a protest party, or else, we're putting up 600 candidates, 'vote for us, we'll have a Liberal government', and it seemed to me neither of these were sufficiently credible in the long run to attract votes for the Liberal Party actually to make progress. I think to be able to say vote for us because we can change the way in which we've been running this country – rather unsuccessfully – we can change it for the better and we will usher in a series of reforms from the electoral system, industrial relations, and so on, is a very much more realistic and attractive prospect; it's changing the nature of the Liberal Party to face responsibility: I don't think that's a gamble, I think it's a change that had to be made.

In this respect, Steel had been absolutely consistent in what he expected to get out of the Pact, constantly imploring his colleagues (who, 'as usual, were difficult and had to be cajoled along') not to harbour unrealistic expectations. Its relative success also hinged upon Steel's capacity for forging political relationships, in this case with the Prime Minister. Therefore the agreement was a product of the two men; as Steel later said, 'it's fair to describe it as a Steel–Callaghan Pact'. Despite 'Liberal carping', thought the journalist John Cole, Steel's performance during the Lib–Lab Pact 'had been a virtuoso one', with the young Liberal leader more than holding his own in the company of older, more experienced political figures.

Steel, however, consistently overstated some of what the Pact achieved, just as his party did at the time by issuing impressive-looking lists of all the concessions it had supposedly gained. Chief among them was that during the eighteen months of the agreement the UK's monthly rate of inflation had fallen from 20 to less than 9 per cent, accompanied by a modest 0.5 per cent increase in unemployment. This was true, but the extent to which Liberal support helped achieve this is a moot point. As Michie and Hoggart concluded in 1978, 'The Liberals cannot fairly claim that their support *in itself* helped to rescue the economy.'

The Pact did, however, mean the Labour government could function without constant threat of collapse, thus enabling ministers to get inflation under control. As Steel somewhat cryptically told Phillip Whitehead: 'I think we had a very marginal influence, positively, but we had a lot of negative influence, and we had a lot of stabilising influence.' But this also brought problems. As Steel himself concluded, the Pact's 'most obvious defect' was that the 'failure and unpopularity of the Labour government' rubbed off on the Liberals. 'We were lambasted for simply keeping in office a government which had outstayed its welcome.' Steel also missed an opportunity to refashion Liberal philosophy as traditional ideological boundaries broke down, his attempts being rhetorical ('I want our party to become the militants for the reasonable man') rather than substantive.

But to Steel abstract ideology and concrete policy concessions were of lesser importance, thus throughout the history of the Lib–Lab Pact, 'no very clear idea emerge[d] of what Steel actually wanted in terms of policies and decisions.' Reflecting on the Pact in 2007, Steel stuck to a realpolitik analysis. 'I have no real regrets, we got a lot out of it,' he told the Liberal Democrat MP Mark Oaten. 'Could we have screwed more out for Liberal advantage? It would have been very difficult. Could we have benefited from a conference for PR? We would have been laughed at if that was what we gained.'

Even the otherwise critical Michie and Hoggart concluded their history of the Lib–Lab Pact with the following qualified praise:

> In 1976, just before Steel took over, the Liberal Party was going nowhere at all. It lacked ambition, it lacked a lot of drive, and it lacked a leader who had any concept of what might be done with the votes and the support that the party had accumulated through the early seventies. What Steel offered was a direction, a purpose and an ambition. Within months of becoming leader he had placed the party absolutely at the centre of British political life, and had made it too important to be ignored by anybody.

The Pact had, at least, 'provided a decisive break with the adversarial two-party system' while, as Mark Oaten concluded in 2007, it had done 'its job, nothing more, nothing less. It allowed a government to govern, and an economy to stabilise.' 'Many Liberals at the time believed that the pact would either bring the party to the pinnacle of power, or else destroy it altogether,' wrote Jeremy Josephs several years later. 'But the truth was far less dramatic. It did neither.'

With the Pact at an end and the Liberals languishing at around 5 per cent in the polls, the party's focus naturally shifted to planning for a general election still expected that October. Steel managed to generate some much-needed press attention, condemning the divisiveness of politics, 'promoted by the confrontation of Labour and Tory parties, financed by opposing sides of industry', while calling for a ban on corporate contributions in favour of limited tax relief on individual donations, a clever way of trying to improve Liberal finances.

He also reasserted his liberal credentials when Mrs Thatcher used the word 'swamped' in relation to immigration, calling her remarks 'really quite wicked'. Steel, judged *The Economist*, 'seems to have recovered his form as a constructive scourge of the two parties. With Liberal support still flagging badly, he will have to keep it up until polling day.' He spent summer at home planning for the election, although the arrest of Jeremy Thorpe and the death of his mentor John P. Mackintosh ('a major influence on my political life ever since my school days') 'cast a shadow' over his spirits. 'This is probably the last letter I shall write to you, assuming an October election,' he told Liberal candidates on 20 August. 'There is *no* question of a Lib–Lab pact being re-created to extend the life of this Parliament. In my view the country has (rightly) come to expect an election and it would be damaging to the economy, the government and to us to seek to postpone it.'[67]

But it was not to be. In what Steel later called 'his greatest misjudgement', Callaghan 'decided not to hold an election … but to hang on for better times which never came'. The Prime Minister had spent his summer analysing previous election results and had concluded he could not secure a majority. Indeed, Steel and John Pardoe later admitted to Bernard Donoughue they had only ended the Pact because they assumed an autumn election 'and the PM never guided them otherwise'. 'If he had told them he was going on till 1979,' noted Donoughue in his diary, 'they would have continued the Lib–Lab pact!' When Steel saw Callaghan three weeks after the announcement, he registered his 'annoyance directly', adding in his memoirs that he never forgave 'the mistake of failing to go to the country at that moment'.

With the benefit of hindsight, however, Callaghan's prevarication was actually good for the Liberals, for it gave the party another six months in which to distance itself from Labour and rebuild its profile as an independent party. At the 1978 Liberal Assembly Steel said the UK was 'badly governed', 'badly governed because its political institutions are antiquated and undemocratic'. 'This

---

67 LIBERAL/19/1, David Steel to Liberal candidates, 20 August 1978.

crucial weakness', he continued, 'is at the very root of Britain's continuing economic and social decline.'

But the Assembly was memorable for another reason. Having been charged formally with conspiracy to murder on 3 August, Jeremy Thorpe had been sacked as Foreign Affairs spokesman and warned to stay away from Southport. Steel thought he had agreed, but on the last day of the Assembly, just after delegates approved the slogan 'Break with the Past', Banquo's ghost turned up at the Liberal feast. 'He didn't just appear,' recalled Steel, 'but, with his usual showmanship, the doors of the back of the hall were flung open and he marched down the crowded aisle with Marion [his second wife] to a half-standing ovation.' When Thorpe reached the platform, Steel had little choice but to escort him 'to his seat amidst a mixture of embarrassed silence and applause, as the platform party contemplated their shoes'. 'I don't think my feelings were printable at that point,' Steel later told Phillip Whitehead. 'I knew the whole thing would be dominated by him.'

By the beginning of 1979 Steel had managed to disassociate the Liberals from an increasingly unpopular Labour government, especially useful with the so-called winter of discontent at its coldest. A key figure in bolstering Steel's position during this period had been John Pardoe. Although, as a defeated leadership contender, he could have caused plenty of trouble, instead Pardoe had applied himself – however erratically – to the Lib–Lab Pact and, importantly, killed off any speculation that he planned to oust Steel as leader.

'John Pardoe was absolutely crucial,' recalls Steel.

> My main weakness in terms of politics and political discourse is my lack of economic background; I had no training in economics whatever. John not only made up for that but he established himself as an authority on economics so let me off the hook! He was happy to do it and became known as deputy leader of the party. There was no such post, but I happily accepted that he was.

Pardoe also held the fort when Steel was abroad, as he was in early 1979 on a delayed tour of southern Africa. Shortly before departing for warmer climes, Steel had a three-hour lunch with Roy Jenkins at his East Hendred home. 'He is very agreeable, sensible and curiously mature,' Jenkins wrote approvingly in his diary.

> He perfectly understands that there is no question of me or anybody else joining the Liberal Party. He equally is anxious to work very closely, and possibly, if things went well, to consider an amalgamation after a general election. He would like the closeness at the time of the election itself to take the form not merely of a non-aggression pact, but of working together on policy and indeed sharing broadcasts, etc. He says that for this point of view he has overwhelming support in the Liberal Party.

This was, of course, the SDP–Liberal Alliance in embryonic form. 'Altogether,' Jenkins wrote in his diary, 'a thoroughly satisfactory talk.'

A Liberal Party political broadcast at the end of January expanded on the theme of cross-party co-operation, recapping the record of the Lib–Lab Pact before Steel asked in rhetorical terms:

> How is Britain to be governed? Is it by the law of the jungle, with the government abdicating all responsibilities? Are envy and bloody-mindedness to be allowed to feed upon themselves? Are we all to regard each other with suspicion? Is the basis of civilised life to be undermined? Once the rush of the Gadarene swine is on no one wants to be left out. That's what a free-for-all means.

'There's something rotten in our political life,' continued Steel gloomily. 'It isn't corruption or deceit. It's a kind of smugness and a hardening of the political arteries. A reluctance to face up to facts and an assumption that the party game must be played at all costs and all issues, that national leadership is something to be talked about but not provided.'[68]

---

68   Margaret Thatcher Papers THCR 2/1/3/17, transcript dated 31 January 1979.

But the game of politics was becoming increasingly hard to play. Labour had effectively been crippled by a series of strikes, while the devolution referendums held on St David's Day added to the government's woes. In Wales there was a clear majority against devolution, while in Scotland most voters said 'yes', just not the 40 per cent of the total electorate required by the Scotland Act. Steel, who by his own admission had played 'a rather small role' in a 'disunited and dispiriting' campaign, met Callaghan a few days later to discuss ways forward. Callaghan was optimistic, telling Steel he was 'quite sure that it was better to carry on if he could: he had no doubt that the sun would shine shortly'. But when the Prime Minister asked for Liberal help to postpone an election until that autumn, Steel said 'they could only offer to help for the purpose of bringing devolution forward.'[69]

Following dinner the next day with Steel and John Pardoe, Bernard Donoughue recorded a perceptive character sketch of the Liberal leader and his Treasury spokesman:

> It was an interesting relationship between Pardoe and Steel, the former attractively ebullient and imaginative and always exaggerating ... and the latter, a true son of the Scottish Kirk, prim and boyish, easily embarrassed, cautious in his statements, a bit short on political imagination, but sensible and realistic in all his attitudes, and clearly an attractive and deeply honourable man. It is sad that such people get lost in the pathetic Liberal Party and do not get near to power. They have so much more to give than so many of our clapped-out middle-rank ministers.

A week later Mrs Thatcher finally won the no-confidence vote she had coveted since the Lib–Lab Pact had been formed almost two years earlier. As Callaghan took his case to the country, morale among Liberal MPs was low, with few of them expecting all fourteen to be back after the election. He opted for an early manifesto

---

69   PREM 16/2201, minute dated 6 March 1979.

launch, the centrepiece of which was a shift from tax on earnings to spending, cutting the top rate of income tax to 50 per cent and the basic rate to 25. Pardoe, meanwhile, spelled out that a commitment to PR would be a pre-condition for any pact or agreement. The manifesto, usefully, was well received by the press.

An astonishing Liberal victory in the Liverpool Edge Hill by-election – the 'community politics' of candidate David Alton having increased local support – also provided a perfectly timed morale booster. The former Liberal MP Peter Bessell said it was the 'equivalent of a dying man receiving a successful heart transplant'. By wide consent Steel fought an attractive and clever campaign, an important element being his 'battle bus', converted by Parks of Hamilton and co-ordinated by Pratap Chitnis, the 'heroic' agent at Orpington whom Steel had persuaded Callaghan to elevate as a crossbench peer.

Liberals gradually began to rise in the polls, and even Mrs Thatcher feared 'a last-minute upsurge of Liberal support'. By design, mean-while, Callaghan and Steel were 'mutually very admiring' during the campaign. Two days before polling day Bernard Donoughue told the Prime Minister not to 'make a hasty resignation', urging him to talk to Steel and the smaller parties before taking any decision. Ken Stowe concurred, and even arranged 'for an aeroplane to stand by to fly David Steel down from Scotland' in the event of a hung Parliament. Steel, however, was not directly engaged with that prospect. 'About ten days before polling day I told David it was quite possible the Tories wouldn't have an overall majority,' recalls Steel's adviser William Wallace, 'so we'd better think about this and set up contacts with the Conservatives so we don't end up like Jeremy Thorpe in February 1974. David said: "If you want to do that, go ahead," so I called Chris Patten [then director of the Conservative Research Department] and he was clearly thinking along the same lines. We needed a negotiating team but David wasn't really interested.'

Yet in his introduction to the 1979 Liberal manifesto, Steel spoke of political reform as a 'starting-point'.

Until we break the two-party strangle-hold, until we get away from
the adversary class politics which are embedded in our parliamentary
structure, we cannot successfully tackle the problems of economic
weakness and industrial mistrust, of misspent resources in housing,
of uncertain management of the public sector and of mishandled
relations with our neighbours abroad.

Confidential party strategy was more explicit, stating that Liberals
were 'willing with appropriate safeguards, in principle, to share
power with either party in the next Parliament', something Steel
reckoned the party had agreed to in February 1978 'with remarkable acquiescence'. Publicly, Steel spoke of creating a 'powerful
wedge' (he predicted twenty or more) of Liberal MPs in the next
parliament. A 'brilliant series of posters' designed by Adrian Slade
also played on this theme, one depicting Steel between gun-toting
images of Callaghan and Thatcher. 'THE REAL FIGHT IS FOR BRIT-
AIN,' it declared. 'GO LIBERAL AND THEY'LL HAVE TO LISTEN.'

The Liberal leader's last campaign broadcast emphasised his
family-man credentials, featuring his son Rory playing in the background. Steel recalled speaking 'slowly, directly and persuasively' in
the short film, an election study later judging it 'one of the most
powerful heard in an election'. All of this appeared to have an effect.
Liberal support rose to 14 per cent in the polls, and on election day
eleven Liberal MPs were returned on marginally less than that share
of the vote. In Scotland, the collapse of the SNP (whose strength
Liberals had feared two years earlier) aided the party's showing,
while in the Borders Steel's majority reached an all-time high
of 10,000.

His vindication, however, also marked the final chapter in his
predecessor's career. In North Devon Jeremy Thorpe was heavily
defeated, his scandal also helping unseat John Pardoe, who was
caught in the 'regional backwash', in North Cornwall.[70] Although

---

70 Gallantly, Pardoe had spoken on Thorpe's behalf during the campaign,
    while Steel sent only a tape-recorded message.

Steel was genuinely upset at the latter's defeat, 'choking back tears' when he heard the news, he was understandably relieved by the overall result. Usefully, as David Dutton assessed, 'the seemingly remorseless process of electoral decline had been arrested and reversed. In a remarkable comeback, the party had, against the odds, confirmed its permanent position on the British political landscape.' It was also no exaggeration to say that had it not been for Steel's leadership the party would have suffered more serious losses. 'It was the most successful of the three election campaigns I was involved in,' recalls Steel. 'In the other two [1983 and 1987] we flat-lined all the way through in the polls.'

'Eleven of us were returned to the House,' reflected Steel in his memoirs. 'A forecast catastrophic disaster had been turned into a slight setback – not nearly as bad as the 1970 result – and therefore seemed almost like a triumph in comparison. We had survived, but the Thatcher era had begun.'

6

PREPARE FOR GOVERNMENT

Politically, if not chronologically, the 1980s began with the election of Margaret Thatcher in May 1979. And while it would take the Iron Lady a few more years to show her mettle, that election was also the making of David Steel as a politician. He had fought his first general election as Liberal leader and emerged with his profile consolidated – if not boosted – by the campaign, while delivering what was, in the circumstances, a creditable outcome.

'Overall, the campaign averted the widely predicted disaster,' was Steel's private assessment, 'was coherent and more effectively organised at the centre than previous campaigns.'[71] Tudor Jones later wrote that Steel, like Jo Grimond and Jeremy Thorpe (who was acquitted on 22 June 1979) before him, had fought 'a skilful national campaign, proving himself an effective communicator of the Party's appeal as a positive third force'.

How that third force was to be deployed would preoccupy Steel for much of the next decade, a period of grandiose schemes of realignment that occasionally owed more to wishful thinking than political reality. At Reginald Maudling's memorial service during the election campaign, he had caught up with Roy Jenkins, President of the European Commission since 1977, and a few weeks after polling day Jenkins invited Steel to have lunch in Brussels. Jenkins left the following impressions in his diary:

---

71 David Steel Papers STEEL/A/2/7, undated memo.

He was pleased with his election campaign, although disappointed with the votes obtained, and went rather out of his way to tell me that, as a result of it, he had become a major public figure, possibly the best known after Callaghan, Heath and Mrs Thatcher. In other words, he was, I think, underlining in the nicest possible way that in any future political arrangement he wasn't to be treated as an office boy. Very strongly anti-Thorpe. Anti-Mrs Thatcher, still rather pro-Callaghan.

Far from being offended, however, Jenkins was pleased to discover that he and Steel were on the same wavelength when it came to 'any future political arrangement', by which Jenkins meant co-operation between a new centre-left party and the Liberals. 'Roy and I agreed', recalled Steel, 'that some new organisation founded mainly on a mass exodus from the Labour Party but linking up in alliance with us would stand the best chance of "breaking the mould" of British politics.' His reasoning combined realism with ambition, recalling in his memoirs that 'we as a party were still not cracking the Labour strongholds. Something "extra" was needed to achieve that. Roy and his colleagues, I thought, could provide it.' Steel realised the Liberal Party – on its own – could not hope to challenge the dominance of the two-party system.

In almost every respect Steel's politics aligned with those of Jenkins. Both babies of the House following by-elections, in the 1950s Jenkins had helped liberalise the law in relation to obscene publications, a reform echoed by Steel's abortion legislation (supported by Jenkins) the following decade, while the two men had also been mutually admiring during the 1975 European referendum campaign. 'It was of considerable importance to their relationship that they belonged to different generations,' observed the authors of the standard text on the Social Democratic Party (SDP), Ivor Crewe and Anthony King. 'Steel, eighteen years younger than Jenkins, could defer to the older man without in any way demeaning himself. Jenkins, for his part, took an almost avuncular interest in Steel. They were in no sense rivals.'

Indeed, Judy Steel wondered if her husband saw 'some parallel in their early political lives'. As Jo Grimond was said to
have observed, Steel was essentially a social democrat (Bernard
Donoughue had made the same observation during the Lib–Lab
Pact) while Jenkins was an Asquithian Liberal; he had even writ-
ten a sympathetic biography of the former Liberal Prime Minister.
Both also enjoyed the good life. Stuart Mole, who worked for
Steel until the 1983 election, still remembers his boss's instruc-
tion when Roy visited the Liberal leader's office: 'Cigar for Mr
Jenkins, Stuart.'

Having forged an uncle–nephew relationship with one older
centre-left politician, James Callaghan, during the Lib–Lab Pact,
Steel had now formed a similar bond with Callaghan's former Home
Secretary. Furthermore, the pair trusted each other completely. As
Hugh Stephenson wrote in his book on the SDP, *Claret and Chips*,
'they had the luxury of being able to concentrate on the strategic
aspects of the battles, safe in the knowledge that – whatever else
might be happening – the understandings and confidences between
them were secure'.

Steel also knew Jenkins well enough to realise there was no question of him joining the Liberals. 'We did discuss it,' recalls Steel,
'and he said if something new didn't happen then he would join, but
not be very active.' As he later told the journalist Hugo Young, while
having 'Roy on the team would add enormously to Liberal credibility', more unhappy Labour MPs were likely to join a new party
rather than his very old one. Therefore Steel did not push the point,
something for which he was later criticised by fellow Liberals (John
Pardoe – in 1987 – said it amounted to 'gross betrayal'). 'He never
rejected any suggestion of mine that I should become a Liberal,'
recalled Jenkins in his memoirs. 'He did not have to. But he had a
wider view of his role than that of being a recruiting sergeant. He
wanted to be a general, not necessarily a commander-in-chief but
one as decisive as, say, Blücher, who turned the course of history.'

But at this stage General Steel was not telling his troops very
much at all, preferring to keep his own counsel at such a sensitive

stage in the battle. As Crewe and King observed, the Liberal Party 'was a difficult one to lead'.

> It lacked organisational or ideological cohesion or even an ethic of cohesion. The MPs were their own men: the party structure was devolved and federal; the constituency associations were almost wholly autonomous. The pervading spirit was one of participation and parochial rights, not one of compliance and collective solidarity. Without patronage or electoral success to bestow, Steel's only resources were persuasion and his legitimacy as the party's elected leader.

In other words, he had to tread carefully. 'I don't think either of us was thinking in terms of a new party which would be equal in status to the Liberal Party,' Steel later told the historian Phillip Whitehead, but 'a new party which might ... conceivably get up to maybe 100 candidates ... working right from the beginning clearly with the Liberal Party and frankly rather under its umbrella'. Jenkins most likely concurred, later writing that it 'did not occur to me that if we were to launch any effective centre movement we should begin by fighting to the death with the Liberals for the right to be the third party'. To have done so with such a similar party, he added, 'would have been lunacy'.

What became the Alliance, therefore, was very much the product of Jenkins and Steel, just as the Lib–Lab Pact had been the product of Callaghan and Steel. Indeed, Jenkins actually believed Steel to be the driving force. 'He showed real political quality,' he wrote in his memoirs, 'and if one man made the Alliance it was he.' Nevertheless, when Steel later wrote up their June 1979 meeting as the decisive moment in what became the Alliance, Jenkins reckoned he had 'imbued' it 'with more significance than it deserved, later meetings being much more important'. Even so, Jenkins's 'regard for him, never low, went steadily up ... [David] was steady under fire from his own party, and he always delivered when he said that he would.'

Steel had also been contacted by another former Labour MP and academic, David Marquand, for 'a long talk about the prospects of a social democratic breakaway from the Labour Party and its possible relationship with the Liberals'. Later it emerged that Steel had actually dissuaded Marquand from joining the Liberal Party,[72] although the meeting led to Marquand urging Jenkins to 'toughen up the draft of what was to become the Dimbleby Lecture, to make it more a call to action and less an academic disquisition on the history of the party system'.

Steel had seen a draft of Jenkins's lecture in advance, and 'Home Thoughts from Abroad' was finally delivered on 22 November 1979, reinvigorating debate on the potential 'realignment' of the UK's left-of-centre forces. Jenkins bemoaned the decline of the 'radical centre' and, significantly for Steel and other Liberals, proposed proportional representation as a key element of his proposed solution (Steel said this made 'it possible to talk turkey' with any new party). Although it had a major impact, the lecture, as Matt Cole has observed, 'was easily regarded as the musings of an erudite but elder statesman on the sidelines'. The former Labour MP Shirley Williams dismissed the idea of a new party, although Jenkins's intervention had at least meant the concept was seriously discussed.

As was the new party's potential leader. When *The Times* polled on this very question at the beginning of 1980, Steel came top, well ahead of Jenkins, who noted in his diary that he would have no problem serving under a younger man in a future government. Congratulating him on the poll, the Labour MP and diarist Tony Benn (a staunch opponent of the Lib–Lab Pact in 1977) warned Steel not to have Jenkins in the Liberal Party because he would 'wreck it'. 'All decent Liberals join the Labour Party – like my dad – and end up on the left,' Benn joked to Steel, 'because the right wing of the party is so bureaucratic and authoritarian.'

Steel had name-checked Benn's father William in a pamphlet

---

72   The SDP MP Robert Maclennan also considered joining the Liberals but was 'strongly discouraged' from doing so after speaking to Steel.

published that year, *Labour at 80 ... Time to Retire*, which urged
Labour's social democrats to

> recall the example of those who went over from the Liberal Party to
> Labour fifty years ago or more, putting their commitment to reform
> and radicalism above party loyalty. What Haldane, Wedgwood-
> Benn, the Mallalieus and others did then, they should do now,
> helping to build up a broad-based reform movement rather than
> patching up a creaking and internally-divided party structure.

Indeed, most of the pamphlet amounted to a searing indictment of
a party Steel suspected was 'structurally impossible ... to reform'.
Dismissing the 'ambitious like Roy Hattersley or David Owen',
he wrote glowingly of Jenkins, Williams and Bill Rodgers: 'If
they had the courage of their convictions they could help change
British politics.'

Yet Steel was gloomy, fearing that 'old allegiances and political
careers well sunk into traditional grooves will persuade many of
them to go down with their sinking ship rather than strike out for
the lifeboats.'

> If we need a new start and new policies with a complete change in
> our national priorities, as I believe we do, we must first change our
> politics. A movement of reform coalescing around a resurgent
> Liberal Party is the first step. A great national government of reform
> is where it should lead. There is room in both for socially responsi-
> ble Conservatives and radical Socialists alike. Indeed their support
> is essential.

It was, argued Steel, the 'Liberal intellectual tradition' that would
prove 'ultimately attractive' to members of other parties, a point
he repeated at the 1980 Liberal Assembly, when he called for a
'meeting of minds ... around principles and policies. Our aim is
a discussion about political philosophy and programmes, not pacts
and personalities.'

Although this was a little ironic in light of how the Alliance would play out, Steel consistently talked up Liberal prospects while playing down those of a new, autonomous, third (or rather fourth) party, telling the same Assembly that without 'Liberal leadership, a Liberal agenda, and Liberal commitment, their efforts are doomed … With us they could make a formidable contribution. Without us they will perish.' As he wrote in *A House Divided: The Lib–Lab Pact and the Future of British Politics*, his strategically timed account of the events of 1977–8, 'During this parliament I intend to demonstrate that the only genuine alternative to the narrow policies of Tory dogma is the modern Liberal Party.' While he realised this would require 'friends and allies', Steel acknowledged in a BBC interview that 'it is very difficult to get people to leave one political party and join another. It is easier to talk in terms of forming new alliances, new groupings, with the Liberal Party as the basis of them.' The number of Labour MPs who would actually switch, added Steel, 'will be very small'. This appears not to have been a 'line' designed to encourage more defectors, for he repeated it in private, telling Hugo Young it would be 'foolish to think that more than one or two Labour MPs will come across to Roy'.

But in terms of rejuvenating Liberal philosophy and actually *making* the party more attractive to voters and, indeed, members of other parties, Steel was not at his best. Asked by interviewers to cite philosophical influences, he often looked and sounded uncomfortable, resorting to anecdote, invoking the Liberal legacy of Keynes and Beveridge and name-checking rather predictable gurus like John Stuart Mill. Theologically, Steel's liberal Church of Scotland background had left him with little regard for doctrinal exactitude. Ideologically, therefore, Steel's was a broad church.

On the right, he approved of Thatcherite moves like trade union reform (on which Hugo Young judged Steel to be a 'hawk') and fiscal responsibility. He even casually put it to Young that perhaps the time had come 'to *abolish* local gov[ernmen]t', which Steel considered 'a farce'. On the left, meanwhile, Steel was instrumental in reorientating Liberal policy on the Middle East. In the autumn of 1980 he met with Yasser Arafat and, in a far-sighted move, essentially backed the creation of a Palestinian state. The move infuriated the Liberal (and pro-Israel) peer Lord Byers, who protested that Steel had shown 'immature political judgement' which would not help 'the credibility of the Liberal Party or its leader'. Steel was firm in response. 'The report [published after the trip] is a thorough, workmanlike document', he told Byers, 'which does credit to the credibility of the party in international affairs.'[73]

But while Steel had a certain feel for foreign affairs, economics – as he freely admitted – was a policy blind spot. His adviser Richard Holme once warned him not to speed up while speaking about fiscal and monetary policy 'because it shows you are not really interested'. His plan for economic recovery – launched in January 1981 – advocated a contradictory mix of policies either already being pursued by the government or having shown themselves to be unworkable. Nowhere, judged the historian Brian Harrison, 'did Steel show how difficulties could be overcome; still less did he show how his compendium of desirable objectives could be combined with three other dimensions of his strategy: lower interest rates, a lowered exchange rate, and international cooperation'.

Even the normally loyal Jo Grimond despaired of Steel's vague assertion that he believed in a 'balanced, sustainable economy' (something John Pardoe, had he not lost his seat in 1979, might have helped flesh out). 'Does this mean that control of the money supply will be slackened whenever some powerful interest threatens?' asked Grimond rhetorically. 'Does it mean a certain amount of government interference, a certain amount of government investment? If so, what amount? According to what principles? Decided by whom?'

When the broadcaster Robert McKenzie put it to Steel that Liberalism could be seen as right wing, his response was muddled:

---

73   STEEL/B/1/7/3, Lord Byers to David Steel, 13 November 1980; David Steel to Lord Byers, 13 November 1980.

It is not that the Liberal Party is opposed to equality. Far from it. We
are an egalitarian party. We are opposed to uniformity and there is a
very important distinction between these two which I think moulds
us ... I don't see why we shouldn't have greater experimentation in
the state sector.

None of this, of course, was necessarily incompatible with social
democracy and although, as one historian of the Liberal Party has
written, Steel's 'near equation of Gaitskellite social democracy with
his own conception of Liberalism' irritated Liberals like Michael
Meadowcroft, nevertheless it 'deserved to be more closely noted
than it was'. Steel, meanwhile, believed privately that even purists
like Meadowcroft could find common cause with social democrats
such as Jenkins.

This, along with Steel's belief that he had 'overwhelming support
in the Liberal Party' for an arrangement with a new party, was
clearly overstating the actual position. There was what he called
a 'troublesome' meeting of the Liberal Party Council in May (the
Liberal activist Michael Steed recalled the 'dominant feeling' as one
of 'cautious willingness'), while Meadowcroft used a 1980 Assembly
fringe debate with David Marquand to warn that key objectives
of social democracy and liberalism were in fact mutually exclusive, one centralist and statist, the other localised and libertarian.
Fears also grew among many activists about the likely effect of a
new centre party on the Liberals. Tony Greaves and the left-wing
Association of Liberal Councillors (ALC), for example, regarded
a right-leaning breakaway group of Labour MPs as not only ideological enemies, but unwelcome competition.

Thus press reports, such as that by Simon Hoggart in *The Guardian*
in February 1980, referred to 'tactical preparations for a marriage of
interests' between Jenkins and Steel. Speaking privately to Hugo
Young, Steel dismissed this story as 'quite untrue', although he
acknowledged his willingness to consider an electoral pact. He was
also concerned the Dimbleby Lecture had come 'too soon, before
any follow-through c[oul]d be done', while as 1980 wore on even

Jenkins (who considered Steel 'a remarkably buoyant young man') entertained doubts when the journalist William Rees-Mogg posited that Liberals did not offer much to build on, the main 'reservoirs of opinion' in British politics remaining divided between the two main parties. 'The Liberals had none of the bottom of either of these groups,' noted Jenkins in his diary, 'and would therefore, whatever Steel's personal qualities, be a particularly ineffective support for decision-making in a government. Maybe there is something in this.'

'In the end,' Steel told Hugo Young over lunch, Jenkins 'wants to be PM, or else to have changed the shape of Br[itish] pol[itic]s.' So Jenkins continued to plot, albeit rather slowly. 'Like you,' Steel told the Labour MP Neville Sandelson in December 1980, 'I am fearful of procrastination.'[74] Dining with Steel the previous month, however, Jenkins found Steel 'not unduly discouraged by continuing hesitancy, and understanding of my desire to wait some time, but not indefinitely, for the Gang of Three'. This trio consisted of the Labour Party's leading social democrats, Bill Rodgers, Shirley Williams and David Owen, although they – unlike Jenkins – remained wary of Steel and the Liberals. Only when Labour moved to oppose EEC membership and increase the power of constituency activists over councillors, MPs and the party's leadership did they act, rejecting the idea of a centre party (proposed by Jenkins in a recent press gallery speech) but envisaging 'a new democratic socialist party'.

Spotting his opportunity, Steel penned an open reply in the same newspaper calling on Rodgers *et al* to 'end your dialogue with the deaf and start talking to us'. He continued:

Given the limitations of our electoral system, there would be nothing worse than the emergence of two or three competing

---

74 Hugo Young Papers HJSY/2/6, notes dated 25 November 1980; Neville Sandelson Papers SANDELSON/9/13, David Steel to Neville Sandelson, 4 December 1980.

progressive parties, each with overlapping philosophies and policy proposals, all appealing to the same sections of the electorate. That would guarantee another Conservative victory, even on a reduced proportion of the vote. We are forced therefore to combine if we would succeed.

Steel signed his letter 'Yours fraternally', but none of the Gang felt compelled to respond. 'It only confirmed to me his superficial approach,' sneered Owen in his memoirs. 'Its aim was publicity ... and inasmuch as we had any view it was one of irritation. For the three of us, rightly or wrongly, the Liberal Party was low on our agenda.' Steel, however, continued with what he called 'chivvying', aided by his advisers' – Richard Holme and William Wallace – talent for drafting letters. 'Throughout the entire birth process of the SDP,' he recalled in his memoirs, 'my approach was publicly to embrace them, smother them with kindness and assume a putative alliance.'

In November 1980, Michael Foot replaced James Callaghan as Labour leader, and when Tony Benn proposed committing the party to nuclear disarmament, a return to nationalisation and withdrawal from Europe, the Gang of Three (now, with Jenkins, the 'Gang of Four') issued their famous 'Limehouse Declaration' on 21 January 1981, thus named after the area of London inhabited by Owen. This called upon Labour's social democrats to join a Council for Social Democracy (CSD) and ended with the phrase, at Jenkins's insistence, 'we believe that the need for a realignment of British politics must now be faced.'

The Declaration, and indeed its language, was music to Steel's ears, and he wrote another open letter ('Its style was pre-emptive,' recalled Owen, 'its tone patronising') while using a party political broadcast to flag up a golden opportunity 'to do what so many of us have dreamt for years' – that is 'to break the mould of a failed political system and to produce a realignment of the progressive and hopeful forces in Britain'. 'If the social democrats' valuable experience of government is added to our nationwide community campaigning experience,' added Steel, 'I believe we could prove an unstoppable combination.'

But there was still no formal shape to that 'unstoppable combination', and having coaxed and cajoled the Gang of Three/Four via journalism and speeches since the end of the previous year, Steel wanted co-operation – and he wanted it quickly. He set an Easter deadline, warning that otherwise he could not prevent local Liberal associations from adopting candidates in constituencies the new party (as yet unformed) might want to fight. Beyond that, Steel hoped to agree a deal before the 1981 Liberal Assembly, although his zeal undoubtedly upset many in his own party. As Crewe and King observed accurately, 'Steel occasionally seemed more concerned with pursuing his personal political vision than with the feelings of his flock.' One Liberal sheep, Cyril Smith, put it most bluntly when he said any new party ought to be 'strangled at birth' considering the threat it posed to the Liberal's third-party status.

Steel's closest advisers (Richard Holme, William Wallace, Stuart Mole and Lord Tordoff), meanwhile, were 'seemingly aloof from the Liberal mainstream' and thus hardly served as a check on Steel's ambitions. As Hugh Stephenson put it, there was 'a widespread feeling in Liberal circles that he had made quite unnecessary positive advances in the direction of a Jenkins centre party which did not yet exist'. 'David played his cards very close to his chest when it came to the Alliance,' recalls Sir Alan Beith. 'Most of us knew nothing about the conversations David had had with Roy Jenkins.' And as had been the case during the Lib–Lab Pact, Steel was much more interested in the *idea* of an alliance than any policy it might deliver.

Meanwhile, the CSD had attracted fourteen MPs and around 25,000 supporters, and thus kept its distance from the Liberals. While Steel knew Shirley Williams and Bill Rodgers from the 1975 European referendum and Lib–Lab Pact, he did not know Owen, the Gang's most mercurial member, at all. When the two Davids made an 'edgy appearance' on the BBC's *Question Time*,

the Conservative minister Peter Walker noted their lack of familiar-
ity. On air, Owen appeared reluctant to engage with the Liberals,
bluntly saying an electoral pact was all that interested him, while
Steel held out for 'an alliance of hearts and minds', predicting that
he and Owen could reach agreement on most policy areas.

When, on 26 March 1981, the SDP was born, it was dismissed
by the two main parties and welcomed only by Liberals who shared
Steel's enthusiasm for a new force in British politics, but it made a
huge media and political splash. In a private Liberal letter leaked to
The Guardian, Steel revealed his intention

> to pursue the possibility of a Liberal and Social Democratic Alliance
> in which we would each retain our separate identities, structures
> and detailed policies while having in common a programme of
> national priorities and, if possible, agreement not to have opposing
> candidates in any one constituency.

These, it should be remembered, were heady days, not just for the
new SDP, but also for Steel, who consistently polled as Britain's
most popular party leader and the second most popular choice as a
future Prime Minister. Unsullied by government, he was clearly an
attractive choice; a *Sun* poll in early 1981 had even suggested that
a combined Liberal–Social Democratic party led by Steel, Jenkins
and Williams could attract more than 50 per cent of the popular
vote. With an increasingly unpopular right-wing Conservative
government in Downing Street, and an increasingly left-wing
Labour Party in opposition, a new third force was proving to be an
attractive alternative for many disillusioned voters.

At this stage Crewe and King judged Steel – who turned forty-
three just days after the SDP launched – to be

> an assured, confident, straightforward politician, a man without
> any very firm grasp of policy, especially economic policy, but with
> clear ideas about the broad direction in which he wanted British
> politics to go. He had the additional advantage of being unusually

skilful at communicating his ideas, whether on public platforms, in newspaper articles or on television.

Yet Steel's character contained what Walt Whitman called 'multitudes'. The journalist James Naughtie noted that despite his televisual confidence, he was in actual fact a 'very private man'. Peter Bartram, who published an authorised biography of Steel at around this time, reckoned he was 'not so much shy as reserved'. He continued:

> The private Steel, relaxing with friends, can be quite different from the rather buttoned-up, earnest politician the public see on their television screen. He is an amusing and entertaining conversationalist, but he will try not to dominate a gathering in an egotistical way, like some eminent men. He can be more amusing in private than in public, when he knows that the nuances of his utterances are not going to be analysed by political commentators and other pundits. But this is not to suggest that Steel behaves like two different people in public and in private. Rather, the public and the private sides of him emphasise different features of the same character.

'Although he is certainly a politician of the times,' judged Bartram, 'on a personal level he runs counter to many of the trends in modern-day society.'

Steel was certainly stylish, buying his trademark two-tone shirts from Harvie and Hudson on Jermyn Street, although they made him appear younger than his years (and often prompted much teasing). 'Steel might have looked like a schoolboy,' noted Shirley Williams in her memoirs, 'but he had the judgement and sagacity of a statesman.' David Owen was less impressed, and resented Steel's continual chivvying on the basis of his – rather than the SDP's – timetable. All he would discuss with Steel were constitutional and industrial commissions 'in very broad outline', and he considered talk of a policy document in July, and indeed a formal alliance, to be 'premature' (although parliamentary co-operation had begun in February and generally went well).

Writing on the thirtieth anniversary of the SDP in 2011, Owen reflected that it was 'hard to recall exactly what we hoped for'.

> I never thought the SDP would govern alone in its own right or that we would be able to batter our way through to power quickly. But I did hope that we would be part of a coalition government within my working lifetime and that I might have the opportunity of being in charge of a department again.

The Liberals, in other words, were peripheral to Owen's vision but central to Steel's, a fundamental tension that would only be resolved in 1988. From the beginning, Steel and Jenkins viewed an alliance as the first step towards the formation of a single party ('We preferred two rivers flowing together,' was Jenkins's classical simile, 'like the Tigris and the Euphrates, with a common delta'), while Owen *et al* saw it as little more than an electoral arrangement between two distinct parties. Owen believed he was taking his cue from the general public, who 'perceived the Liberals, loaded down with all their historical baggage, as representing failure', while he thought Steel 'was playing a bad hand very astutely'.

This view extended beyond Owen. A paper by the SDP MP Mike Thomas concluded the new party was 'credible personally and politically', while the Liberals were 'widely disliked and discredited (with the sole exception of David Steel)'. Too close an association with the Liberals, he argued, would 'gravely damage' a distinct SDP identity, thus he proposed a 'firm and public rebuff for the Steel tactics of constantly setting us deadlines and some (again public) distancing of ourselves from the idea we are being bullied or swept along by this'.

On the other hand, when SDP MPs met to plan tactics the Leicester East MP Tom Bradley reckoned 'David Steel should be given some encouragement. The longer we delay the weaker position we will be in.' Neville Sandelson also wanted to 'try to help David Steel', while David Marquand felt Steel 'needed some indication that the SDs were willing to work with the

Liberals. There was a middle way.' Roy Jenkins summed up the discussion thus:

> [B]oth parties should retain their separate identities – there was no idea of a merger; that there must be an arrangement before the next general election; that the Liberals were a loose body and varied in their support in different areas throughout the country; that there was too much negotiation being carried on in public by the Liberals. He felt that the S[ocial]D[emocrat]s should acknowledge that David Steel has been a very determined supporter of an alliance with the SDs. We should return to him constructively. He did not see why we shouldn't ask him for something in return – they should endeavour to have a moratorium of adoption of candidates during this period … It was not in the SD's interest to have an adversarial relationship with the Liberals.[75]

Bill Rodgers and Shirley Williams were asked to communicate this view to Steel, but Owen continued to be irritated that certain meetings had not been discussed collectively, a case in point being an April jaunt to Königswinter for an annual meeting of the Anglo-German Association, attended by Rodgers and Williams as well as Steel and his adviser Richard Holme. Williams recalled setting off with Steel

> on a walk up the Drachenfels, one of the range of hills above the Rhine, followed by Bill and Richard Holme. On that walk, he and I agreed that the parties would have to work together, produce an agreed policy statement and support one another on an equivalent basis when there were by-elections for Parliament. Bill and Richard reached the same conclusions, and all of us returned to Britain feeling pleased with what we had accomplished.

Less pleased was Owen, who noted that 'a trend had been set in

---

75   David Owen Papers D 709 3/1/1/14, SDP minutes dated 7 April 1981.

motion which was to prove impossible to reverse,' later writing that
the relationship between the two parties had gone 'critically wrong'
between 3–5 April in Germany. 'It was clear that David Steel had
foreseen the opportunity for a serious discussion with us,' recalled
Bill Rodgers in his memoirs. 'With typical sense of occasion, he
had even tried to hire a motor launch to ensure publicity for the
event.' The result was the so-called Königswinter Compact, drafted
by Richard Holme on green paper and promising an alliance that
would fight the next election 'as distinct parties but offering the
nation a government of partnership'.

Steel, meanwhile, was adamant that the priority was returning
Jenkins and Williams (who had lost her seat in 1979) to the House
of Commons. A by-election in Warrington appeared to provide
Jenkins with that opportunity, and although he lost on 16 July,
that he had come within 1,759 votes of winning had a transforma-
tive effect, convincing Steel that it exceeded anything the Liberals
could have managed alone in what had been a safe Labour seat.
The campaign also endeared Jenkins to Liberal activists, coach-
loads of whom had descended upon Warrington to 'support' his
SDP candidature.

It also increased Steel's chances of securing Assembly support for
an alliance, and to that end he and Shirley Williams had launched
a joint 'statement of principles' in June. Keen to emphasise the
word 'alliance' at every opportunity, Steel wanted to call it 'A New
Alliance for Britain', although this was toned down to 'A Fresh
Start for Britain'. Steel and Williams were photographed looking
like a pair of what Hugh Stephenson called 'superannuated student
lovers' on the grass at Dean's Yard, Westminster Abbey; Williams
reckoned it 'looked like an advertisement for vitamins for the
middle-aged', although 'it served its purpose'.

At the Llandudno Assembly, momentum was on Steel's side. A
modest fringe meeting on the eve of the alliance vote turned into
a mass rally, addressed by Jenkins and Jo Grimond. Unlike Owen,
Jenkins assiduously courted the Liberals, flattering them and their
history and even crowning Grimond as 'father of the alliance' while

reminding the audience that he too had argued for realignment in the 1960s. Grimond's presence and later speech also helped reassure rank-and-file Liberals uneasy about being bounced into another pact by Steel. 'I beg of you to seize this chance,' implored Grimond. 'Do not get bogged down in the niceties of innumerable policies. I have spent my life fighting against too much policy in the Liberal Party!'

The following day only 112 delegates out of more than 2,000 voted against an electoral pact with the SDP. Unusually for Steel, he allowed a rush of blood to the head to produce a quixotic climax to his Assembly speech:

> Now at last we have the reality in our grasp. We must have the nerve and courage not to let it slip. I have the good fortune to be the first Liberal leader for over half a century who is able to say to you at the end of our annual Assembly: go back to your constituencies and prepare for government.

Steel had come to the Assembly with that speech already written, and while it received a rapturous reception in the heat of the moment, it made him look – particularly after 1983 – more than a little foolish. Steel subsequently claimed the phrase had been 'regularly taken out of [its coalition] context and used against me', although the earlier line 'When our Alliance government takes office' did not sound like a pitch for coalition government.[76] 'I still believed that it was possible for us to go straight in and confront the Conservative government with an alternative prospectus,' Steel later told Phillip Whitehead. 'I was wrong in that, but I was right in the sense that we were able to inflict grievous bodily harm on the Labour Party.'

---

76 Jenkins's speech at Llandudno had not been far removed from Steel's own exhortation. 'Be in no doubt,' he said, 'there is now a perfectly feasible prospect of a Liberal–Social Democrat government after the next election.'

Nevertheless, the Llandudno Assembly was a personal triumph for Steel and his planning over the previous eighteen months. 'Llandudno propelled the whole thing,' he recalls; 'there was no way the party was going to roll back after that,' having clearly foreseen that four parties – two of them in alliance – were better than three. He had also played the long game, and played it well. By referencing the 'bumpy road' line from his first Assembly speech in 1976, Steel had reminded delegates that his was not a new strategy: the Lib–Lab Pact had been the first bump in the road, an alliance with the SDP was another. The Alliance, meanwhile, would allow the Liberals to move from the wings to centre stage, while enabling the SDP to be more than just a novel flash in the pan.

For the media, however far-fetched some Alliance expectations turned out to be, this all made good copy; *The Economist* captioned an ebullient photograph of Steel, Jenkins and Williams as 'Her Majesty's new opposition'. Not in the picture was Owen, who continued to argue that 'we should guard against our two-party Alliance becoming before the next election, *de facto*, a single Alliance Party'. An October by-election in Croydon North West, however, highlighted tensions within the Liberal Party rather than between different elements of the Alliance. As soon as the sitting Conservative MP died, Steel saw it as an opportunity to increase the Alliance's momentum, albeit at the expense of his own party.

Bill Pitt, who had fought the seat for the Liberals in 1979, turned out to be (in the words of Owen) 'a bearded Liberal activist, extremely affable, but a libertarian militant'. Steel took a similarly dim view of Pitt, who, as he pointed out, had fought and lost the seat several times under the Liberal banner. Rather Steel believed the SDP's Shirley Williams should have a shot at fighting the seat. But in attempting to engineer the switch Steel faltered, his repeated arm-twisting simply serving to build up an image of 'plain Bill Pitt' holding out against the machinations of the big boys. Steel was forced to U-turn and, when Pitt took everyone by surprise by being elected on 22 October, cheerfully greeted him on his first day in the House of Commons.

Shirley Williams did not have to wait long for another by-election and won Crosby just a month later (although Steel was irritated by her failure to consult him about her decision to stand). The Alliance could now boast two MPs (Pitt and Williams) as proof of public support for a non-socialist alternative to the incumbent government. And while Mrs Thatcher mocked Steel as 'a sort of man for all fusions', she was well aware of dire private polling and the potential for significant Tory defections (in the event only one Conservative MP, Christopher Brocklebank-Fowler, joined the SDP). The fact that Williams had overturned a Tory majority of 19,000 also shot a hole through the government's depiction of the Gang of Four as socialist front. With the government's survival already looking precarious, three by-elections in the second half of 1981 had transformed the political scene. In December the Alliance peaked at over 50 per cent in the polls, while Steel's net approval rating stood at +48 (compared with –41 for Thatcher and –24 for Michael Foot).

Ever the realist, Steel told his confidant Pratap Chitnis at the end of 1981 he was 'not so wildly optimistic' about what the Alliance could achieve, but 'even if the wind is not far behind us, the next election is far more than the usual battle for the survival of Liberal values: it presents the first genuine opportunity since the war of a real return to Liberal power in politics.'[77] Steel's public line was more positive, having set out his thinking in a September 1981 article for the Liberal journal *New Outlook*:

The question then immediately arises: could not the Liberals achieve the breakthrough on their own? I believe the answer is 'No – not at one general election ... The leap from a handful of MPs to a party of government is one which few people consider at all likely and it is a problem of credibility ... I do not deny that my role, as I saw it, in encouraging a social democratic break-out from the Labour Party and the formation of a new party was, and

77   STEEL/A/2/6, David Steel to Pratap Chitnis, undated.

is, a high-risk strategy. But I also believe that it is the approach
which provides us with the only chance to break the existing two-
party system and present the electorate with a credible alternative
government, in one move, at the next general election.

It is difficult to fault Steel's rationale in this respect, and his ability
to derive maximum advantage from minor political opportunities impressed (while also frustrating) both Liberals and Social
Democrats. Given the character of his party, judged Crewe and
King, 'Steel not unnaturally adopted a hands-off, detached, somewhat secretive leadership style,'

> avoiding direct dealings with his party workers wherever possible
> and relying instead on a small group of advisers to act as fire-fight-
> ers and intelligence agents. He kept out of internal party disputes,
> did not cultivate any faction and handled dissent by means of
> manoeuv-ring and fixing. He chose to communicate his views
> through the national media or *Liberal News* – or via his lieutenants
> – rather than face to face. It was a style that protected him from
> the snares of faction but could also cut him off from his party's
> thinking. Usually it worked – but not always.

Bouncing his own party into strategic decisions was one thing,
but adopting the same approach in relation to the SDP – leaking
private meetings and publicity stunts – irritated otherwise friendly
Social Democrats like Bill Rodgers. 'In fact, it was the habit of a
lifetime,' he reflected in his memoirs, 'seen as no less appropriate in
the new circumstances in which Liberals found themselves.'

Nevertheless, Steel's importance to the formation of the Alliance
could not be overestimated. The academic Vernon Bogdanor judged
in a 1983 book, *Liberal Party Politics*, that 'it is not over-estimating
his influence to argue that, under different leadership, either the
Alliance might not have come into existence at all; or alterna-
tively its shape would have been very different.' And whatever the
view of grassroots Liberals, Bogdanor reckoned Steel had 'already

influenced the party at least as much as Jo Grimond and more than any other leader since Lloyd George'.

Buried in the Liberal Party's collective memory was the 'coupon election' of 1918, in which Lloyd George's Liberals and the Conservatives had carved up seats between themselves in order to fight as a governing coalition. More than half a century later, tensions within the Alliance over candidate selection emerged early on, becoming one of the issues that, as the historian Matt Cole has observed, 'exemplified differences of culture and approach between the two parties'. Established Liberal candidates were understandably reluctant to relinquish long-cultivated constituencies in favour of Social Democrats they regarded as lacking campaigning experience.

Steel's attempt to oust Bill Pitt in Croydon North West had demonstrated this issue in high-profile terms, and indeed Pitt's victory had if anything emboldened certain Liberals against Steel's plea for sacrifice when it came to allowing prominent Social Democrats a free run in hitherto Liberal territory. When the Labour MP for Greenock, Dick Mabon, defected to the SDP in October 1981, it further exacerbated the problem. Existing guidelines clearly entitled Mabon to fight the seat at the next general election, but local Liberals – who had a strong local government presence – insisted only they could win the seat with a Liberal candidate.

Predictably, these localised battles were soon replicated in every region of the UK mainland (neither Liberals nor the SDP contested seats in Northern Ireland). Steel had always envisaged the Liberals having the upper hand in terms of total seats fought, with the SDP tackling no more than a hundred, a view (for once) shared by grassroots Liberals such as Michael Meadowcroft and Tony Greaves of the ALC. The SDP, however, sought parity with around 300 seats, and frustration among Liberals grew as it became clear Steel was more willing than them to compromise.

Also frustrated was Bill Rodgers, the SDP's lead negotiator on seat allocation, particularly when Steel's proposed guidelines appeared in the press during August 1981, warning Steel by letter that if they gained general currency then the SDP would 'be obliged to begin stating our own terms'. Steel, in turn, repeated his 'doubts about whether you [Rodgers] will be able to find 300 adequate organisations within the next two years. Any public insistence – on either side – on a target of seats could prove embarrassing later.'[78]

Between July and October 1981 Rodgers's team frequently met with Steel's, which included Alan Beith and David Penhaligon. 'Successive drafts of the guidelines were scrutinised and interpreted with an intensity and precision more appropriate to the Dead Sea Scrolls,' remembered Rodgers in his memoirs. After one particularly fraught meeting on 1 October, Steel wrote to Rodgers at length (and in his own hand) from his home in Ettrick Bridge. Instead of progress having been made on the draft guidelines, he lamented, there now seemed to be 'wider disagreement'. Steel continued:

> I cannot understand your choice of team. Mine were chosen because they were people both with experience and with a determination to make the Alliance work, *not* because they were thought to be the people most likely to get the best bargain for the Liberal Party. If that had been the aim I would have included Cyril Smith, Michael Meadowcroft, Councillor Tony Greaves etc. who start from the proposition that we should possibly let you stand in 100 seats.

Mike Thomas for the SDP, wrote Steel, was 'insufferable', while Matthew (later Lord) Oakeshott, although 'highly intelligent', was 'still contemplating divisions based on academic analysis of the psephology and demography of each constituency'.

> On the overall picture I have told you consistently that I am quite happy to accept your 300 seats as a *target* but not as a *principle*. It makes no sense to elbow aside a working Liberal organisation

---

78   William Rodgers Papers Box 28, David Steel to Bill Rodgers, 1 September 1981.

simply to reach a notional parity if there is nothing to put in its place. That will not make the Alliance more effective.

It was only to be expected, continued Steel, that the Liberals would 'have slightly more seats than the SDP (but not overwhelmingly more) simply because of our superior organisation'; equally it was 'natural that if we form a government you will have the larger share in any cabinet because of your superior experience. Neither of us should be frightened of these realities if we are going to fight a successful campaign together.'

Steel ended his letter by regretting 'that the trust and goodwill, and indeed friendly optimism, which was so apparent between our two parties at Warrington and Llandudno was [now] markedly absent ... and I do trust you to do something about it'. Rodgers did not reply, at least not by letter, and the atmosphere did not improve. Greenock posed particular problems ('Greenock is becoming tiresome,' Rodgers told Steel, 'or, to be precise, your people in Greenock are'[79]), as did Derbyshire, and Rodgers argued, with some justification, that both were crying out for Steel's direct intervention. Steel, however, repeatedly refused to get involved, arguing that local difficulties ought to be resolved locally.

Determined that Steel 'not be allowed to get away with it', Rodgers tried again on 31 December, warning that an 'impasse' was being reached. 'In both cases your people are clearly at fault,' wrote Rodgers. 'You have made this plain to me in private, but have not used your authority in public. Frankly, this is bound to undermine confidence. The overall negotiations cannot proceed further in such an atmosphere.'

Deciding a public airing was necessary, Rodgers took a leaf out of Steel's book and tipped off *The Observer*'s Anthony Howard, who splashed the story. Steel was 'stunned' and, putting on what Rodgers called his 'disapproving son-of-the-manse face', was

---

79   Rodgers Papers Box 28, David Steel to William Rodgers, 1 October 1981; Bill Rodgers to David Steel, 30 December 1981.

interviewed from his home in the Borders. 'I think', said Steel, 'Bill Rodgers may have had one or two too many mince pies.' The impasse eventually ended over lunch rather than more mince pies, Steel and Rodgers agreeing to more flexibility to overturn previous understandings, and that parity of representation was a common goal.

Although this led to what Steel called 'a general improvement in progress',[80] it appeared to contradict his pre-Llandudno pledge that it would be 'unreasonable' for any Liberal candidates who 'have energetically been building up their local organisation and support over several years' to be asked to stand aside. Even so, by March 1982 Steel and Rodgers were able to announce that two thirds of the seats in Britain had been allocated, which, according to Rodgers, 'was only a slight gloss on the figures'. Roughly speaking, the Liberals got the lion's share of what were termed 'golden seats' (where they had done well in 1979), while the SDP were given priority in the next tranche of 'silver seats'. The whole business, reflected Steel in his memoirs, had been 'frankly wearisome and debilitating'.

At the end of that month Roy Jenkins fought and won the Hillhead by-election in Glasgow, marking his triumphant return to the House of Commons following an absence of nearly six years.[81] Steel had actually cautioned Jenkins against contesting the seat, believing it to be an 'unacceptable gamble' due to the SDP's relative weakness in Scotland. Nevertheless, he campaigned on Jenkins's behalf four times, referring to him as a man of 'rare experience and vision' in a campaigning letter. Steel was also concerned the SNP would choose a strong candidate who might put the very English (though Welsh-born) Jenkins on the defensive. 'Behind the scenes Roy shows a terrible weariness,' Steel told Hugo Young. 'It is taking so much out of him.' He also reckoned the consequence of defeat

---

80   Rodgers Papers Box 29, David Steel to William Rodgers, 21 January 1982.
81   Chic Brodie, who stood aside as the Liberal candidate following a conversa-
      tion with Steel, later defected to the SNP and was elected an MSP in 2011.

would be 'terrible', 'causing a lot of personal frictions and difficulties'.[82] Privately, David Owen also feared the press would be 'ready to pounce on us like hounds' if Jenkins did not pull it off.

Defeat would also have halted the Alliance's momentum, which had already suffered due to the ongoing row about seat allocation. Jenkins's victory in Hillhead, however, did not resolve that. Interviewed together on Granada's *World in Action*, Owen reckoned it would 'come down to about a hundred [seats] that might be difficult', while Steel joked that there remained 'great potential for 635 rows' (the number of Westminster constituencies). This was an early television outing for what Owen called 'the two Davids', and indeed both men had the ability to express themselves well, as the *Times* journalist Geoffrey Smith put it, 'sounding decisive even when they have nothing to say'.

Although Steel was seen as having negotiated a good deal for his party by some commentators, it did not look that way to many Liberals, who needed constant reassurance that he was not sacrificing their interests to wider goals. As Michael Steed put it, 'because the SDP was the newcomer, it felt to Liberals as if they were being required to do all the giving,' which was particularly the case in seats where the sitting Labour MP had only defected to the SDP through fear of deselection ('Defect and Survive' ran a spoof SDP slogan, after the government's booklet *Protect and Survive*, then being distributed, on what to do in the event of a nuclear attack).

Another part of the problem was Steel's impatience to reach a deal, not to mention his boredom with the minutiae of local negotiations. This led Steed to identify another constant feature of his leadership style during the period 1981–7:

> He sought the interests of the Alliance rather than, as urged on
> him, the interests of the Liberal Party. But in so doing he severely
> damaged the cause of the Alliance within his party. Liberals seeking,
> quite justifiably, the application of the guidelines to their cases were

---

82   HJSY/2/8, notes dated 25 March 1982.

labelled anti-Alliance in the pressures that the leadership brought on them – a self-fulfilling prophecy as they and others who took their side lost commitment to the Alliance.

Nine months of debilitating rows, argued Steed, 'sapped energy, damaged the confidence of many Liberals in their leader's judgement and ... cut David Steel off from the rest of his party'. 'The price,' he concluded, 'was not only the public standing of the Alliance, but the internal harmony and effectiveness of the Liberal party.'

'Increasingly, the argument ceased to be between myself and David Steel,' reflected Bill Rodgers in his memoirs, 'and became between each of us and local activists in our separate parties.' Writing to Steel in April 1982, Rodgers repeated his concern that 'negotiations may drag on indefinitely' and raised the prospect of independent arbitration at the end of May. 'We are all getting pretty tired of negotiations. I doubt whether either party has anything fresh to bring to it. An independent and authoritative point of view would come as a relief.' Steel, meanwhile, was 'wholly sympathetic', telling Rodgers his team had no 'wish to encroach on eternity'.[83]

By July 1982, however, the negotiations reached their final, critical stage. At this stage Roy Jenkins's authority was crucial, while even Steel, as Bill Rodgers noted, 'threw his full weight behind the solution of difficult problems and was entirely fair in seeking a satisfactory outcome for both parties' (come the election, Steel also refused to campaign in any seat where Liberals had failed to reach and respect an agreement with the SDP). It was, however, the SDP's turn to feel aggrieved at what this outcome looked like. Writing to Jenkins on 7 September, Mike Thomas emphasised that it was 'actually about preserving the capacity of our own party to survive and develop, and thus contribute to a genuine alliance'. In another angry letter two weeks later, Thomas railed against what he by then took to be a 'done deal'.[84]

---

83 Rodgers Papers Box 39, David Steel to William Rodgers, 26 April 1982.
84 D 709 3/11/1/1, Mike Thomas to Roy Jenkins, 7 September 1982; Mike Thomas to Roy Jenkins, 20 September 1982.

Jenkins was acutely aware of the need for finality. 'It is vital that you and I put our full weight behind the agreement and be prepared to ensure that it sticks,' he wrote to Steel on 18 September.

> We have agreed that you will tell me on Monday whether you are able to accept this package to bring the negotiations to an end. If it is not acceptable, I feel that we will merely muddle on through the autumn with no greater hope of settlement in individual cases but considerable damage to the impact of the Alliance.[85]

Usefully, Steel was happy with the agreed allocation in which the SDP would fight 311 seats and the Liberals 322, putting his party in a modestly superior position. It was this deal he put to delegates at the 1982 Liberal Assembly in Bournemouth and, although contentious, Steel deftly won the crucial vote, proving he was – as *The Economist* observed – still 'in control of his party'.

'When eventually the history of the Social Democratic Party is written,' reflected David Owen in an *aide-mémoire* dated 24 September 1982, 'historians may have to decide at what point it became inevitable that it merged into the Liberal Party and of all the thresholds and of all the turning points it may be that they will conclude that it was this week that the final determination was made.' Jenkins, he believed, had finally 'tipped the seat negotiations across a threshold which could be fatal for the independence of the party', while Steel would now 'push Roy Jenkins very hard indeed'.

> I am the victim of the politics of edging at which both Roy Jenkins and David Steel are very great exponents. Issues are never confronted directly. There is often very little discussion about what should be done but steps are taken unilaterally and often publicly which remorselessly carve out a position.

---

85   Rodgers Papers Box 30, Roy Jenkins to David Steel, 18 September 1982.

Having challenged Jenkins for the SDP leadership in July 1982 and lost, Owen felt understandably diminished within the Alliance hierarchy (although his standing had increased during the Falklands War, of which more below). Steel, meanwhile, was relieved, realising that a defeat for Jenkins would have put his vision of the Alliance in danger. Indeed, the fact that 44 per cent of SDP members had been prepared to back his more robust view of the party's long-term independence did not augur well for the future. The BBC's John Cole believed Steel talked up Jenkins chiefly in order to ensure Owen's defeat, thus increasing the prospect of completing the merger of the two parties. Even so, Steel was keen to avoid what he called 'another year of constitutionitis' and realised the priority was 'projecting our forces to the electorate'.

'Roy is uniquely equipped to lead the Alliance,' Steel had told the journalist Hugo Young in March, who also noted his thoughts on future leadership structure:

> What D[avid]S[teel] is beginning to favour is a steering committee jointly chaired by himself and Jenkins, which at some point makes clear that Jenkins will be Prime Minister if they win. It is quite delicate. Clearly Steel is an electoral asset, and it would be counterproductive to submerge him under Jenkins. He must remain the clear leader of the Liberals at the elections, and indeed hopes to perhaps take the lead in television etc. They may also have to select a shadow team – itself a delicate task.

Steel admired Jenkins's ability to 'obliterate disagreements with the sweep of his hand'. 'It's his manner, and his experience, and his past, and his weight,' Steel told Young. 'He'd be much better than me at running the show if we got in – but I have fought an election campaign as a party leader, which none of them has done. And it is a very difficult thing indeed to do.'[86]

Indeed, when an autumn poll ranked Jenkins behind not only

---

86   HJSY/2/8, notes dated 25 March 1982.

ABOVE David Steel greets Jo Grimond at Edinburgh University's Old College. The relationship Steel forged with the Liberal leader after nominating him as the university's Rector was a crucial event in his early political career. © Johnston Press

THIS TIME

David Steel

LEFT Steel's election address for the Roxburgh, Selkirk & Peebles by-election in 1965. His was a modern, energetic campaign which propelled Steel into Parliament aged only twenty-six. The *Daily Express* hailed him as 'The Boy David'. © Scottish Liberal Party

David and Judy Steel with their first child Graeme, born during the defining battle of Steel's early parliamentary career – a Private Member's Bill to liberalise Britain's abortion laws.
© Johnston Press

Steel and Jeremy Thorpe welcome John Bannerman to Parliament following his appointment to the House of Lords in late 1967. Although Steel had supported Thorpe as Liberal leader after Jo Grimond resigned that year, he quickly became disillusioned.
© Johnston Press

John Pardoe and David Steel during the 1976 contest to succeed Thorpe as Liberal leader. The campaign was not particularly edifying, with Grimond memorably remarking that it risked becoming a competition as to who was 'the biggest bastard'.
© Rex Features

Printed by the Government Printer, Salisbury

Form No. I.F. 5

RHODESIA

IMMIGRATION ACT, 1966

NOTICE TO PROHIBITED IMMIGRANT

To .....DAVID   HARTIN   Scott   STEEL..................

at ....SALISBURY..

    TAKE NOTICE that permission to enter Rhodesia or to remain therein is refused on the ground that you are a prohibited immigrant by reason of the operation of—

    *(a) paragraph (*H*) of subsection (1) of section 5 of the Immigration Act, 1966;

    *(b) subsection (5) of section 5 of the Immigration Act, 1966;

    *(c) section 6 of the Immigration Act, 1966;

    *(d) section 30 of the Immigration Act, 1966, in that you have *entered/remained in Rhodesia

        in contravention of the provisions of ....;

    *(e) subsection (3) of section 23 of the Immigration Act, 1966.
    *Immigration officer to delete or complete as appropriate.
You are notified that, in terms of the Act, you may appeal to the nearest magistrate's court –

    (a) on the grounds of identity, as provided in section 10 (1) of the Act, if you have been alleged to be a prohibited immigrant by reason of the operation of paragraph (a) or (b) of subsection (1), or of subsection (5) of section 5 of the Act; or

    (b) to determine whether or not you are a prohibited immigrant if you have been alleged to be a prohibited immigrant by reason of the operation of any other provision of the Act.

    Such appeal must be noted within three days after this notice has been given, and shall be made on form No. I.F. 6, which may be obtained from any immigration officer.

Date ....

Place ....:.............

                          Immigration Officer

    I hereby acknowledge receipt of the notice of which this is a copy, declaring me to be a prohibited immigrant to Rhodesia on the grounds stated therein.

Date.....................................   Signature..

Having been partially raised in Kenya, Africa was a consistent thread throughout Steel's political career. On a 1972 visit to Rhodesia he was detained at Salisbury airport and forbidden from re-entering the country. Courtesy of David Steel

Steel alongside Margaret Thatcher and James Callaghan at the 1977 remembrance ceremony on Whitehall. Mrs Thatcher never forgave Steel for depriving her of an election earlier that year, while Callaghan came to view the Liberal leader with avuncular affection during the Lib–Lab Pact. © Getty Images

A talented campaigner, Steel's performance during the 1979 general election – the first to utilise a Liberal 'battle bus' – was generally credited with saving his party from electoral meltdown. © Johnston Press

ABOVE Liberal and SDP MPs all smiles during the so-called Ettrick Bridge summit at Steel's home in the Borders. What actually happened – an aborted attempt to sideline Roy Jenkins as the Alliance leader – was anything but light-hearted. © Johnston Press

THE RT. HON. DAVID STEEL. M.P.

HOUSE OF COMMONS
LONDON SW1A OAA

2nd July 1983

Dear Alan,

Sorry about the enclosed, but there it is.

I do urge you __not__ to circulate it to colleagues.
Pass copies round and collect back if you wish,
otherwise it will leak.✳

Whatever the precise timing of departure you
agree, the announcement should I think be made
next weekend, certainly before the Executive
and Council the following weekend, which I do
not now propose to attend.

Yours ever,

David

enc

Alan Beith, Esq, MP
House of Commons
London SW1A OAA

✳ This is very important because I do not want
a press circus at the university. I hope I can at
least trust my colleagues to respect confidentiality
in this. DS.

LEFT Steel's hitherto unseen covering letter to certain Liberals during his attempted resignation in the wake of the 1983 general election. He was disappointed, exhausted and far from certain he wanted to lead his party into another election. © Sir Alan Beith MP

Steel sporting some questionable knitwear alongside David Owen during the troubled 1983–87 parliament. 'The two Davids' were novel and popular, but their clashing visions for the Alliance created constant tension behind the public bonhomie. © Sally Soames

Steel comes face to face with his *Spitting Image* in 1992. Although he claimed to see the funny side, internal Liberal polling showed that his depiction as being under the heel of David Owen caused him real political damage. © Rex Features

Steel jokes for photographers on the Bournemouth waterfront during the 1984 Liberal Assembly. As leader, he dreaded his party's autumn gatherings which – particularly Eastbourne in 1986 – were full of political danger. © Michael Ward for the *Sunday Times*

Steel and the interim SDP leader Bob Maclennan manage a smile as they announce that merger negotiations are on hold following the 'dead parrot' debacle. Even had Steel wished to lead the 'Social and Liberal Democrats', his handling of this incident made it almost impossible.
© Rex Features

ABOVE Steel photographed in front of the building that caused him so many headaches during his spell as the Scottish Parliament's first Presiding Officer. Having anticipated a figurehead role, Steel instead found himself virtually micro-managing the Holyrood project.
© Harry Benson CBE

LEFT A 1997 portrait of Steel wearing his Privy Councillor's garb at the National Liberal Club in Whitehall. After leaving the House of Commons at that year's general election, he gave full reign to what Michael Foot called his 'elder statesman' phase.
© Julian Calder

Steel but also Michael Foot in terms of leadership, the Liberal leader appeared keen to emphasise that the top Alliance job was still very much up for grabs. Under media pressure, however, Steel and Jenkins were compelled to come up with an answer. The result, as Shirley Williams admitted in her memoirs, was 'at once pompous and pretentious', not to mention 'presumptuous': Jenkins was to be 'Prime Minister designate', while Steel was to be 'campaign leader' in the forthcoming election. In his memoirs, Steel was careful to disown Jenkins's 'Pooh-bah-like title', with its 'ring of Gilbertian pomposity', having told Hugo Young in 1984 that it had been 'a [David] Marquand idea, which we fell for'.[87]

'There was absolutely no doubt in my mind that if the unlikely happened,' Steel wrote, Jenkins 'should lead our Cabinet but with obviously more power for the Deputy Prime Minister as leader of his own party than was possessed by Willie Whitelaw. On this we were agreed.' In this division of duties, Steel was sincere, respecting – as Richard Holme put it to Hugo Young – Jenkins's 'huge experience'. 'He realizes he's got no ministerial experience at all, no managerial record even,' said Holme, adding that even then Steel probably underestimated 'the appalling difficulties of running governments these days'.

By September 1982, however, the words 'Prepare for government' (from Steel's Llandudno speech) looked very hollow draped across the platform in Bournemouth. A Conservative recovery had begun when the government's unorthodox economic strategy looked as if it might be working, a recovery then given added momentum by the Falklands War, thus the Liberal–SDP Alliance now ranked a poor third in opinion polls. Planning had therefore switched from completely breaking the mould to hoping for the balance of power should neither the Conservatives nor Labour win an outright majority at the next general election.

Very quickly the SDP had become yesterday's news. The media

---

87   HJSY/2/10, notes dated 8 February 1984.

spotlight moved from Hillhead and Croydon to Port Stanley and South Georgia, while candidates fighting their first local elections in May 1982 – as the *Sheffield* and *Belgrano* were sinking – found themselves swamped by patriotic fervour.[88] 'The party had been formed the previous year to heal the divisions in our society,' wrote Dennis Outwin in his history of the SDP, 'but now these divisions were being healed in a different way – by Galtieri and the Argentine junta.'

General Galtieri's invasion of the Falklands, recalled Steel much later, 'robbed us of real political triumph', while 'there was never really any serious chance that we would recover the ten or so percentage points which we had tumbled in the opinion polls.' This had obviously not been part of the plan, and when the Alliance trailed the Conservatives by more than 4,000 votes in a by-election at Mitcham & Morden (which had been an SDP seat) in June, the effect on its electoral prowess was clear. Returning from a meeting at the United Nations, Steel admitted the Falklands had dominated the agenda, unconvincingly adding that he had also been 'struck by the enormous public interest in the Alliance, and in the challenge Liberals and Social Democrats are mounting to our present class-based system of politics in Britain'.[89]

Publicly, Steel was supportive of the government's military action but not uncritical; only when the jingoism kicked in did he let off steam: 'I have to confess a real sense of repugnance', he told the Bournemouth Assembly, 'at the way the Prime Minister has tried to use the heroism of British servicemen to the greater glory of herself and her party ... by wrapping herself up in the Falklands bunting.' ('How remote', sneered Thatcher in her memoirs, 'politicians can seem at these times of crisis.') The subsequent Franks Report (into the causes of the war), to Steel and Jenkins's disappointment, offered little ammunition, and instead the Alliance's

---

88   In the May 1982 local government elections the Alliance secured net gains of 150, although these were modest compared with what might have been.

89   STEEL/B/1/7/5, press release dated 16 May 1982.

recovery depended on events outside its control: whether the economic recovery was sustainable and whether the left and right of the Labour Party remained at each other's throats. 'I can count on both,' was Steel's confident prediction.

As a result, Steel realised the importance of a united front, having learned from his experience of the Liberals in the 1960s and early 1970s that however unpleasant it was to choose between two unpalatable decisions, the choice had, as he told Hugo Young, 'to be made *together*'. It was, he added, an 'absolute prerequisite', although the 'SDP have yet to understand this'. Although Steel disagreed with Jenkins on certain issues (chiefly defence and law and order), he believed there was agreement on almost everything else, 'on how to get into incomes policy, how to run a mixed economy, etc.'.

Nevertheless, the SDP did couch many of its policy positions in vague terms, arguing they were 'sensible' or 'common sense' without giving many details. The same could have been said of the Alliance, although Steel reasoned that while it was true it lacked 'precise policies in some areas', he did not think people wanted 'precise policies'. 'They are interested in attitudes rather than details,' he told Hugo Young, and 'the attitude of the Alliance is known well enough.'[90]

Defence policy, however, illustrated that Steel was being more than a little complacent. While Steel and the Liberal Party accepted the case for a NATO-controlled nuclear deterrent against the Soviet Union, it did not see any need for the Polaris missile system (then being phased out) to be replaced with Trident. In short, the Liberals did not agree with an independent (British) nuclear deterrent, while the SDP did. Both parties, however, were opposed to Trident. 'We both accept that Polaris has a limited life,' Steel told *The Times*, 'and therefore the only point we have to discuss is one of timing.'

Steel had touched upon UK disarmament in a speech following his election as Rector of Edinburgh University in May 1982, telling

---

90   HJSY/2/8, notes dated 25 March 1982.

students that 'the case for an abandonment of independent nuclear deterrence at this stage is a powerful one in principle.' He expressed a preference for collective European action to achieve *détente* and, ultimately, global disarmament, and while Steel and Jenkins held this admittedly shaky line up until the 1983 general election, it was to become a running sore in the next parliament and of crucial importance to the future of the Alliance.

David Owen, meanwhile, remained passionate that the 'SDP mustn't just look like another Liberal Party'. '[He is] determined not to be an Alliance party,' noted Hugo Young after lunch in November 1982. 'Thinks Steel is finally understanding this.'[91] Owen also despaired of Jenkins, whose politics he considered 'rooted in the 1960s' (as indeed were Steel's). Indeed, the Alliance's policy prospectus was, according to Ian Bradley, 'little more than a rehash of that cosy, corporatist, social democracy which nearly sank this country in the 1960s and 1970s'.

Aware that the Alliance had lost momentum, in a Christmas message Steel spoke of the need to campaign with 'renewed vigour and determination'. At a relaunch event at Westminster, meanwhile, Shirley Williams promised fun as well as idealism and hope. And when she appeared alongside Steel on a Christmas edition of Thames TV's *Afternoon Plus*, Williams was true to her word. Invited to do a musical number, Steel changed the words of the 1916 song 'If You Were the Only Girl (in the World)', and crooned 'If you were the only Shirl in the world and I was the only Woy'.

In the midst of the media silly season, it got huge press coverage. Less successful was Steel's much-ridiculed rap single, 'I Feel Liberal – Alright!' 'You can help me to change the face of British politics,' intoned Steel with full New York funk-rap backing, 'let's pull our country together instead of tearing it apart' (it also came with instructions for dancing the 'Steel-Step'). Steel was later teased about this on the BBC programme *Have I Got News for You*, although he protested at the time that it was 'meant to be fun,

---

91   HJSY/7/2/1, notes dated 17 November 1982.

tongue-in-cheek, and geared to the young'. 'I think it's quite a good tune,' he added. 'I've actually had one or two fan letters.'

Steel certainly remained very popular at the end of 1982, whatever the state of the wider Alliance. Posters urged students and members of the public to 'Come & Hear David Steel: Britain's most popular leader', while Shirley Williams even introduced him at one meeting as the 'most popular politician in the country'. Still deferential to Jenkins, Steel did his best to boost his co-leader's profile, but voters simply refused to believe the claret-drinking former Chancellor was one of them, even when Jenkins talked up his (relatively) modest background. Liberals, therefore, urged Steel to claim seniority but he deliberately held back, provoking more damaging internal squabbling. Both Jenkins and Steel appealed for discipline, the latter asking his colleagues to resist the temptation of 'confiding their views in the nearest journalist, microphone or camera'.

The Liberals' spectacular by-election win in Bermondsey on 24 February 1983 simply made things worse, Simon Hughes's victory (in an admittedly grubby campaign) taking Steel's approval rating to 65 per cent. 'The better the polls,' judged Jeremy Josephs in his book *Inside the Alliance*, 'the more Liberals became convinced not only that their leader's modesty was excessive, but, more importantly, damaging to the interests of the Alliance.'

But if Bermondsey signified a revival for the Alliance, it was short lived, for in Darlington the following month the SDP candidate came third after a disastrous campaign, which Steel considered a vivid demonstration that the Liberals knew 'more about third-party politics' than the Gang of Four.[92] Aware of the need to appease the Liberals, Roy Jenkins made it clear he 'would serve under Mr Steel if we jointly judged that it was the right position for the Alliance'. It was, however, all very confusing for the electorate, who would, within a few months, be asked to cast their votes for an Alliance that appeared less than unified. The SDP, noted Crewe and King, 'went

---

92   HJSY/7/2/1, notes dated 27 April 1983.

into the election hopeful and determined rather than – as would have been the case in 1981 – positively optimistic'. Steel, meanwhile, believed there was still 'everything to play for'.

The election campaign, believed Steel's adviser Alan Watson (later Lord), ought to be fought with 'maximum polish and drama'. 'There has to be a long march through barren territory if we are to win support for our view,' he concluded, 'and at present we do not seem to have left camp!' Privately, Steel was also realistic, arguing the party needed to stress its 'commitment to end see-saw politics', but wording it in a way that conveyed 'our capacity to do this … if we don't actually achieve government, while retaining government as our aim'. Publicly, Jenkins and Steel said the Alliance would be prepared to do a deal with either main party, while privately Steel believed the SDP should attack Labour and Liberals the Conservatives, 'exposing their insensitivity, authoritarianism and incompetence'.[93]

Crewe and King concluded that while both possessed impressive qualities, Jenkins and Steel were instinctive politicians who preferred 'to fly by the seat of their pants', neither being a strategist in the sense that he paused occasionally 'to examine the changing terrain in which he finds himself in order to assess the best means of achieving those goals'. As a result, the Alliance message in 1983 was virtually identical to that in 1981, echoing Jenkins's Dimbleby Lecture with its broad themes of national unity and avoiding extremism on left or right. By constantly stressing moderation and reconciliation in the changed circumstances of 1983, Jenkins and Steel 'ran the risk of appearing dated and faded, of seeming to be ever so slightly out of touch'.

Proportional representation, on which the Alliance was united, was central to the two leaders' strategy for the election. William (later Lord) Wallace, one of Steel's advisers, prepared a memo on 'The Constitutional Position, if no party has a majority', while Steel – determined not to repeat the mistakes of the Lib–Lab Pact –

93   STEEL/A/2/6, paper by Alan Watson, 8 February 1983.

dropped heavy hints to the Labour right. 'An interesting conversation with David Steel on Thursday evening,' recorded Giles Radice
in his diary during March 1983. 'He says that, if there is to be a
coalition with Labour, he wants the support of Labour MPs. I say
that conference's support would also be essential.'

Lunching the previous November, David Owen had told Hugo
Young he wanted to go into the election 'pledged to a referendum,
as second best solution to PR. i.e. if SDP–Libs hold a balance, they
will demand a referendum in six weeks on PR'. Also speaking to
Young in April 1983, Steel presciently predicted that the Alliance
vote could be close to Labour's, albeit with a 'vast discrepancy'
in seats. Still, Steel reckoned this would convince many Labour
MPs to see the merits of PR, which he saw as the Alliance's 'single
biggest demand'. When Young asked Steel about Owen's desire to
push for a referendum within six weeks, he thought it a 'bit daft to
set so short a time' although 'again, it all depends on the numbers'.
Although the Alliance would 'have to act decisive[ly] and hard',
being prepared to oust Thatcher and Foot, it would 'depend on
how strong our PR case really looked like to the public'.[94]

In truth, as Steel probably realised, PR elicited little enthusiasm from British electors, although initially, at least, the Alliance
campaign seemed to go well. The manifesto – the boldly titled
A Joint Programme for Government – combined core Liberal
commitments like constitutional reform with Social Democrat
economic policies, and was generally well received, albeit seen as
a little backward looking. The Alliance's first broadcast, featuring
Steel and Jenkins praising one another, was also judged a success,
while neither leader committed a gaffe or contradicted the other in
public. Steel, meanwhile, took delivery of his 'Mark 2 battle bus',
which, unlike the 1979 model, was equipped with a rooftop platform for open-air meetings and, added a press release breathlessly,
'two television sets and a video-tape machine'.[95]

---

94   HJSY/7/2/1, notes dated 27 April 1983.
95   STEEL/B/1/2/2, press release from April 1983.

Joining Steel on the campaign trail, the *New York Times* noted the bus's 'Day-Glo signs in Liberal orange'. Sometimes, the report noted, 'things go hopelessly wrong', as they did when Steel visited Shirley Williams in Crosby:

> His speech never took place; the supermarket that was to have provided a crowd had not yet opened for business. Desperately improvising, he lifted the hatch in the bus's roof and told the driver to tour the town while he stood and waved and talked through a loudspeaker. But it was lunchtime, the streets were deserted and a high-tension wire nearly throttled him. Mrs Williams said bravely to a tiny knot of people, 'We're delighted to see so many supporters'; Mr Steel said later, when she had left, that the Social Democrats had a lot to learn about organising things.

For the duration of the campaign both the BBC and ITV had agreed to give the Alliance almost as much airtime as the Conservatives and Labour, while most newspapers did the same. 'I tried to concentrate on the longer television interviews which more easily absorbed my "ornate gothic constructions" as [Steel] later friendlily described them,' recalled Jenkins in his memoirs, 'while leaving him [Steel] to do the shorter clips at which he was much better than I was.'

Even so, many Liberals remained unhappy about Steel's subordinate position. As Michael Steed put it, Jenkins was hardly a doorstep asset and, with hindsight, Steel's 'greater televisual appeal was the asset to be exploited'. Crewe and King reckoned 'Steel was fluent and relaxed as a campaigner' while Jenkins, by contrast, 'was almost always ponderous and ill at ease'. Worse, millions of viewers watched Jenkins perform poorly during major interviews on *Weekend World* and *Panorama*, while one poll showed that Steel easily outpolled him – both among Alliance supporters and among voters generally – in terms of who would make the best Prime Minister.

The tipping point, however, was a 24 May Audience Selection survey that dramatically revealed that a Steel leadership would add nine points to the Alliance's showing. A MORI poll also showed that 85 per cent of voters could identify Steel, higher than both Jenkins and Owen. Liberals inevitably got jumpy, and reports surfaced that Steel was coming under increasing pressure to sideline Jenkins for the good of his party, the Alliance and indeed the election. 'The pressure was certainly on,' recalls Steel. 'The main protagonist was Richard Holme, who said to me, "You've just got to do this." I was troubled by the fact that we were getting the wrong images across, while I had made a tactical error at the beginning of the campaign by saying Roy could do the opening broadcast.'

The fact that Holme and other senior advisers, such as Alan Watson and Stuart Mole, were fighting marginal seats added a certain *frisson* to the advice making its way to Steel. 'Some of the key people from my office were expected to become MPs,' he recalls, 'so at the very moment I needed them, they weren't around.' Steel, meanwhile, consulted Owen during a visit to Plymouth. 'I agreed he was right on the issue,' recalls Owen, 'but I made it clear David had to sort it out with Roy in private, then we'd all ratify it.' Publicly, Steel told journalists it was not in his 'nature to push people aside'. 'Obviously, we will have to look at our campaign over the next week,' he added, 'to see how best we can project the idea that this is not a presidential campaign.'

At several points in the week beginning 23 May Steel sounded out Jenkins in private. 'He telephoned early on the morning of 24 May and spoke with embarrassment and imprecision about the issue,' recalled Jenkins in his memoirs. 'He reverted to the subject at an unfestive breakfast (normally our common meals were enjoyable) which we had together the next morning. I said I would think about it during the day.' After thinking about it, however, Jenkins concluded that to change tack at this point in the campaign would smack of disarray and, worse, not actually benefit Steel. 'It is often easier to be admired as number two than as number one,' reasoned Jenkins; Steel 'might well find himself dangerously exposed after he had removed the protection of having me as the more vulnerable one of the partnership'.

On 27 May Steel informed journalists that leading figures in the
Alliance would be meeting at his Ettrick Bridge home on Sunday
29th, the purpose being 'quite simply to reassess strategy in view of
the collapse of the Labour Party'. Steel phoned Jenkins the following day to say he planned to raise the leadership issue once again
although, curiously, he told David Owen 'that nothing could be
done. Ousting Roy against his will was out of the question.' As
Owen flew north from Norwich he read the *Sunday Times*'s speculation on the coup, complete with denials from Jenkins ('absolute
nonsense') and Steel ('the subject is not on the agenda').

On the same flight was John Pardoe, who Steel had drafted into
the campaign at the last minute. He recalls making it quite clear
to Owen that he planned to raise the Jenkins issue. 'The Alliance
wasn't working in the election campaign,' he recalls, 'so it was no
good shilly-shallying about – David was leader of the Liberals and
had to lead the whole thing.' Pardoe, however, denies any large
degree of co-ordination with Steel (Crewe and King imply the
contrary). 'I had formulated a view with myself that this had to
be resolved at Ettrick Bridge,' recalls Pardoe, 'that there had to be
one leader.'

What then unfolded in the combined kitchen/dining room at
Ettrick Bridge was, in the judgement of Crewe and King, 'one of the
more bizarre episodes in recent British political history, with more
than faint echoes of the second act of *Macbeth*'. Steel sat with one
or two others in a window seat while his advisers and the Gang
of Four arranged themselves more or less randomly around the
dining table. Significantly, perhaps, Owen sat at the far end of the
table from Steel. Shirley Williams pointed out that the window was
open, so it was closed (the press were outside), 'but the atmosphere,
for a time, remained casual,' noted Crewe and King. 'Judy Steel
hovered in the wings. The Steels' dog wandered in and out.'

After some general chat, it was Pardoe who raised the leadership question and Jenkins's performance. Before anyone in the
SDP had a chance to respond, an 'extremely uncomfortable' Steel
produced a draft press release (Bill Rodgers called it 'an abdication

statement') to the effect that Jenkins would be taking a back seat and concentrating on Hillhead while Steel took personal charge of the campaign. When David Owen tried to change the subject, arguing that there was plenty to discuss beyond the leadership question, Owen recalled that Steel 'persisted, with extreme toughness'. 'I ought to make it clear', said Steel, 'that I've had many representations from the Liberal Party and from the constituencies saying that they have very little faith in the current leadership and that there's a lot of unhappiness about.'

By then it was clear the whole thing had been planned in advance by the Liberals present; as one later admitted, 'We came not to bury Jenkins, but to embalm him.' Bill Rodgers, who remembered Jenkins looking 'bruised and embarrassed', attacked John Pardoe for his clumsiness and was strongly supported by Shirley Williams. 'His [Pardoe's] denunciation of Roy's role in the campaign was brutal,' recalled Williams. 'He told him in short order to relinquish his leadership position. Sitting across the table from Roy, I could see him gradually yielding to this extraordinary battering. I kept mouthing "No! No! No!" at him, fixing him with an unblinking stare in an effort to attract his attention.' Those present also remember Roy's wife Jennifer doing her best to scupper the coup attempt. Owen, meanwhile, said nothing, believing the joint leadership to be a matter for Jenkins and Steel to sort out privately.

'In the end,' recalled Rodgers, 'Steel and Pardoe gave up.' As everyone broke awkwardly for lunch, Jenkins and Steel put together a statement giving the latter a higher media profile and attended a relatively gentle press conference at the local village hall. When a reporter asked Steel if anyone had suggested that Jenkins step down, Steel simply lied, replying, unequivocally: 'No.' Remarkably, not a word about the attempted coup made its way into the newspapers. 'It was not written up as an attempted assassination,' recalled Owen in his memoirs. 'The television coverage on Sunday night had even looked pretty good – a relaxed group; friendly politicians being nice to each other!' Or, as Steel later put it, 'We got away with it.'

En route back to London, Bill Rodgers remembered Owen's

response as they went over the morning's events: 'I didn't know he had it in him!' 'I glanced at David in the passenger seat beside me and caught a half-smile of genuine admiration,' Rodgers wrote in his memoirs, 'perhaps his first and last for David Steel in the six years of Alliance.' Indeed, Owen essentially agreed with what Steel had attempted to do, privately commending Steel's 'efforts' after the meeting while having 'no doubt that there would have been some electoral return – perhaps as much as ten to fifteen extra seats'. Several years later, however, Owen changed his tune, telling the journalist Kenneth Harris that he had never 'seen such a ruthless and savage deed'. 'The whole thing', concedes Steel, 'is an episode of which I'm not particularly proud.'

Those present at Ettrick Bridge could hardly believe their luck on reading the following day's newspapers. Even better, there was an apparent surge in the polls. Steel's 'sober' estimate was that the Alliance would win 27 per cent of the popular vote although that, he admitted to Hugo Young, would not result in 'any big improvement on the present position' in terms of seats. If it managed 29 or 30 per cent, however, 'then no one can tell what the effect in seats will be.'[96]

In a private strategy paper entitled 'OPERATION BREAKTHROUGH', Steel argued that if Liberals did

> not shoot for the higher target with the credibility and momentum that implies, we may not reach the lower base, on which our prospect of holding the balance of power and achieving proportional representation demands. Equally, if we achieve 29–30 per cent without converting that level of support into solid gains in our best prospects, the tide will recede leaving us no stronger than we are now and demoralised as well.[97]

It was a prescient prediction, for it must have occurred to Steel

---

96   HJSY/7/2/1, notes dated 27 April 1983.
97   STEEL/A/2/6, undated memo.

that any realistic prospect of the Alliance achieving what Jeremy Thorpe had called 'total breakthrough' had vanished as soon as an Argentinian flag was planted on British soil. Had it simply been too much to expect an awkward pact between one old and small party and a new and untested party to go from a theoretical third force to a party of government with no intervening period? As Jeremy Josephs concluded before the election, not doing well 'would surely be the end' for the Alliance, Steel having instructed his troops to 'prepare for government' rather than a slaughter.

'Ever since I became leader of the Liberal Party seven years ago,' said Steel in an eve-of-poll Alliance broadcast, 'I have urged the building of a political movement capable of uniting our country in a spirit of co-operation and partnership in a way the Tories and Labour simply cannot by their very nature do.' 'The country has been yearning for this,' he added, 'and I believe that it must happen and that it will happen. We have waited long enough.' Indeed, Steel hoped the 1983 general election would vindicate everything he had argued for since 1976.

Privately, Steel told Hugo Young that 'a mere twenty-five seats' would 'not be the breakthrough which we are looking for', although on the other hand 'even a relatively small' Alliance tally could 'still form the basis of something worth staying around for'. But, added Steel with a hint of melancholy, 'I have been leader for over seven years now ... if it did seem to have failed, there'd be a lot of people who opposed what I have done [and] who w[oul]d want me out fast.' Under that scenario, concluded Steel, he 'would not hang around'.[98]

---

98   HJSY/7/2/1, notes dated 27 April 1983.

7

THE TWO DAVIDS

The 1983 general election was both a triumph and a disaster for the Liberal–SDP Alliance. A triumph because it polled 25.4 per cent of the popular vote, the most for a third party since 1923 and only 676,000 votes behind the Labour Party, but a disaster because under the UK's first-past-the-post electoral system this returned just twenty-three Alliance MPs compared with Labour's 209. It introduced, as the *Sunday Times* put it, 'a new order of unfairness', but then no one had ever claimed British politics was fair.

For the Liberals, at least, there were glimmers of comfort. Instead of twenty-nine SDP MPs and thirteen Liberals, as before dissolution, there were now only six SDP representatives but seventeen Liberals. Would the Alliance have overtaken Labour had Steel been its single, acknowledged leader? Ivor Crewe and Anthony King judged that 'the evidence in favour' of this was 'not strong', although Steel would certainly have handled the key television interviews with more aplomb. Whatever the rights and wrongs of the Ettrick Bridge coup, it had occurred too late in the campaign to effect any major change.

Watching a seven-year leadership project come crashing to a halt at polling stations around the country cannot have been a pleasant experience. Steel was also exhausted, not just from seven busy years leading his party, but from a gruelling national campaign. Unsurprisingly, Judy Steel remembers her husband returning home 'in the most hurt and despondent of moods, determined to resign as leader'. A leader, observed the journalist James Naughtie two years later, 'for seven years and nothing to show for it, except the hopes for next time. The thought that he might [wait] another five weary years for the same result was intensely depressing.'

Facing his first parliamentary meeting six days after polling day, Steel's mood cannot have improved. Led by Cyril Smith and supported by David Alton and Simon Hughes, those sceptical of both the Alliance and Steel's leadership style (which included Michael Meadowcroft, newly elected in Leeds West)[99] subjected him to 'a barrage of criticism' and circulated a strategy paper calling for the Chief Whip and a deputy leader to be elected by the Parliamentary Party – a clear attempt to curtail the leader's power. Steel also detected a lot of resentment regarding who had and, more to the point, who had *not* been present at the Ettrick Bridge summit. 'It was a very bad-tempered meeting,' recalls Steel, 'with lots of bruised egos. I thought to myself, "I've had enough of this; there must be better things to do."'

Also weighing on Steel's mind had been the resignation of Roy Jenkins as SDP leader two days before. Although understandably anxious about his weak performance during the campaign, Steel had reassured himself that for as long as Jenkins remained at the helm then there was a strong chance the two parties would merge and, considering Jenkins was nearly twenty years his senior, Steel could reasonably expect to take over as leader. The election of David Owen, who succeeded Jenkins unopposed, diminished this likelihood considerably. And although he had told the journalist Hugo Young before the election that he was 'not much interested in a parl[iamen]t which contains fifteen Libs and five SDP MPs', Owen was now determined to consolidate his grip on the SDP and fend off any moves towards merger. 'Roy would have tried to push through joint selection [of Alliance candidates] at the September conference so I had to oust him before then,' Owen admits. 'I just

---

99   More happily, Steel had the satisfaction of seeing his former aide and friend Archy Kirkwood gain his neighbouring constituency of Roxburgh & Berwickshire.

wanted what I called an "amicable divorce", but when I consulted the other SDP MPs it was clear I was in a minority of one.'

When Steel met Owen shortly after the election, he put the prospect of a merger to the new SDP leader. This, recalled Owen, allowed them to 'discuss the pressure ... quite frankly', although he made it clear he would 'oppose it tooth and nail', conceding only – as Shirley Williams recorded in her memoirs – 'that the Alliance would remain in existence at least until the European Parliament elections of 1984'. Owen, however, agreed to limit what he would say in public, as did Steel, while both agreed not to exploit temporary changes in party and personal fortune. 'I considered myself bound by that conversation thereafter,' recalled Owen, 'and never once tried to oust David Steel from our joint leadership.' Two beaming Davids then posed for the cameras, leaning on a five-barred gate.

So that was that. Steel, meanwhile, sought to repair his rather strained relationship with Jenkins. When Steel remonstrated with him for not giving him advance warning of his resignation he got, as Jenkins put it in his memoirs, 'a pretty sharp answer'. Beyond that, Jenkins attributed the Ettrick Bridge interregnum 'to an error of judgement rather than of motive'.

Meanwhile, soundings taken by Hugh Jones at Liberal HQ indicated that although there was disappointment and some criticism, Steel was still in a strong position as leader. 'I told him all this as he sat in my office,' recalled Jones in his memoirs. 'I think he took it in, but I was not sure. He made no comment except to thank me for it. He seemed almost concussed.'

Ten days later, in what Jones called 'a fit of gloom', Steel addressed a letter of resignation to party president John Griffiths, having already said publicly (in a radio interview on 14 June) that he was by no means committed to staying on and leading the party into the next election. The letter covered four main complaints:

1. The Parliamentary Party – two MPs (probably Cyril Smith and David Alton) 'for whom I have particular personal regard' had

refused to accept frontbench duties, making 'their decision all the more painful for me'.

2. The Association of Liberal Councillors (ALC) – this, wrote Steel, was 'how the militant tendency started', adding that it was in danger of becoming 'a party within a party'.

3. Assembly resolutions – Steel found attempts to remove his right of veto over the Liberal manifesto 'irritating', and moves to transfer responsibility for party political broadcasts to a Liberal Party committee 'preposterous'. No matter what other criticisms people had, argued Steel, this aspect of his leadership had been 'one area of triumphant success'.

4. Party units – Steel could not accept that regional, city and constituency Liberal parties adopting strategy at odds with the Assembly and executive was 'a virtuous characteristic of Liberalism'. He also referenced his 1976 Assembly speech about not wishing to lead 'a nice debating society'. 'I certainly do not intend', he added, 'to lead a nasty one.'

Individually, concluded Steel, none of these complaints justified resignation, but taken together they added up 'to a picture of a grave lack of purpose and discipline which has to be put right'. Judy had tried to persuade him of a wider responsibility to the party, but he simply could not 'find the mental or physical energy to begin to cope with a bout of internal argument'. He wanted to spend more time with his family and 'repair ... the Steel finances'. But Steel did not intend 'to sulk in my tent'; he would accept a party brief in the autumn and, 'having spent seven years largely on Liberal strategy, devote more time to writing and speaking on Liberal philosophy and policy'.

In a covering letter to Alan Beith on 2 July, Steel added the following:

Dear Alan,
    Sorry about the enclosed, but there it is.

I do urge you not to circulate it to colleagues. Pass copies round
and collect back if you wish, otherwise it will leak.*

Whatever the precise timing of departure you agree, the
announcement should I think be made next weekend, certainly
before the Executive and Council the following weekend, which I
do not now propose to attend.

Yours ever,

David

* This is very important because I do not want a press circus at
the university [see below]. I hope I can at least trust my colleagues
to respect confidentiality in this. D.S.[100]

Steel had clearly made up his mind, although many who saw the letter
believed it bore all the hallmarks of mental and physical exhaustion.
'Physically he was near a breakdown,' judged Dennis Outwin in a
1987 book on the SDP (Graham Watson later accused the SDP of
spreading rumours to that effect), while in his memoirs, Alan Beith
stuck to the official line that Steel had 'become ill with post-viral
depression and exhaustion'. Judy Steel, along with Archy Kirkwood,
played a key role in persuading him to change his mind, with the
latter even retrieving Steel's resignation letter from an Ettrick Bridge
post box. Others, such as Beith, weighed in by telephone. 'Nearly all
of us at the top of the party believed that neither the timing nor the
reasoning for a change were right,' recalled Beith, 'and that David
Steel was in no state to be taking the decision.'

Nevertheless, Steel was adamant he must take a break – later termed
a 'sabbatical' – of at least two months, 'not just because he physically
needed it', recalled Judy, 'but to make a point with his colleagues in
parliament and the party at large'. As Judy also admitted, it was not
exactly clear 'what that point was; but it was of consuming importance
to him'.[101] Graham Watson (later Sir Graham), who replaced Stuart

---

100 Sir Alan Beith Papers (private collection), David Steel to Alan Beith, 2 July 1983.
101 Steel later admitted his 'sabbatical' had been 'somewhat over-publicised
       and exaggerated'.

Mole in Steel's office after the election, remembers the inspiration for
the sabbatical coming from a Scandinavian politician who had taken
a similar break from frontline politics. 'He thought it would appeal
to the electorate,' recalls Watson, 'making a show of taking some
time off, winning support among the public and allowing the party
to have a think about the future.'

Part of the point was also to spend more time with his wife and
children. Billy, whom the Steels had adopted in 1976, needed a lot
of attention, although he had developed a close relationship with
David.[102] 'Billy had a deeply disturbed background,' recalled Steel
in his memoirs, 'and this continued to show up through his teens in
many traumatic ways, exacerbated by intrusive press interest.'

When Billy accompanied his father to a ceremony marking the
'patriation of the constitution' in Canada in April 1982, he gave
Steel 'an excited goodnight hug' before sampling every drink in his
hotel room minibar. The following morning, Steel having failed to
rouse him, the hotel authorities had to gain entry to his room using
a master key, finding him 'lying in bed semi-conscious'.

On leaving school Billy attended the Arts Educational School in
London, sharing Steel's rented flat in London (as Catriona did later
on). His presence in the family, however, had a negative effect on
Graeme (as Steel had predicted), creating yet more tension in the
family home. By nature a private person, Steel was not inclined to
air any of this publicly. Only in his memoirs, published in 1989,
did he describe any of this, while his wife's (published in 2010),
included an even franker account of the challenges she faced as
Steel's spouse. In 1982 Judy had told *Woman* magazine that even
after seventeen years as an MP's wife, when in London she felt like
'an observer, an outsider and completely out of my element'. '[H]e
has built up a life, a circle of his own in London,' she reflected.
'And when I come south, I barely touch it. In London, I only exist
as David's wife.'

---

102 There are a few quite personal letters (dated 1980) from Billy to Steel among
the latter's papers at the National Library of Scotland.

As Peter Bartram wrote in his biography of Steel, while David was 'quiet, tough, slightly shy, and disciplined', Judy was 'vivacious, bubbling, out-going and somewhat chaotic'. Even so, as the 1983–7 parliament progressed, Judy would often be 'unfavourably contrasted' (as she recalled in her memoirs) with Debbie Owen, 'the slim metropolitan wife who was a successful literary agent, while I was a frowsy careerless bumpkin'. In terms of family life, added Judy, she 'found the years of his [David's] leadership much the hardest'. Although a growing interest in theatre acted as 'a kind of therapy', she found coping with a family largely on her own 'dreadfully stressful'. 'I had the feeling that I was neither an adequate mother nor an adequate partner to David,' she admitted in her memoirs. 'I spiralled downwards, feeling more and more impotent.' Steel was of course supportive, but it was an added pressure at an already stressful period in his career. 'As the years roll by, Steel has become even more aware of the missed family life,' his biographer Peter Bartram had written in 1981. 'He is now far more likely to dig in his heels and insist to his staff that they avoid official appointments which clash with family birthdays or special occasions.'

Alan Beith, meanwhile, took over as acting leader of the Liberal Party,[103] while Steel took it easy until the new parliamentary session began in the autumn, only interrupting his rest to make three visits to Penrith & the Border for a by-election (caused by Willie Whitelaw's introduction to the House of Lords), as well as his duties as Rector of Edinburgh University. Indeed, in a quatercentenary lecture at the university just a few days after Steel's aborted resignation, a little of his post-election mood is easily identifiable:

Those of us engaged in politics, whether of the national or student variety, cannot press gang the rest of the population to share our own absorbing interests. The average citizen has his views, demands

---

103 Had Steel gone through with his resignation, Beith would probably have competed with Truro MP David Penhaligon for the succession.

to be able to choose – and, more importantly, to fire – his representatives, and will choose them more on his perception of their
general demeanour and attitudes than on a detailed analysis of a
collection of policy resolutions.

It was a clear repudiation of the 'community politics' beloved of
Liberals such as Tony Greaves and the policy obsessions of delegates
at Liberal Assemblies. Indeed, by this point Greaves (via the ALC)
was pushing to remove Steel's veto over manifesto pledges in an
internal row that was to rumble on until the autumn. The Liberal
leader, he commented publicly, now had a 'dictatorial, Thatcher-
type' style.

David Owen considered Steel's sabbatical 'an incredible situation', not least because the main opposition party, Labour, was
leaderless (Michael Foot having resigned after the election) 'and
the Liberal Party leader was resting'. Owen, ironically, benefited
from this leadership vacuum, the internal balance of the Alliance
tipping in his favour. 'It left space for me,' recalls Owen. 'The only
reason we [the SDP] were able to survive was because I had zest
and we won the battle of ideas. In 1983 and 1984 even Margaret
Thatcher fell back, so I had the field almost to myself.' Speculation
about Steel's future also refused to disappear. In August *Private
Eye* depicted the Liberal leader behind bars with a speech bubble
saying: 'If there's any more talk about me threatening to resign
– I'll resign.'

By the time Steel returned to the fray for the September Liberal
Assembly, the press was full of speculation that he had lost control
of his party. Steel, however, successfully fought off Greaves's attempt
to remove the leader's right of veto, aided by Jo Grimond (who had
been wheeled out over the summer) and his wife Laura, who argued
in a memorable speech that it would be absurd for Steel to be forced
to admit on television that there were aspects of his manifesto with
which he disagreed. At the SDP conference in Salford, Owen also
shored up Steel's – and by extension the Alliance's – position with a
warm tribute. 'Friendship holds the key to it all,' said Owen. 'That is

why I will never allow the press and media, who only want to report divisions, to drive a wedge between David Steel and myself.'

In his end-of-Assembly speech – an important one given speculation he was no longer interested in politics – Steel joked about the 'few days' he had taken off that summer ('But I'm back now and I must say you're all looking a good deal better for it') before embarking on a lengthy defence of the Alliance. As had become the custom, he referenced his first speech as leader:

> I said that the road I intended us to travel back to power would be a bumpy one. And indeed we have climbed some rough terrain together. But look where we've got to. We have established for the first time in fifty years a really secure base camp. We are ready to begin the final assault on that summit.

It was fighting talk and, usefully, Steel sounded as if he meant it. Otherwise his demeanour over the past week had attracted some attention. The *Radical Bulletin* had described him as 'remote' and 'somewhat arrogant', while the BBC's John Cole later recalled his 'extraordinary style'. 'He holds court in his suite,' wrote Cole, 'goes out to lunch and dinner with journalists, and shows a certain distaste for his followers.' As Monroe Palmer, the Liberal treasurer, had felt compelled to tell Steel before the 1982 Assembly, 'I think the party would accept your decisions, attitudes, policy preferences etc. if you would waste a little more time buttering up certain group leaders. People like to be flattered and consulted.' It would, he added, make 'people feel that they were part of the decision'.[104]

Several tensions associated with the first phase of the Alliance, namely policy and leadership, also remained during the 1983–7 parliament. Seat allocation was, at least initially, just as problematic. When a dispute arose early on over North Bedfordshire, Bill Rodgers told Steel they would have to agree 'on a suitable channel

---

104 David Steel Papers STEEL/A/1/1, Monroe E. Palmer to David Steel, 5 September 1982.

for dealing with these matters urgently'. 'Presumably you don't wish to be involved as you were before,' added Rodgers. 'But an effective channel with authority behind it is absolutely vital.' Steel concurred, firmly indicating his desire not to 'get involved in seat negotiations again', although he would 'discuss the necessary machinery with David'. Owen, meanwhile, told Steel of his concern at 'the number of Liberal seats that are going ahead and selecting candidates'.[105] The use of 'joint selection' in strongly disputed seats (whereby Liberals and Social Democrats all voted on a joint candidate) did not necessarily make things easier, with Owen regarding the process as a 'stalking horse' for merger.[106]

The election of the modernising Neil Kinnock as the new Labour leader (with the moderate Roy Hattersley as his deputy) on 2 October 1983, meanwhile, increased the pressure on both Alliance leaders. The challenge for what inevitably became known as 'the two Davids' during the 1983 parliament was threefold: articulating a non-Labour/socialist alternative to resurgent Thatcherism, maintaining good relations within the Alliance and, crucially, convincing the electorate that casting a vote for the Liberals and SDP would not be wasted at the next general election.

David Owen, as Messrs Kinnock and Hattersley would have known, could be a difficult character, disliked by as many of his former colleagues as he was by Liberals within the Alliance. MP for Plymouth Devonport since 1966, the former GP had risen quickly through the Labour ranks, becoming an under-secretary at the Ministry of Defence in 1968 and, from 1974, minister of state at the Department of Health and Social Security (DHSS) and the Foreign

---

105 Bill Rodgers Papers Box 8, Bill Rodgers to David Steel, 29 September 1983; David Steel to Bill Rodgers, 5 October 1983; David Owen Papers D 709 3/11/5/3, David Owen to David Steel, 3 October 1983.

106 Later in the parliament, relations between the SDP's Dick Newby and the Liberals' Andy Ellis were good enough that not only were Owen and Steel relatively uninvolved in seat allocation negotiations, but in the 1987 election no Liberals opposed SDP candidates in any seat.

Office. Finally, following the death of Tony Crosland in 1977, Owen
– aged only thirty-eight – became the youngest Foreign Secretary
since Anthony Eden.

Widely regarded as talented, Owen could also be conceited and
arrogant, to the extent that he even quoted Denis Healey's verdict
in his memoirs, that 'the good fairies gave the young doctor almost
everything: thick dark locks, matinee idol features, a lightning
intelligence – unfortunately the bad fairy made him a shit'. Roy
Jenkins likened him to the poisonous Javanese upas tree, which
extinguished all life around it (a line also quoted by Owen in
his book). The Labour MP Giles Radice, meanwhile, considered
Owen's personality 'abrasive'. 'He could be charming to older politicians or younger acolytes,' he wrote. 'With his equals he was all
too frequently rude, moody and suspicious.'

Even the mild-mannered Steel found Owen a handful, privately
telling Robert Mugabe that he was harder to deal with than
Mugabe's rival, Joshua Nkomo. Publicly, Steel said Owen was
'not the easiest person in the world to work with. He never has
been in any post he has held.' Owen, in turn, said his initial relations with Steel were 'edgy but civil', while his memoirs fluctuate
between charming and damning. 'I never underestimated David
Steel's manipulative skills,' wrote Owen in the latter vein, 'if they
had been matched by an interest in the policies best suited to our
country, he would have been a formidable force.'

In other words, Owen did not regard his Liberal counterpart
to be 'a serious figure', which for him, as the SDP MP John
Cartwright recalled, 'was ... absolute damnation'. Paddy Ashdown
also suspected Owen of not believing that Steel had 'the stuff of real
leadership in him'. This disdain grew stronger when it came to the
wider Liberal Party which, according to Jenkins, Owen essentially
regarded 'as a disorderly group of bearded vegetarian pacifists'.

That said, Steel too was arguably 'not as nice as he looks' and
could, according to the columnist Alan Watkins, be impatient with
subordinates. Recounting the story of one aide who left his room
without closing the door properly, Steel snapped: 'I don't mind if

the door's open, and I don't mind if it's shut, but for God's sake make up your bloody mind.' As Watkins noted, Steel said this in his hotel suite 'when he was under some strain at a party assembly' and indeed, such incidents were rare. The Liberal leader, wrote Peter Bartram, was 'slow to criticise, but ... also slow to praise', driving his small staff of two aides and two secretaries 'as hard as himself', although none of them complained. Interviewed jointly with Owen by John Tusa in mid-1984, Steel gesticulated at Owen and joked: 'He's the nice one and I'm the nasty one.'

Steel's temper, however, was nothing as compared with Owen's. Richard Holme later put the Owen–Steel relationship in marital terms, describing 'one partner who is given to periodic explosions of temper and throwing crockery but then calms down and goes sulky, and one partner who smiles and carries on'. Private polling appeared to back this up. When, in mid-1984, the Liberals commissioned image research, analysis revealed that the words most often associated with David Owen were 'aggressive', 'egotistical', 'hasty' and 'divides', while those associated with David Steel were 'controlled', 'healer', 'modest' and 'brings together'.[107]

Roy Jenkins thought part of the problem was that the two Davids were contemporaries, of a similar age and even looked 'superficially alike'. 'At least Steel and I were incapable of being confused with each other and therefore, in a sense, of being rivals,' wrote Jenkins. 'We would never have appeared together cable-stitched. I would always have been less sportingly dressed, and he would always have had the advantage of looking leaner and keener.' The relative youth of the two Davids, however, also presented a vigorous image which even Margaret Thatcher conceded was 'at first attractive' (although later, 'increasingly ridiculous'), so much so that the Prime Minister instructed Norman Tebbit to find a new chairman, 'someone young, to counter the Steel–Owen image'. (The solution was the 43-year-old John Selwyn Gummer, who was slightly

---

107 STEEL/A/4/2, minute of Joint Leaders Advisory Committee dated 25 July 1984.

younger than both Owen and Steel but had the misfortune to look older.)

For his part, Steel generally played down any conflict with Owen, saying 'There was no personal animus between [us] however much the press played that up,' while Owen maintains the relationship was 'as good as it possibly could be in the circumstances'. Indeed, while both men were perfectly capable of a maintaining an adult relationship, what really divided them was, as Matt Cole put it, 'their completely divergent agendas for the future of their parties'. 'On policy matters they shared a good deal of common ground, even where elements of their parties were at odds,' judged Cole, 'but on merger they were irreconcilable, and suspected one another of manipulation in pursuit of their respective agendas.'

While Steel constantly pressed for measures that would bring the two parties closer together, Owen remained determined to maintain the separate identity of the SDP. Lunching separately with both Davids during February 1984, the journalist Hugo Young found Steel relatively upbeat, but Owen gloomier. The SDP leader complained about too much 'bickering, too much scrutinising of the relationship, too little pride in the Alliance and the fact that it's two parties'. Owen also criticised 'too feeble a leadership of the Liberals', adding (unconvincingly) that this was not a criticism of Steel. 'But the fact is that he has left a lot of areas too free for the troublemakers,' Owen told Young. 'Lib[eral]s can be led in the right direction if the leadership tries hard enough.' If Steel resigned, however, Owen thought it would be 'a catastrophic loss'. 'There's no doubt he's gone down, and it's not just due to my arrival on the scene,' reflected Owen. 'Something much much deeper [Owen did not elaborate, noted Young, but 'I suspect he half knows']. But he will, I hope, recover his steam and ground. He is irreplaceable. After him there's literally nothing.'[108]

Even before the 1983 general election, Bill Rodgers had detected a 'clearer view of David Owen's strategy'. 'Put simply, it was to

---

108 HJSY/2/10, notes dated 29 February 1984.

keep the Alliance together only long enough to win proportional representation for Westminster,' he later wrote, 'and then for the SDP and the Liberals to go their separate ways.' Steel's aides, meanwhile, had pushed him to make a bid for merger in December 1983 but he had declined, wanting to make it 'clear that any break-up of the Alliance is D[avid]O[wen]'s fault'.[109] Publicly, however, the two Davids enjoyed good relations. Owen and his wife Debbie even stayed with the Steels at a snow-covered Ettrick Bridge during the Christmas of 1983, with the Owens later providing reciprocal hospitality at their cottage in Wiltshire.

On 13 April 1984, Steel sent Owen a hitherto unpublished memo 'on the state of the Alliance as I see it, to serve as the basis for a serious discussion on where we are going'. While he believed the Alliance would survive until the summer (sustained by 'various elections') thereafter Steel feared 'it will be open season for every freebooter in both our parties.' There were, he argued, several factors, although chief among them was 'a perceived obduracy on your part about the growing-together of the Alliance'. Progress on this count required tackling both parties' 'internal self-protecting empires' and building 'a small nucleus of Alliance organisation' ahead of the next election, the Joint Leaders Advisory Committee (JLAC) being an 'inadequate command structure for a national campaigning force'.

Steel had similar concerns about policy development, highlighting as 'absurd' the existence of two 'quite separate Health Service campaigns'. 'Like you I am against creating a vast corpus of detailed policy,' wrote Steel. 'We need at least to do more work in the area of incomes policy and industrial partnership, but just as I am becoming attracted to some of Meade's ideas I fear that you are moving away from them.'[110] In terms of seat allocation, Steel described increasing resentment 'at our inflicting apartheid on the

---

109 David Thomson's notes for *Against Goliath*.

110 James Meade (1907–95) was a Nobel Prize-winning British economist famous for his economic 'growth theory'.

constituencies'. 'You have always explained very fairly to me your objection to joint selection, and I am seized of your argument,' conceded Steel. 'But I now think that it is over-weighed by the damage caused to our momentum through lack of joint action, especially on selection.'

But it was the strategy of the Alliance ('a real minefield') that exercised Steel the most:

> Fairly or unfairly you are perceived as blocking *any* integration within the Alliance, and I am perceived as letting you do this and not bothering about it. Well, I am worried about it, and not just because of probable trouble ahead as I described at the beginning … If at the time of the Liberal Party Assembly that year [1981] I had envisaged that the SDP would have an eventual existence separate from and competitive with the Liberal Party I should not have wished, nor would I have been able, to 'sell' the Alliance to my party.

Steel then outlined four options:

1. Merger. 'You have steadfastly and consistently opposed this. I am also against it during the present parliament, though not so vehemently. But because I recognise your strong commitment I do not wish to open this up for discussion.'
2. 'A growing-together leading to possible union in the indeterminate future. This is my preferred option.'
3. The status quo. 'I simply do not think this is workable, and it will lead to increasing disaffection not just in my party but in yours as well. It will also diminish our public impact.'
4. 'Dissolution of formal Alliance while continuing friendly co-operation in Parliament, by-elections and encouraging electoral pacts where they are desired by the constituencies.'

Number four would, argued Steel, at least be 'workable and defendable in logic', although potentially damaging to both parties. 'But at least both parties would be free to develop their own campaigns and identities as they wish, if that is what you really prefer.'

Steel made it clear he remained 'committed to the objectives of the Alliance' and would 'stick with them through to the next election, whichever course we decide to take'. Steel concluded with a final warning: 'I am sure we can keep the Alliance going in some form, but I do really see the storm clouds gathering if we don't take a new initiative.'

Owen took more than two weeks to reply to Steel's dark (although realistic) take on the Alliance's prospects. He showed the memo to Shirley Williams, who agreed that 'merger now would be divisive in both parties, and would absorb an awful lot of energy needed for other things.' 'You and David [Steel] are the Alliance's most precious assets ... I am amazed at the sheer workloads you both carry,' she added soothingly. 'But here too lies one of our greatest problems. The Alliance looks like a two-man band.' On 'relations with the Liberals,' warned Williams, 'I think we face trouble.'

Finally replying on 1 May, Owen said his 'perceived obduracy' existed in both parties, stemming from the perception, 'perhaps mistaken, but nevertheless sincere of what is in the interests of our Alliance'. 'It is a judgement moreover held,' added Owen a little defensively, 'by many of us who took the greatest risk with their political futures and held with total consistency.'

On policy development, Owen noted acerbically that it was 'no accident that those enthusiastic for joint policy making in each and every policy area are also the most ardent advocates of merging. If one loses the ability to create policy as a party one has lost one's separate identity.' All Owen conceded was a willingness to have 'more joint meetings of our two parliamentary parties', though he protested that the JLAC had 'worked quite well'.

Owen then recalled putting two questions to Steel about the 'nature' of an Alliance party, 'would it still have to have the word "Liberal" in its title?' (Steel had said 'yes') and would 'it still have to give total independence to the local associations or parties' (again, Steel had answered 'yes'). Owen argued, rather petulantly, that attending constituency dinners as the guest of Liberal MPs was 'hardly the action of someone who wishes to block the further development of the Alliance'. 'Nor', he added, 'was the restraint we in the SDP showed in the aftermath of Etterick [*sic*] Bridge, your sabbatical, the policy shifts at Harrogate away from the joint platform on which we all fought, the actions of people who wished to block the Alliance.'

Clearly getting into his stride, Owen then raked over recent history in order to make the point that Steel too had clear ideas about what he wanted from the Alliance:

> You pushed publicly for an early break from the Labour Party, you then pushed publicly for a very close relationship between the new SDP and the Liberal Party, without giving us time to build up our own identity. You made it quite clear that you wished Roy Jenkins to be our leader. You argued for a single leader and despite your doubts, which you know I thought well founded, you effectively made Roy Prime Minister designate. You then felt it necessary to go back on that for understandable reasons, actually in the middle of the campaign.

'I mention all this not to argue that was the right or the wrong course,' continued Owen, 'but merely to remind you that you had and still have your own views about both the SDP and the Alliance and in my judgement while some have been proven correct, some have been wrong. None of us are infallible.'

Had he realised the eventual aim of the Alliance was merger then Owen 'would not have helped form the SDP and nor I suspect would the majority of our MPs either'. So Owen did 'not understand' Steel's four options. 'If the creation of the SDP was not a con on its own members, there was never any agreement explicit or implicit to merge,' argued Owen. 'Nor was the Alliance founded on that basis.' He questioned why Steel felt compelled to 'mirror the conventional political pattern' when all his efforts should be focused on taking 'pride' in the Alliance. 'Perhaps the SDP is too homogenous but equally the Liberal Party is perhaps too diverse,' mused Owen. 'Our cohesion as an Alliance depends on our capacity to learn from each other. Our partnership depends on it being equal.' He continued:

> If I thought at this stage in our history, Option 1 – a merger – could bring this about best of all your options, I would go for it for all its other difficulties, but I do not. I believe that only you – David Steel – have the authority and capacity to bring about that transition within your party and furthermore to be blunt I only believe you will be able to do this if the SDP points the way from time to time by holding firmly to the politics of an alternative government. I suppose if either of us were to cease being leaders of our respective parties, the dynamics might change but the political difficulties would remain and the task of presenting the Alliance as a governing force would be even harder. I see no viable alternative than to continuing an equal partnership between our parties and between you and me as leaders.

Owen ended his sprawling memo on an optimistic note, arguing that if the Alliance could 'hang on until 1986' then it might see a return to the situation in 1981 when both the Conservatives and Labour were deeply unpopular. 'If by then the Alliance looks credible in terms of policy and is active on the ground, we could once again take off.'[III]

Thus nothing had been resolved. As Owen's moratorium neared its end (the deadline set after the 1983 election had been the June 1984 European Parliament election), Steel continued to push for merger, or at least movement in that direction, while Owen baulked at any such suggestion. Less than a year into the Steel–Owen joint leadership, the Alliance had reached an impasse. It did not bode

---

III   D 709 3/11/5/3, David Steel to David Owen, 13 April 1984; Shirley Williams to David Owen, 25 April 1984; David Owen to David Steel, 1 May 1984.

well for the remainder of that parliament, the next general election
or, indeed, its aftermath.

Relations between the two Davids at this point were clearly civil,
although hardly friendly. When a child's letter asking what Owen
would do if he knew the world was going to end was sent to the
wrong David's office, Steel passed it on, as Owen recalled, with 'a
barbed note ... suggesting that the end of the world was more my
department'. And when this found its way into the press, Owen
quipped that if he knew the world was going to end then he would
join the Liberal Party.

'About this time David wrote me a letter whose implications
were all too clear,' recalled Owen in his memoirs, 'he would make a
move to dominate the Alliance if we failed to win the Portsmouth
[South] by-election, something he clearly expected to happen. It
was like a black cone warning of a storm ahead.'[112] In the event,
however, Mike Hancock gained what had been a safe Conservative
seat with a majority of more than 1,300 on 14 June 1984. In elections to the European Parliament held the same day, the Alliance
polled a respectable 19 per cent of the vote.

A few days before William Wallace, one of Steel's advisers, wrote
in a memo that Owen 'tries to reserve all policy initiatives within
the SDP to himself and disregard his party and his own constitutional channels'. 'He is, as we all know, extremely impatient with
the requirements of party democracy,' added Wallace, 'and would
prefer the Alliance to operate quite straightforwardly from the top
down.' The same critique, of course, could also be applied to Steel,
and throughout the 1983–7 parliament both Alliance leaders, as Bill
Rodgers recalled, 'preferred to make decisions together rather than
find themselves bound by any joint committee of the two parties'.

---

112 It is possible that Owen was confusing this 'letter' with Steel's memo of
     13 April 1984. But the sitting MP for Portsmouth South, Bonner Pink,
     died on 6 May, so the memo could not have been connected with the
     by-election.

Replying to Wallace, Steel said he entirely agreed with concerns about 'authoritarian leadership'. 'After all, Jo [Grimond] had a "Leader's Committee" covering everything, which he appointed himself,' he added. 'I don't think I would get away with that nowadays, and have no wish to try!'[113]

Steel, however, was under pressure not just from Owen's leadership style, but also from his own party. Ahead of the September 1984 Liberal Assembly, *Liberator*, the journal of the party's left, wrote that Steel was 'tired and burnt out', as had been suggested, 'by last summer's mystery illness'. (A *New Yorker* profile of Steel that year concurred, observing him 'do no more than go through the motions' at constituency functions.) Steel dismissed *Liberator* as 'a rag', but came under further pressure from Simon Hughes, the MP for Bermondsey, and Paddy Ashdown, a rising Young Turk already jockeying for the leadership, to elect a single Alliance leader ahead of the next election.

Steel hit back by challenging his critics to field a candidate against him. 'We have an open system in our party,' he told ITN. 'If anybody wants a leadership election, they have only to ask for it and it can happen.' Covering the Assembly for *The Guardian*, Hugo Young judged that Steel had 'no great love for his party, nor it for him'.

When he made his first appearance in Bournemouth, he sat through the ninety minutes of a question-time for the Parliamentary Party with little-concealed disdain. In eight years as leader, he'd seen it all before. He could predict every question and every answer. The smoothly immobile countenance and loftily distanced eyes recall Ted Heath in his late leadership phase, gazing out with weary displeasure at a party which might just possibly be getting bored with him.

---

113   STEEL/A/4/2, William Wallace to David Steel, 8 June 1984; David Steel to William Wallace, 12 June 1984.

Despite differences between the two Davids and, more to the point, between Steel and his own party, by the end of 1984 the Alliance had recovered its standing, maintaining a regular polling presence of between 25 and 33 per cent of the vote. But as Christmas gave way to a new year, this improved poll rating only increased Steel's frustration. 'I honestly do not believe that your approach of "You look after the Liberal Party and I'll look after the SDP" is at all an adequate approach to leading the Alliance,' Steel wrote to Owen on 15 January 1985, 'as we shall be storing up trouble if we do not discuss any differences regularly between us.' He continued:

> Do you realise that until today we had not spoken for a month? Even allowing for Christmas, etc., this just is no way to keep the show on the road. As I indicated clearly to you on the telephone a number of grievances have been building up, and unless we discuss them frankly and amicably we risk losing what I genuinely believe is a golden political opportunity now presenting itself.[114]

Two days before, Steel's private feelings had also spilled over into the public domain. 'Our mission is not to represent "Thatcherism with a human face", promising a better-managed Conservatism,' he warned in a speech. 'We stand for different values and a better way for Britain. We will not do it by presenting ourselves as crypto-Tories, that is why our style of campaign and of leadership as well as our policies must be seen to differ fundamentally from Mrs Thatcher's.'

Steel's speech was probably a coded reference to the ongoing miners' strike, which had dominated UK politics since March 1984. Owen's instinct had been to oppose the strike and, while the SDP leader courted the National Coal Board boss, Ian MacGregor, Steel was more sympathetic, meeting the (non-striking) Nottinghamshire miners and criticising Mrs Thatcher's strident rhetoric (as well as her appointment of MacGregor). Clumsily, the two Davids had

---

114   D 709 3/11/5/3, David Steel to David Owen, 15 January 1985.

failed to co-ordinate their statements as Steel was attending the Democratic Party convention in San Francisco.

The wider problem was that Steel believed Owen was alienating Labour voters, observing 'tartly' to the BBC's John Cole 'that at a time when there was a revolt against Thatcherism and the Thatcher style, it was odd that Owen had become the hero of the *Express* and *Sun*'. Set alongside Steel's generally more pro-Labour statements, this inevitably led to confusion. As the broadcaster Brian Walden put it, 'What we don't know is who the Alliance is gunning for … Is the Alliance in business to replace the Labour Party or the Tories?'

But in the aftermath of the 1983 general election Owen no longer saw any point in appealing to the moderate centre ground. 'If we could simultaneously break right on the market and left on social policy,' he explained in his memoirs, 'I believed we could find an electorally attractive political mix.' This was Owen's so-called social market idea, which he had been exploring since 1981. Viewed as sub-Thatcherite by suspicious Liberals, the historian Duncan Brack has argued that it was little more than a slogan designed to differentiate Owen from his predecessor, Roy Jenkins, and also Steel, whose centrist interventionism he disliked (Liberals, as Steel and others pointed out, had long accepted the market). Indeed, during a December 1983 meeting with Owen, Steel had got the impression he was 'more and more Thatcherite, more and more at odds with his party'.[115]

Steel's concept of Liberal philosophy, never very deep, was firmly orthodox, embracing the free-market liberalism of the nineteenth century and the social (interventionist) liberalism of Lloyd George. Roy Jenkins had characterised Asquith's instinct as 'the maximum of radical result while arousing the minimum of conservative opposition'. Steel in that respect was Asquithian and had been since his 1960s activity in relation to abortion and apartheid: radical, but not so much so that it might upset moderate Tory opinion.

When it came to actually crafting policy, however, Steel's lack

---

115   David Thomson's notes for *Against Goliath*.

of interest was well known, to the despair of both Liberals and
Social Democrats. 'The problem with the Liberal Party', Owen
apparently told the Liberal MP Michael Meadowcroft, 'is that you
have a leader who isn't interested in policy.' The SDP MP John
Cartwright, meanwhile, remembered attending 'a number of
policy meetings where it was quite clear that Steel hadn't read the
papers'. 'Steel wasn't terribly interested in policy,' he added, 'and
that I think Owen found very difficult to get along with.'

Indeed, Owen was a one-man policy machine, regularly reeling
off five-point plans and releasing them to the press in a matter of
hours. Steel, by contrast, made no secret of his belief that detailed
policy development was an unnecessary indulgence. Voters, he had
argued in January, were put off by 'theological lectures about the
difference between Social Democrats and Liberals'. And although
he introduced a Freedom of Information Bill in the House of
Commons during 1984, it was more to flag up a standard Liberal
demand than effect any tangible change.

Following Gary Hart's campaign for the Democrat nomination
during May 1984, Steel was struck by the candidates' use of prima-
ries to 'sketch out the kind of America they would like to see in the
year 2000'. 'Whether in education, social welfare or protection of
the environment,' Steel wrote in *The Guardian*, 'what we have is a
discussion of the future and not, as happens with so much British
political debate, a constant dissection of the past.'

Steel had sought to rectify this the previous month by initiating a
series of 'Britain 2000' seminars, inviting Liberal-friendly individuals 'eminent in their own field to present a paper on the conditions
likely to prevail at the end of this century and how Liberals might
influence these and respond to the challenges they present'.[116] Steel
saw this not only as a useful exercise in its own right, but also as
a source of ideas for the next Alliance prospectus and, perhaps, a
useful foil for criticisms that he was not interested in policy.

---

116 Liberal Party Papers LIBERAL PARTY/2/32, David Steel to Liberal
colleagues, 12 April 1984.

'In my view politics over these last twenty years had become too much the servant of economics, and politicians the slaves of economists,' wrote Steel in an introduction to what was published as *Partners in One Nation*. 'As a Liberal and pluralist I believe in a panoply of diverse measures all of which contribute to the same end – the creation of a partnership society in Britain.' This had been a Steel refrain since the Lib–Lab Pact, a desire to nudge the UK from a wage-orientated to a share-income economy. As Steel wrote in a 1986 paper on profit-sharing (introduced on a modest scale by the 1978 Budget), 'I am convinced that a widespread adoption of this new "third way" forward could bring about an era of cooperation, success and shared reward for our companies and those who work in them.' (The partnership concept also dominated Steel's 1985 Assembly speech.)

'The result is a mixture of complaints about Thatcherism, provisional manifesto drafting and genuine argument from first principles,' observed *The Times* in a review of *Partners in One Nation*. 'Steel's book is remarkable for the rarity of its reference to Liberal history and tradition.' Published at around the same time, Ian Bradley's book *The Strange Rebirth of Liberal Britain* was laced with similar implications that the Steel-led Liberal revival lacked an intellectual base, although it did acknowledge that Steel had taken up such issues as the Falklands War, overseas aid and freedom of information in order to 'express his own innate radicalism and deep attachment to the politics of conscience and moral principle'.

In a foreword to Bradley's book Steel was, at least, offered the opportunity to defend himself. He refuted Bradley's view of the Liberal Party as having had an 'over obsession with tactics'. 'In my view he is wrong,' argued Steel. 'The change of recent years has been to rescue Liberalism from the fireside of Oxford studies to be once again a relevant movement appealing to a mass electorate.'

Inevitably, friend and foe alike used Steel's twentieth anniversary as an MP as an opportunity to assess his performance and political prospects. The journalist James Naughtie reckoned both had improved over the past year. 'He is making more – and better

– speeches outside the Commons than he was then', he wrote, 'and perhaps more importantly his work behind the scenes in the Alliance has lost the lethargy which marked his attitude for at least a year after the 1983 general election.'

> But he still suffers from the assumption that he is somehow a man whose moment has passed, and who is in league with one – Dr David Owen – whose moment has yet to come. Like all such impressions at Westminster it is hard to dispel once it has taken hold. He still faces criticism from Liberal activists that the SDP leader appears to be able to shuttle more efficiently from television to radio studio and back again than their own man, and is ready with the crisper instant comments.

The two Davids had, of late, been meeting more frequently, and their correspondence from that period is markedly less tetchy. Steel, however, continued to pester Owen about a merger, alerting him in May to a likely Assembly motion on the need for one Alliance leader. 'Realistically I do believe that after the next election the merger option will be up for democratic decision and I do not even know what my own attitude to it will be then,' replied Owen. 'I suspect a lot will depend on what has happened within the Alliance on the policy front. How good a programme for government we managed to agree; how well that held up during the election and how likely it looked like holding after the election.' As for having a joint leader, Owen could not 'imagine a more damaging scenario than to have a leadership election across parties. They are divisive enough when conducted within the constraints of a single party. Take that constraint away and there could be untold damage done to the Alliance.'[117]

At this point Steel was busy campaigning in the Brecon & Radnor by-election, caused by the death of the Conservative MP Tom Ellis Hooson (a cousin of Emlyn Hooson, Steel's former

---

117   D 709 3/11/5/3, David Owen to David Steel, 21 May 1985.

Liberal colleague). It was the Liberals' turn to field a candidate (the two Alliance parties took by-elections in turns), Richard Livsey, and, usefully, he won with a slim majority of a little over 500. 'I was glad for David Steel,' reflected Owen in his memoirs. 'He had had a rough year and this result gave him great heart and balanced the SDP success in Portsmouth. If the partnership were to thrive, the more we could keep it in balance the better.'

From this point the Joint Leaders Advisory Committee became the Alliance Strategy Committee, chaired jointly by the two leaders and meeting regularly to discuss and sometimes resolve problems between the parties. In early meetings, recalled Bill Rodgers, there 'was a desultory attempt to raise merger until it was seen to be fruitless'. In private, meanwhile, Rodgers tried to persuade Owen not to rule out merger and, indeed, becoming leader of that merged party. 'He never dismissed this out of hand,' he recalled, 'but a major obstacle was plainly his contemptuous impatience with much of the Liberal Party which he thought of as jejune and ungovernable. There was no song in his heart about the prospects for the next parliament.'

In July there was also a joint conference of candidates in London where both Owen and Steel (probably reluctantly) emphasised the dual leadership approach. Just weeks later, however, Steel reopened the leadership issue after scrutinising a *Daily Telegraph* poll which suggested Steel as sole Alliance leader would produce a 4–5 per cent lead. 'On reflection, I may have been misled by my own Parliamentary Party and national executive,' wrote Steel.

It is one thing to convince political activists of the possibility of dual leadership, it is quite another to saddle the electorate with yet another complication on top of all the new ideas of power sharing, coalition and electoral reform we are pressing on them. They want to know who's in charge.

As in his 1984 merger memo, Steel set out three (rather than four) possible options for future action:

1. 'nothing'.
2. 'we have a leadership election. I remain opposed to this for the
   reasons we have both agreed. There is a particularly idiotic idea
   canvassed by some [in the] SDP last Saturday that we should
   choose one leader on the eve of the election. I can think of nothing more upsetting.'
3. say 'no need for a single leader in this parliament ... [but agree] to
   end uncertainty and unnecessary speculation that D[avid]S[teel]
   will lead Alliance MPs either in government, or opposition, or
   whatever position of power sharing we achieve'.

Steel recognised that option three would require Owen to go much
further than he had in discussing this 'probability', but he could
think of no 'other way of avoiding both the "Prime Minister designate" fiasco, and the continued exploitation by our opponents of
repeated polls'. Could Owen, Steel wondered, 'come up with any
other suggestions?'

Remarkably, Steel did not receive a reply for another month,
Owen having only received his letter after visiting his Wiltshire
cottage on 30 August. He finally replied on 3 September from his
home in Limehouse, 'baffled by its context and amazed by your
conclusion which is diametrically different to the view you advocated so effectively on *Newsnight* on 24 July ... Why have you so
shifted your position from 24 July to 3 August?'

> You cannot expect me to seriously believe that it is the result of
> having read one Gallup poll. If we were to shift around the strategy
> of the Alliance on this basis then we might as well forget breaking
> through against the formidable opposition we face ... The argu-
> ments for a merger are and always will be wholly legitimate – I do
> not dismiss them, how can I? It is and always will remain an option
> to be taken by our members at any time, but that is their choice, it
> cannot be pre-empted by either or both of us.

Owen dismissed the *Telegraph* poll, saying that 'neither I nor others whose opinion I value agree ...We must maximise our appeal, broaden it, not narrow it and fragment it.' He repeated his line about reconsidering merger (with which Owen clearly conflated joint leadership) after the next election and, based on 'objective criteria', chiefly 'how effectively the joint programme had worked during the election campaign'. 'We must obviously talk soon,' concluded Owen. 'But why throw this firecracker into the pot when we are doing well and consolidating our position? It's all too reminiscent of Ettrick Bridge Mark II but at least it's private and let's keep it this way.'

Steel replied breezily a couple of days later, joking that if they exchanged any more hand-written letters, then they would 'fall out over which of us has the more indecipherable handwriting – I claim it is you!' Steel then refuted the notion that he had changed his mind on the basis of 'one poll', arguing that follow-up coverage of the *Telegraph* story had been less substantial than he had expected. He conceded, however, that Owen's allusion to Ettrick Bridge was fair. 'It is precisely to avoid that that I raise the issue now privately,' wrote Steel. 'What happens if after a year of our best efforts the polls still show a demand for one clear leader post-election?' 'We must', he added, 'keep this under watch.'[118]

Both Davids, meanwhile, continued to consolidate their joint, or 'tandem leadership', agreeing a timetable for a joint policy document and a joint leaders' office, while it was agreed the two leaders would address their respective conferences as a matter of course. Owen even went so far as to say that 'after the next election the issue of merger or of a closer relationship will come back on the agenda and rightly so', while Steel pushed the line as much as he could, telling TV-*AM* in February 1986 that 'on balance' he thought merger would be 'a good idea'.

---

118   D 709 3/11/5/3, David Steel to David Owen, 3 August 1985; David Steel Papers
      TD 3431/41, David Owen to David Steel, 3 September 1985; D 709 3/11/5/3,
      David Steel to David Owen, 5 September 1985. Curiously, neither Steel nor
      Owen quote from their 1984–85 correspondence in their respective memoirs.

By early 1986 both Davids would have been conscious that a
pivotal Labour conference at Bournemouth the previous autumn
had subtly altered the political terrain. There, Neil Kinnock had
taken on his party's militant left ('you cannot play politics with
people's lives'), marking a clear turning point for the Labour Party
and therefore, in Owen's view, for the Alliance's prospects. As the
Liberal activist George Binney warned Steel in a letter, 'The danger
is that the media and the public will once again feel that only
Labour provides an alternative government to Mrs Thatcher's.'[119]

Giving Steel his private thoughts on strategy a few weeks later,
Sir Russell Johnston implored his leader not to lose sight of the
bigger picture as he considered policy and tactics. 'A final point,
which may seem pompous, but I don't care,' he wrote. 'Let us
remember that all our efforts should be not on our own behalf, but
to enable the creation of a more skilful and humane society ... in
our country. Otherwise why are we here?'[120]

Steel attempted to answer that question in a well-received
Channel 4 broadcast in February 1986. *David Steel's Britain* was
an hour-long state-of-the-nation personal perspective, and as
good a statement of his political outlook as anything in print. The
programme opened in Steel's Borders constituency, which he took
as a starting point for his beliefs about 'the other Britain', a 'complex
mixture of history, tradition, politics, art and everyday life'.

Other parts of the programme were filmed in Toxteth (scene of
the 1981 riots), the Baxi factory near Preston (run on a partnership
basis) and outside Gladstone's family home in Liverpool. 'For the
last few years the left have been in control in Liverpool,' said Steel.

They seek simple answers to our decline as an industrial nation,
ignoring the actual people involved. They see the triumph of one
class, or one set of economic principles as the solution. This idea

---

119 STEEL/A/1/1, George Binney to David Steel, 5 October 1985.
120 STEEL/A/4/6, Sir Russell Johnston to David Steel, 11 November 1985.

that life and politics are a ceaseless struggle is exactly what is wrong
with our country.

'It was an effective testimony,' lamented Steel in his memoirs, 'lost
in the Sunday-night Channel 4 ratings.' A few weeks later Steel
had a long lunch with Hugo Young, during which he ruminated
at length about Owen, the Alliance and the next general election.
By this point, both the Liberals and the SDP had long since abandoned, at least privately, any hope of 'breaking the mould' and
forming a government in their own right; instead they focused
Alliance energy on gaining enough seats to hold the balance of
power in a hung Parliament.

Steel had clearly given this a lot of thought, explaining to Young
that the Alliance expected the other parties to get 'rattled' as this
scenario became more likely, allowing them to exploit the resulting
'splits and confusions'. On the 'theology' surrounding coalitions,
contended Steel, the 'Alliance will be the only party which has its
act together, having thought through a united front'. A key lesson
he had taken from the Lib–Lab Pact, meanwhile, was that 'a pact
was much less good than a coalition'. If the Alliance won only thirty
MPs, then they would have to settle for a pact, but if they got more
('and he is very confident that they will', noted Young), Steel would
favour coalition government, preferably for a five-year term and
contingent, of course, upon achieving proportional representation
(PR).

The two Davids, however, were split over how to actually get
PR in the first place, crucial as it was to the long-term prospects of
the Alliance as a third force in British politics. Although Steel realised it could not be achieved by anything other than 'a substantial
Alliance presence', Owen thought it best secured by a referendum
while Steel preferred to make it a precondition of any pact or coalition, agreed by the necessary Parliamentary Party. Nevertheless, he
was keen to emphasise to Young that the disagreement had been
'overplayed'.

Although the Alliance's polling average in 1985/86 had been

the best since its 1981/82 heyday, in mid-1986 it dropped to 25 per cent, its lowest level since April 1985 and only one point short of its 1983 election showing. There was, however, a general assumption that support would rise during an election campaign as a result of media coverage balanced more evenly between the two main parties and the Alliance. An 'unresolved problem', meanwhile, was how many joint appearances the two Davids should make. Steel believed it was a good idea, not only because it would remove 'from the interviewer the possibility of concentrating on what the other has said elsewhere', but also because it 'evidently pleases the folks'.

Steel told Young he had favoured a series of 'double-acts' on major television shows during 1985, while Owen had been 'more reluctant'.[121] Steel was particularly sensitive when Owen was interviewed solo. Complaining to London Weekend Television's Brian Walden about the SDP leader appearing alone 'yet again' ('peppered with questions about *my* statements and attitudes!'), Steel argued that recent Liberal council gains had been 'an ideal opportunity to have us both in, so that we could be *seen* to be speaking – as we do – with one voice'.

This sensitivity was a product of a sense of drift. 'We were marking time and like Mr Micawber we were waiting for something to turn up,' reflects Archy Kirkwood. 'To some extent it was by-elections and opinion polls which kept the show on the road,' agrees Sir Graham Watson, 'which gave the appearance of success and the appearance of momentum.' Steel felt this most acutely of all. 'We put up quite a good show in Parliament and around the country,' he says, 'it just wasn't moving forward; that was the trouble, it was stuck.'

> What else could I do? If the other leader [Owen] wasn't willing to
> move the Alliance forward then we were stuck. It was frustrating,
> but I just had to live with the reality. I was scared of having a bust up
> with Owen and there was no point in the two of us falling out – it

---

121   HJSY/2/12, notes dated 19 March 1986.

would have been disastrous – so we maintained good relations. Any discussions on merger were pointless if Owen wasn't playing ball.

By-elections, meanwhile, continued to sustain the Alliance. On 8 May 1986 the Alliance (fielding Liberal candidates) gained Ryedale from the Conservatives with a majority of nearly 5,000 and missed taking West Derbyshire (also from the Conservatives) by just 100 votes. Two months later, however, Steel marked his tenth anniversary as Liberal leader by making it clear he considered merger inevitable. In his memoirs, Owen recalled taking 'no exception to this speech, apart from wishing that we could get headlines on policy rather than on internal arguments'.

Internal Liberal polling showed that both leaders enjoyed similar approval ratings (15.9 per cent for Owen; 15.6 per cent for Steel), Steel's highest individual rating being 26 per cent for his understanding of ordinary people, and Owen's for his handling of foreign affairs. The Liberal leader, however, was down from a 'most able' rating of 24 per cent in June 1983 to just 16 per cent in May 1986. Supporters of the Alliance generally rated Steel's leadership abilities far higher than the electorate as a whole, although 49 per cent still considered him a 'likeable' person, 'competent primarily because of his long experience as his party's leader. He is able to get his views across effectively, is thought to be reasonable and intelligent and to know what he is doing.'

Unfortunately, added a pollster in a briefing note, 'the *Spitting Image* image of the Steel–Owen relationship appears to have taken root'.[122] Indeed, many commentators have argued that the popular perception of the two Davids was established by Luck and Flaw's popular 1980s puppet show. While Owen was depicted as suave and rather brutal, Steel was diminutive and victimised (though rarely, as many appear to remember, physically in Owen's pocket). 'I often said to myself, it must be awful to have that,' reflected Owen later.

---

122   STEEL/A/4/7, paper dated 1 July 1986.

'I think *Spitting Image* was a ghastly thing to happen for him [Steel] and he handled it with great dignity.'

'David was almost fatally wounded as a political figure by [that] representation of him week after week,' reflected Judy Steel in her memoirs.

> The caricature was well short of the truth, but it was what people saw, and what they believed. I could hardly bear to watch it, and often left the room: David always sat through it. I suppose he needed to know what they were saying, and his marvellous, resilient humour even allowed him to see the funny side.[123]

There is a shred of truth in most satire, and *Spitting Image*, although a caricature of the real relationship between the two leaders, reflected not only the two Davids' approval ratings but also Liberal perceptions of their leader's relative influence within the Alliance. To an extent, Steel had become – in some quarters – a figure of fun. Constantly mocked and heckled by Dennis Skinner and other Labour left-wingers in the Chamber, he even had to have a special microphone installed so he could be heard above the din. As someone who took himself and his politics seriously, this must have been a lot for Steel to stomach.

Also suffering by 1986 were Steel's relations, never very good, with the grassroots and Parliamentary Party, which continued to view their leader as far too willing to defer to Owen on policy issues. On 15 July the Montgomeryshire MP Alex Carlile alerted Steel to the first meeting of the 'June 9th Committee', which comprised all the Liberal MPs elected just before, at, or after, the 1983 general election. Signed by Carlile, Malcolm Bruce, Paddy Ashdown, Simon Hughes, Jim Wallace, Michael Meadowcroft, Archy Kirkwood and Richard Livsey, the committee declared itself 'extremely anxious'

---

123 'However, when I too was given a puppet,' adds Judy Steel in her memoirs, 'I rather liked it: she had a strong Scots accent and spent all her time knitting and soothing.'

about the state of the Alliance, believing it would be 'totally wrong to allow the present unsatisfactory situation to linger on, without evidence of progress towards a far greater cohesion between the two parties'.

In a covering note, Carlile apologised to Steel for the letter's 'pomposity', before making it clear the group was not exactly singing from the same hymn sheet ('Simon Hughes and Michael Meadowcroft are opposed to the idea of an Alliance front bench,' wrote Carlile, 'Michael is opposed to joint leadership'). Steel replied saying he was reluctant to meet the group as it 'could be misconstrued as divisive' by other colleagues, although his tone was constructive rather than antagonistic.[124]

While Steel could, as the former Liberal Party president Des Wilson reflected in his memoirs, act impulsively ('often when his patience was strained too far by a minority in the party'), he was normally inclined – particularly in situations like this – 'to find a solution acceptable to everybody, rather than just demand his own way'. As Sir Graham Watson recalls, 'Whenever there was trouble in the Parliamentary Party David would take the aggrieved party out for dinner and talk them round; it would then fizzle out.' In terms of relations with the wider party, however, relations were strained. 'He could occasionally be unappreciative of the enormous voluntary input of many Liberals,' wrote Wilson, 'probably less from ingratitude than a failure, from his Westminster perspective, to be fully aware of it.' Rather he remained closest to his aides and circle of advisers and, conceded Wilson, you did not have to spend more than an evening 'in the slightly chaotic, homely and warm base of the Steel family at Ettrick Bridge to see why'. It was obvious to most that Steel was more relaxed on home turf than he was in London. (This was in spite of family trouble. In 1985 Graeme Steel had been ordered to do seventy-five hours' community work for his part in a shop raid in which cigarettes, lager and groceries had been stolen.)

---

124 STEEL/A/1/2, Alex Carlile to David Steel, 16 July 1986.

Key to Steel's inner circle was Richard Holme, who, as Steel recalled after his death in 2008, 'regularly came into my office early, read and digested the main newspapers before I arrived and then departed for his employment'. As a result, Steel probably grew a little too dependent upon Holme, while his advice did not exactly motivate the Liberal leader to develop any great affinity with his members. 'He and others told Steel that his job was to lead, tell the party what to do and that they should do as they were told,' recalls Chris (later Lord) Rennard, then a young Liberal activist. 'Advisers like Holme and Alan Watson were contemptuous of the party's grassroots; they would tell David "They're all riff-raff, don't bother with them, they don't respect you enough", so inevitably there was a disconnect with the wider party.'

'A certain amount of resentment did grow up,' admits Steel, 'but I took the view that my advisers were people of substance who knew what they were doing.' He had expected, after the 1983 election, to be surrounded by confidants who were also MPs, but when Holme, Stuart Mole, Watson and Menzies Campbell failed to win their seats, Steel was instead left to rely on unelected advisers. By this point, meanwhile, Steel had virtually given up on attending meetings of the Liberal Party Council and National Executive Committee (NEC). 'The Liberal Party structure was really pretty chaotic,' he recalls. 'I simply concluded there was absolutely no point in my going to these things.'

Something Steel could not avoid was the annual Liberal Assembly. 'We had a date with destiny every autumn because of the Assembly,' recalls Archy Kirkwood, 'and we were at the mercy of the conference agenda committee.' Indeed, Steel had come to envy the Conservatives, who – unlike Labour and the Liberals – did not have to manage what he saw as an excessively powerful party conference. All of this, together with Steel's infamous lack of enthusiasm for policy development, was about to come to a head.

The Alliance debate over defence policy was twofold. First, the stationing of short and intermediate-range 'Cruise' missiles in western Europe, including at Greenham Common, was opposed by many Liberals; and second, the question as to whether Polaris, the 'independent' British nuclear deterrent, ought to be replaced when it reached the end of its shelf life. On the latter point, the two parties were split: David Owen wanted to retain a British deterrent at all costs while many (but not all) Liberals wanted rid of it. Steel, though admitting to 'some emotional sympathy' with unilateralism, had no particularly strong views on defence policy, and to him the details were even less important. His chief aim was to find enough common ground to craft a common Alliance position; defending the views of his own party came a poor second.

To Owen, however, not only was defence important (not least in his Plymouth constituency), but having witnessed Hugh Gaitskell's battle over unilateral disarmament in the late 1950s and early 1960s he was absolutely determined not to compromise. Furthermore, Owen believed the Alliance could not tackle Labour on defence without having a clear line of its own; Steel saw the logic of this, but had a harder game to play in terms of managing his party.

'The Liberal left or radical wing grew in confidence with each Assembly,' observed Matt Cole, the 1981 gathering having opposed the deployment of Cruise missiles, 'a gulf opening up between leaders who reckoned they knew what was best, and a grassroots behaving increasingly like that in the Labour Party.' Steel was aware of this, but adept, at least then, at developing 'coping mechanisms'. Defence policy had also been deftly managed during the 1983 general election, the SDP and Liberals having reached a deal over Trident and Cruise that Steel regarded as a 'minor masterpiece, however scruffy it looked'.

But when the issue of how, and indeed whether, to renew Cruise emerged during the 1983 parliament, the two parties – mindful of the damage an internal row had done to Labour during the election – agreed the need to compromise as soon as possible. 'If we are going into different lobbies on Cruise we must prepare the ground very carefully to minimise the damage,' Steel had told Owen in October 1983. 'One way of doing this would be to get cracking on a wider defence study. If the Alliance came to power in 1988 Cruise would be a fait accompli, and we must have an agreed defence and arms control policy.'[125]

Thus, in the summer of 1984, the Alliance established a Joint Commission on Defence and Disarmament, which was scheduled to report before the SDP and Liberal Party conferences in the autumn of 1986. It also bought the Alliance time, although not very much. At the 1984 Bournemouth Assembly Steel managed to win support (for the first time) to retain Polaris, while on Cruise missiles he argued for a deployment freeze in what *The Guardian* called a 'courageous and forthright' speech the newspaper likened to Gaitskell's 'fight, fight, and fight again' stand at Scarborough in 1960.

But Paddy Ashdown had other ideas. 'David, this is not about you, it is about unnecessary nuclear weapons,' he said in a speech opposing Cruise missiles. 'We want to get rid of them. But we do not want to get rid of you.' This earned enthusiastic applause from delegates but, as Ashdown recalled in his memoirs, 'a (wholly justified) look from him [Steel] which was clearly intended to turn me to stone on the spot'. Indeed, Steel was not amused. When someone wrote to him describing the Bournemouth Assembly as a 'unifying experience', Steel replied that if that were true, then 'words have ceased to have dictionary meanings. The public certainly didn't think so, and it was not reported as such by anybody.'[126]

In March 1986 Steel told Hugo Young he was confident the Joint Commission would come up with a defence policy acceptable to both the SDP and Liberals. 'The problem will be how he [Owen]', he added, 'sells it to the party.' By then, however, it was becoming known that the commission was likely to suggest that a decision on a replacement for Polaris ought to be deferred, not least because Polaris itself might remain in service until the mid- to late 1990s. Steel then – probably unintentionally – threw a spanner into the

---

125 D 709 3/11/5/3, David Steel to David Owen, 20 October 1983.
126 STEEL/A/4/8, David Steel to Kevin White, 6 November 1984.

works. During a lunch with Martin Dowle of *The Scotsman* he let slip that the commission's report would not advocate a replacement for Polaris, which Dowle took to mean it completely rejected the notion of adopting a new deterrent, rather than the actual recommendation, which was to 'wait and see'.

Owen heard about the story en route to the SDP Council in Southport. The headline, 'ALLIANCE REPORT REJECTS UK DETERRENT: OWEN'S NUCLEAR HOPES DASHED', injured both his pride (the implication he had been outwitted by Steel) and his policy stance (he had warned Steel he would not budge on a UK deterrent), and produced a nuclear reaction. 'No leader of any political party', Owen stormed to delegates, 'can stand before the British electorate and refuse to answer the question' of what to do about replacing Polaris. The 'fudging and mudging' of the commission's position, he added, 'would get and would deserve a belly laugh from the British electorate'.[127] Owen's outburst marked a turning point for the Alliance just months before a general election, Owen having neither checked the reality of the position with Steel nor spoken to Bill Rodgers, who was the Joint Commission's lead SDP member. Roy Jenkins later suggested that 'the Alliance began to die on that wet Southport Saturday morning', while Steel reckoned it 'marked the beginning of a worrying lack of trust at the heart of the Alliance between David Owen on the one hand and me with Roy, Shirley and Bill on the other'.

When the Joint Commission reported on 11 June 1986 it still fudged the issue of whether or not Polaris ought to be replaced with a new British deterrent. 'I believe that when the next election comes we have to have specific answers to these questions,' predicted Steel at a press conference. 'The election is not on us yet' and it

---

127 Owen notes acidly in his memoirs that Steel later wrote to *The Scotsman* saying he had made it clear to Martin Dowle that he had 'yet to see any text or draft' of the commission's report. The newspaper stood by its sources (i.e. Steel) while Owen had no doubt that Steel had 'leaked the report and then tried through the *Scotsman's* letter column to pretend he had not done so'.

would be quite wrong to take up 'cast-iron attitudes now'. It was agreed the two Davids should try and repair the damage by visiting France to explore the possibility of a Europe-wide (rather than solely British) nuclear deterrent, later dubbed the 'Euro-bomb'. Steel, however, was anxious not to be 'portrayed ... wandering round Europe seeking a new range of nuclear weapons', while his adviser William Wallace also flagged up 'considerable scepticism' among Liberal defence experts about the concept of a European solution.[128] Nevertheless, the SDP backed the Joint Commission's report at its conference in Harrogate, and Steel was confident his party would do the same at its Assembly in Eastbourne.

'Politics has a new found terror in requiring the Liberal leader to speak at not one but two party conferences,' wrote Jeremy Thorpe on 17 September, alluding to the requirement that each Alliance leader speak at the other's party conference. 'When we are in coalition, it will probably be three or even four!'[129] Steel had urged Owen to skirt over defence in his speech to the Liberal Assembly, but despite being conscious of 'walking on egg shells', the SDP leader instead treated Liberal delegates to a seminar on the negotiations, deliberately keeping his speech 'excruciatingly dull' in order to avoid a Liberal walkout.

On the eve of the Assembly, most observers expected Steel to triumph over his critics. But warning signs to the contrary were certainly there. Seeing Eastbourne as their last chance to influence Alliance policy, Simon Hughes, Archy Kirkwood and Michael Meadowcroft published a report, *Across the Divide*, which essentially built on the 1984 anti-Cruise Assembly resolution. 'I remember being flabbergasted when I saw the conference motion [which included the Euro-bomb proposal] for the first time,' recalls

---

128 STEEL/A/4/7, Minutes of Alliance Strategy Committee, 17 June 1986; D 709 3/11/2/14, David Steel to David Owen, 1 July 1986; William Wallace to David Steel, 19 August 1986.

129 STEEL/A/5/5, Jeremy Thorpe to David Steel, 17 September 1986.

Kirkwood. 'I just didn't see that it was realistic or had any political value, so I couldn't vote for it.'

Even when made aware of this discontent, however, Steel and his advisers still believed they could carry the day and thus made no attempt to manage the debate. It was a clear sign he had lost touch with his party, failing to understand widespread resentment at Steel's perceived deference to Owen – particularly following his May outburst – over the defence issue. As Duncan Brack observed,

> Steel failed to understand what most Liberals expected the defence debate at Eastbourne to be about. Steel wanted it to agree *Alliance* policy, but most Liberals thought it was going to agree *Liberal* policy, which the two parties would then negotiate about, in the context of the comprehensive joint policy programme that was at the time being constructed.

Paddy Ashdown, for example, told Steel that he and Owen were pushing the 'French option' with 'all the enthusiasm of a drowning man clutching at a life belt'.[130]

The next day, and having U-turned on his 1984 anti-Cruise position, Ashdown made a 'very bad' speech in favour of the leadership line, which, as the debate progressed, appeared to have split the party down the middle. Tony Greaves, representing the increasingly rebellious ALC, said it was about the 'values and principles and the soul of the Liberal Party'. 'If we abandon those what is our contribution?' he cried. 'We may as well join the SDP.' Owen, who watched the debate on television, found it a 'most depressing experience'. 'As I heard opposition ... mounting,' he later told the journalist Kenneth Harris, 'I found myself almost trying to will David Steel to go down to the rostrum and make an impromptu speech to stem the tide.' Similarly, Bill Rodgers was 'very surprised to find David Steel (unlike Gaitskell in 1960) not bringing his persuasive powers to the debate at all'. 'I was caught on the hop,'

---

130 STEEL/A/1/1, Paddy Ashdown to David Steel, 29 September 1986.

admits Steel. 'Had I known it was going to be defeated I could –
and would – have spoken in the debate.'

With the debate at an end, the Assembly voted by 652 to 625 to
give latitude to the leadership in crafting a European defence policy
(as set out in the Joint Commission report), but with a crucial
caveat providing 'that such a defence capability is non-nuclear'.
Not only did it blow a missile-shaped hole in any hopes of a united
Alliance front on defence, it represented a serious defeat for Steel,
who, along with Owen, had invested a lot of political capital in
the contrary position. At a press conference after the vote Steel
shrewdly played down what had occurred, but 'went to bed feeling
that the world was about to fall in'.

Newspaper headlines the following day were appalling: 'ALLI-
ANCE SHATTERED', 'STEEL HUMILIATED' and 'DOCTOR IN DISTRESS'
giving just a flavour of the sub-editors' malice. There was clearly an
anti-SDP subtext to what had occurred, with many delegates determined to make it clear to Owen that he could not have everything
his own way. Bill Rodgers thought it amounted to 'two defiant
fingers up to David Owen', while one of Steel's allies, when asked
what the message of the Assembly had been, said: 'That's easy. The
message of Eastbourne was: "Fuck Owen".' But far from taking
advantage of Steel's difficulties, Owen defended him both privately
and publicly. 'Our friendly working relationship deepened during
this crisis,' he told Kenneth Harris; 'we knew we had to reach agreement and David soon realised that I wanted to help, not hinder.'

'The real David Steel was on display at the press conference the
evening before,' recalls Archy Kirkwood, 'but then his political
advisers went to work.'[131] Indeed, as Des Wilson later recounted,
'somewhere between one and two o'clock in the morning and
seven or eight, David Alton [by then Liberal Chief Whip] went

---

131   Kirkwood later came to regret his involvement with the defence pamphlet.
      'It was the first time I'd had a disagreement with David and it was a blow
      to him, I know that,' he says. 'I shouldn't have got as closely associated with
      that pamphlet as I did.'

completely off the rails,' taking every opportunity to attack supporters of the amendment. Wilson later found Steel 'with his aides preparing an attack on the party', one telling him: 'We intend to crucify them.' And crucify them Steel did, rebuking his party with a stern lecture, receiving cheers, applause, cries of protest but mostly stony silence as he spoke of the Assembly's 'breathtaking misjudgement' at 'temporarily and unnecessarily' putting electoral victory for the Alliance at work. Steel also harked back to his first Assembly speech as leader a decade earlier, reminding delegates of the 'bargain' he had made with them that day. In one particularly eloquent passage, he declared:

> I am not interested in power without principles. But equally, I am only faintly attracted to principles without power. Without power all our resolutions, all our idealism, and all our passion will remain mere intention, mere hope, mere dream. We have so much to do, so much to change, such great tasks to achieve. But we will do nothing, change nothing, achieve nothing unless we can first gain power and then use it wisely.[132]

'The assembled were told by the headmaster that the exam results were not good enough,' was Des Wilson's interpretation of the speech. 'Steel almost fell into his chair at the end of the speech, trembling with exhaustion,' he recalled. 'It *had* been a brave and impressive performance, and, if he wanted to demonstrate authority, authority of a sort he *had* demonstrated.'

Steel's authority was also undermined by other, though lesser, rebuffs. The Assembly insisted that an elected negotiating team, and not just the two Alliance leaders, should fashion any post-election pact, while Steel was finally compelled to accept an elected

---

132 Tony Blair later paraphrased a line from Steel's speech following his election as Labour leader in 1994: 'Power without principle is barren, but principle without power is futile. This is a party of government, and I will lead it as a party of government.'

Chief Whip, something first mooted by David Alton and others in 1983. The only bright spot was the return to the Assembly, after a three-year sulk, of Cyril Smith, who, helpfully, proclaimed his confidence in both the Alliance and Steel's leadership.

Nevertheless, the Eastbourne defence debacle had been a comprehensive failure of party management by Steel, with whom the buck stopped as Liberal leader. As Duncan Brack has written, it need never have happened, particularly the unconvincing Euro-bomb initiative. 'At almost every stage, senior politicians [i.e. Steel and Owen] made serious – sometimes quite spectacular – errors of judgement,' assessed Brack. 'It should have been easy to avoid the rows taking place at all.' But by 1986 Steel was not only increasingly out of touch with his own party but he could not see how worried many of them were becoming about his apparent willingness to defer to Owen.

Owen also had to take much of the blame, not least for his inflexibility over even the mildest compromise. Indeed, Roy Jenkins believed Steel's defeat was a direct result of Owen's own brand of 'unilateralism' at the Southport SDP conference, while Michael Meadowcroft rightly pointed out that the Alliance's opinion poll slide could be traced back to Owen's speech that wet morning. Whatever the case, the slide continued post-Eastbourne, the whole affair damaging the credibility of the Alliance as Mrs Thatcher prepared to wind up the session. Crucially, it also damaged the credibility of the man at the eye of the storm. As the *Daily Telegraph* put it, the date of 23 September 1986 was 'likely to be found engraved on the heart of Mr Steel'. In retrospect, Eastbourne effectively marked the beginning of the end of Steel's term as Liberal leader.

Paradoxically, however, Steel was under no immediate threat. There was no rival leadership candidate and his political and media skills were still widely acknowledged, even by his critics. 'He was not a loved party leader,' judged Des Wilson, 'but there was a simple reason for this – he had no desire to be one, and made no concessions to attract affection. Likewise, for all his popularity with the public, he was not a populist.'

While Steel's approval ratings remained healthy, the gap between him and Owen had been narrowing over the last few months, so that by late 1986 the SDP leader was ranked above him as a potential Prime Minister. Not only did Neil Kinnock's moderate Labourism threaten to diminish the Alliance's *raison d'être*, but Owen looked increasingly likely to eclipse Steel as the coming man of third-force politics.

Although Steel had by common consent recovered much of his pre-1983 energy (Stuart Mole reckoned he had been 'back in business' since 1985), the SDP leader's grasp of detail and policy initiative had always been more substantial and, by early 1987, Owen had become 'consistently the tougher, more incisive performer both in the House of Commons and on television'. Liberals, of course, remained unhappy at the perception Owen had the upper hand. 'It's not in my nature to play second fiddle to anybody,' Steel felt compelled to say at one point. 'I think what we are playing is a very effective duet.'

The impression, of course, was gleefully reinforced by *Spitting Image*. Less than a week after the Eastbourne Assembly it depicted Steel practising his speech in front of a mirror. 'Fellow Liberals, go back to your constituencies and prepare for a bit of a disappointment,' he declared. 'Yes, I think that strikes about the right note.' Acutely aware of the effect on his personal profile, Steel descended into a quiet, but nevertheless deep, gloom.

Responding to a letter from Michael Meadowcroft on 17 October, he noted bitterly that council by-elections and polls had 'damaged my standing as much as the party's', adding that individuals (i.e. Meadowcroft) ought to have 'thought through the political consequences of making an unacceptable amendment to an otherwise acceptable motion before doing so. The party can no longer enjoy the luxury of indulging in "good debates" in a vacuum.' At a meeting of the Alliance Strategy Committee, meanwhile, Steel bitterly observed that the 'hoped for boost in opin[ion] polls did not come due to [the] Eastbourne debate'.[133]

Amid the gloom, however, a solution still needed to be found. Steel tried to get a grip on the defence issue, convening a summit at Ettrick Bridge on 19 October, followed by meetings of the Liberals' policy committee, Parliamentary Party and NEC. The result was a compromise requiring an Alliance government to retain a minimum nuclear deterrent until it could be negotiated away in global disarmament talks. If Polaris became defunct before that proved possible, then it would be 'maintained' (rather than 'replaced') with a system boasting similar firepower. Owen's Euro-bomb idea had already been quietly dropped.

Liberal discontent, however, remained. When *The Times* reported another Liberal scheme for disarmament, Owen blew his top in a letter to Steel:

> I can only warn you in the most private but serious way that I can that if you proceed on this course, you will make yourself and your party a laughing stock, and I cannot see how the SDP can be involved with it. By all means, work out together such an option and put it in if it really will fly. But to expect the SDP to go along with this bounce in this way is really extraordinary, particularly so when you yourself have paid tribute to the patient and quiet way in which almost everyone in the SDP has handled the delicate situation since Eastbourne.

Steel blamed Ashdown for the leak, reminding him by letter that he was not defence spokesman and 'to have such a wildly misleading story appearing in the press in between our two difficult meetings was the very reverse of useful'.[134]

Finally, in December 1986, the Liberal Party Council agreed a

---

133 STEEL/A/1/2, David Steel to Michael Meadowcroft, 17 October 1986; STEEL/A/4/7, minute dated 21 October 1986.

134 D 709 3/11/2/8, David Owen to David Steel, 22 October 1986; David Steel to Paddy Ashdown, 23 October 1986.

detailed defence accord with the SDP. 'It puts the defence debate,'
Steel declared at a press conference, 'internally, to bed.' With minimal compromise by the SDP, Owen had therefore won on Polaris, as
Ivor Crewe and Tony King put it, 'and won decisively'. The electoral
consequences, however, made both Davids potential losers. While
the Alliance had begun 1986 at 35 per cent in the polls, it ended it
on just 23.5 per cent (post-Assembly it had dropped as low as 17 per
cent), a stark illustration of the electoral fallout from Eastbourne.

A couple of weeks later, the Liberal MP Sir Russell Johnston sent
Steel what amounted to an end-of-term report card on his advisers
and parliamentary colleagues. It included shrewd advice in relation
to Richard Holme ('I know he's an old and loyal buddy, a nice
chap and a great help in speech-making, but his judgement and
feel isn't always there'); Paddy Ashdown, who Johnston reckoned
was 'furiously ambitious and … is going around knocking you';
and the defence rebel Simon Hughes, who 'simply has to learn how
these games are played'. 'He's hugely active,' judged Russell, 'but
also strangely clumsily inarticulate for one of legal training. They're
usually only long-winded on purpose!'[135]

The Eastbourne debacle also revived one of the British media's
favourite pastimes – merger speculation. If the two parties could
not agree over defence, then how could they possibly contemplate
becoming the same party? *Spitting Image* captured this latest frenzy
in one of its most memorable sketches, which depicted the two
Davids in bed together *à la* Morecambe and Wise:

Steel: Ah, David? [Owen: Yes, David?] I know it's too ridiculous for
words but, well, what if, just say, supposing [Owen: Yes, David?];
what happens if we lose the next election?
Owen: We'll merge, David. [Steel: Merge?] Yes, into one party.
Steel: Oh, and what will we call this one party, David?
Owen: Well, we'll take one word from your party [Steel: Mmm],
and one word from my party.

Steel: Uh, which words?

Owen: From mine, 'Social Democratic', and from yours, 'Party'.

Steel: Oh, so we'll be called the Social Democratic Party.

Owen: Mmm, has a ring, don't you think, David?

Steel: Oh yes, it's very fair, thank you very much indeed, David. But who will be the leader?

Owen: Again, David, one word from your name and one word from mine.

Steel: I see, and which words?

Owen: Well, from yours, David, I thought we'd take the word 'David'.

Steel: 'David'. And from yours, David?

Owen: Er, what about 'Owen'?

Steel: So, it's David Owen, head of the Social Democratic Party?

Owen: Mmm.

Steel: Well, that's put my mind at rest. Thank you very much, David.

In reality, however, Owen had finally given in to Steel and agreed to joint Alliance spokesmen in the Commons. Negotiations were predictably tricky. The prospect of the SDP's John Cartwright as Alliance defence spokesman, for example, prompted lots of horrified letters to the Liberal leader's office, and Steel had to interrupt a New Year's holiday in Morocco to quell a Michael Meadowcroft-led rebellion. 'Inevitably there will be more Liberals in it than SDP,' he told the Parliamentary Party in a caustic letter, 'but not substantially so.'

> We are *not* a Council group, but a team to fight a general election. There must be rough parity in that … I am appalled at your suggestion that some may find the package unacceptable and say so … This is a time for the exercise of collective responsibility. We cannot proceed at the pace of the latest dissenter … Failure to do so will finish off our general election prospects and our local election ones for May on which those so much depend.[136]

---

136   STEEL/A/4/14, David Steel to Liberal MPs, 7 January 1986 [1987].

If this was further evidence of merger by stealth (the Alliance's 'shadow Cabinet' was unveiled in mid-January 1987), a few weeks before Bill Rodgers and Shirley Williams had discussed going much further, agreeing that if the Alliance did not hold the balance of power following the next election 'merger would then be urgent', although the pair doubted that Steel any 'longer had the will to lead a new party'.

Steel, most likely, had not yet reached a conclusive decision on his political future, although a road traffic accident on 22 December robbed the Liberals of at least one potential leader in David Penhaligon ('You're the obvious successor', Steel had told him recently, 'if I give up after the next election'). Hugely popular in his Truro constituency and indeed beyond, Steel paid tribute to him as 'an instinctive Liberal of the old school' and so, on that sad note, an eventful if unhappy year ended. The Ryedale by-election aside, if any twelve-month period could be described as David Steel's *annus horribilis* – arguably worse than 1977 or 1983 – it was 1986.

On 31 January 1987, the Alliance relaunched with a rally at London's Barbican. Under the banner 'The Time Has Come', the Alliance team and programme for government were unveiled to the strains of Purcell's 'Trumpet Tune in D' ('Perhaps symbolically,' mused Owen, 'it is often played at weddings'). Steel was on good form, in contrast to a rather lacklustre Owen, whose impressive Commons oratory rarely transferred to the conference platform. 'The deliberate decision to produce a slightly rougher Steel,' recalled Des Wilson in his enjoyable account of the 1987 general election campaign, 'and to accentuate his ability to seize the moment, was now vindicated.'

Indeed, the Barbican rally generated significant press coverage (Steel guest-starred on the popular *Wogan* chat show shortly afterwards), while Alliance morale was boosted further following by-elections in Greenwich ('Britain now has three-party politics,' wrote Steel after Rosie Barnes's victory for the SDP on 26 February) and Truro (held by the Liberal Matthew Taylor on 12 March). The 'slightly rougher' Steel was by this point regularly getting stuck into Margaret Thatcher, largely as a means to emphasise his left-wing credentials. During one onslaught on David Frost's Sunday television programme, Owen actually intervened to say Steel had 'gone too far', arguing that 'once we get into the business of telling other parties who is to be leader, that goes down a dangerous course'.

This highlighted a long-running tension between the two Davids: whether to focus Alliance fire on the right or the left. While Owen concentrated on criticising Kinnock, Steel said it was 'highly unlikely, almost impossible, inconceivable' that the Alliance could work with Mrs Thatcher in 'a balanced Parliament'. The Prime Minister was hardly bothered by such comments, deriding the Alliance leaders by quoting from an old music hall song. 'I gather at the next election they are hoping to be asked to give us an encore,' she joked during a speech in March, 'the two Davids in that ever-popular musical delight: "Don't tell my mother I'm half of a horse in a panto."'

Speaking to Hugo Young that month, David Owen had already written off the election, predicting Labour gains of between thirty and forty and only forty seats – in total – for the Alliance. He also appeared to have written off Steel as Liberal leader, speculating that an Ashdown succession would be 'disastrous' and suggesting Alan Beith as, he hinted, a more pliable option. 'Quite a lot of the cutting edge of the SDP has gone in the need to get agreement with the Liberals,' Owen told Young gloomily. 'I can't go on fighting every fight.' Des Wilson, meanwhile, told Young he thought the case for merger post-election would 'become irresistible', a tacit admission that he – like Owen – expected little from the election. But would, wondered Wilson, 'Steel be there to see it through?'

A delicate question. There would have to be a leadership contest, and maybe Steel would win it. Would he actually want to? He has worked out another sort of life, in which he remains a backbencher and elder statesman, writing and journalising. The truth is that Steel would not mind Owen becoming the leader, as long as this didn't come about either through his being beaten on a vote or his manifestly shirking the struggle. Somewhere in there is a path towards Owen becoming leader of the merged party.[137]

Although this proved wide of the mark, Wilson had accurately identified Steel's post-Eastbourne state of mind.

On 11 May 1987 *Newsweek* magazine devoted its front page to a photograph of the two Davids. 'DAVIDS AND GOLIATH,' read the headline. 'WILL THE ALLIANCE BECOME BRITAIN'S MAIN OPPOSITION?' It was a curious echo of the *Economist* cover showing Steel, Roy Jenkins and Shirley Williams ('Her Majesty's new opposition') in 1981, yet illustrated – at best – the survival of the Alliance and – at worst – its failure. From a potential party of government six years earlier, it was now viewed as little more than a potential party of opposition. Although, for the first time, Sir Robert Armstrong extended the courtesy of pre-election talks between the Alliance and the Civil Service, it was little more than a formality.

In relative terms the 1987 Alliance election campaign was slicker and much better prepared than that in 1983. And while John Pardoe proved an effective chairman of the Joint Campaign Committee, there remained areas of weakness. The opening party political broadcast featured, bizarrely, extended soft-focus film of Greenwich by-election winner Rosie Barnes petting a rabbit in a field, while another, in which Steel addressed the camera directly ('The march of the moderates has begun'), was improvised at the last minute.

In the run-up to the manifesto launch, meanwhile, Steel was temporarily derailed after being tipped off that the *News of the World* was preparing to allege an affair between him and Elspeth Campbell, the wife of his (soon to be) parliamentary colleague and friend Menzies. Not only did it demonstrate that the media honeymoon with Steel (who 'felt almost physically sick' at the allegation)

---

137 HJSY/2/13, notes dated 24 March 1987.

was over, but for the next five days ('a complete mess') he spent all his time 'on the telephone to solicitors, press officers and my offended friend and her husband'. It was also hard on Judy, an 'especially bad photograph' of her having been published, as she later recalled, 'emphasising the frowziness of the wife from whom David surely wanted to escape'.

Mercifully, the story went into retreat relatively quickly, news bulletins leading on a 'Steel smeared' line rather than the allegation itself. Opposition politicians also condemned it, while there was minimal public willingness to take it at face value. Within days, both the *News of the World* and the *Daily Star* (which had also covered the allegation) acknowledged the story was based on 'unfounded rumour' and agreed to pay Steel 'substantial' damages. 'Nevertheless, it [had] clearly upset David,' recalled Des Wilson, 'and I felt some of his early buoyancy had at least temporarily gone.' The former US presidential contender Gary Hart (who had faced similar allegations about his private life) wrote to Steel quoting John Paul Jones: 'Damn the (press) torpedoes – full speed ahead!'[138]

The joint Alliance Planning Group, meanwhile, had 'never determined an overall theme or plan for the campaign, largely because neither party leader believed in overall themes or plans'. 'Steel and Owen both regarded electioneering as a form of tactical warfare,' judged Crewe and King, 'consisting of lightning strikes and mobile defence, not of set-piece battles. And both fancied they were good tacticians. The result was that some fundamental strategic questions were never addressed.' Des Wilson (who chaired the Planning Group) concurred, later writing that 'while we presented the country with a coherent set of policies, there was no clear message, no clear theme.'

That 'coherent set of policies' was set out in the Alliance manifesto, *Britain United: The Time Has Come*, at its launch on 18 May. In a joint foreword the two Davids said: 'The task of drawing Britain together again can only be achieved through political, economic

138   David Steel Papers (private collection), Gary Hart to David Steel, 2 June 1987.

and social reform on a scale not contemplated in our country for over forty years.' If the Alliance held the balance of power, they pledged, the Tories' divisive policies would be curbed and Labour's destructive antics halted. But beyond constitutional issues like PR and devolution, *Britain United* was cautious, and therefore not very mould breaking. It skirted over difficult issues (such as defence) and hedged its bets on potential coalition partners. It seems likely, meanwhile, that Steel was not terribly well acquainted with its contents. In his memoirs, Owen claimed that half way through the campaign an SDP press officer had been shocked to discover that 'David had not read all the Alliance manifesto', a memory John Pardoe also shares.

The 1983 election had highlighted three main tensions within the Alliance: ideology, defence and leadership, all of which remained problems – to varying degrees – during the 1987 campaign. On the first, ideology, the argument that the Alliance might be the kingmaker in a 'balanced' Parliament inevitably raised, as the historian David Dutton has written, 'the question of which way the balance was likely to be tipped in the event that the Alliance got hold of it'. Even before the campaign began Owen had grown frustrated at Steel's inability to sustain the impression that there might be circumstances under which he could envisage working with Mrs Thatcher. 'To say David hated her,' remarked Owen in his memoirs, 'was hardly an exaggeration.'

While categorising Steel as left wing and Owen as on the right over-simplified matters, it was nevertheless the prevailing percep-tion among voters. 'So both leaders were constantly trying to correct the other's apparent emphasis on one side or the other,' recalled Des Wilson. 'As a result the whole thing fell apart.'

The split was compounded during a joint interview on the popu-lar *Panorama* programme. 'Do you think that a Tory government would be a greater evil than a majority Labour government?' Sir Robin Day asked Owen. 'Which is the greater evil in your view?' On the basis of its unilateralist defence policy, Owen said Labour was, while Steel was more discreet. 'I don't believe either is capable of providing a government which can unite this country again,' he said, 'and I am not going to be driven to making a choice between the two of them.' When pressed by Sir Robin, Steel said: 'I don't see why I've got to start getting out the measuring rod and saying "Well, one would be slightly better on this one, slightly better on that one."'

Owen, of course, had shown no such hesitation in bringing out the 'measuring rod', but on noticing his gaffe, he admitted to having being 'notoriously indiscreet':

> David [Steel] is much wiser than I am in handling [Steel: You go too far] your attempt to try and get us to decide. The fact of the matter is that for the first time the people of this country are not faced with this horrible choice ... the electorate are going to say they want neither Labour or Conservative.

'The good doctor dropped an almighty clanger,' Steel later recalled, but in truth, as Sir Robin put it in his memoirs, 'my question did not divide the two Davids. It merely served to reveal the division which already existed and which they wished, naturally enough, not to advertise.' No one watching, observed Owen, 'could have failed to notice that we had a very different attitude to the Labour Party's defence policy: for me it was the disqualifying factor for being the government, for David it was one very good issue to measure Labour by, no more and no less'.

Although by May 1987 East and West were engaged in bilateral talks that would halt, if not reverse, the global arms race, Labour continued to exploit the Eastbourne split during the campaign, asking: 'Whose defence policy? Owen's or Steel's or the Liberal Party's?' (Owen later claimed this had been 'an albatross around our necks throughout the 1987 election campaign', although it had not been apparent at the time.)

This fed into the third tension of the campaign, the question of leadership. The 1983 election, which had culminated in the fractious Ettrick Bridge summit, had revealed the difficulties of dual leadership yet, despite Steel's best efforts in 1984–5, the mistake was repeated in 1987. During the campaign the two Davids held joint morning press conferences at the National Liberal Club and public 'Ask the Alliance' meetings in the evenings, both designed to reinforce the impression of unity. But it did not work, producing what one academic commentary diplomatically described as a 'blurred image'. At least in 1983 there had been some clarity as to who would lead an Alliance government; in 1987 there was none.

The press, recalled Pardoe, 'inevitably alighted on the question of who was the real leader, [so] we never succeeded in getting the leaders to complement each other. In fact each diminished the other during the course of the campaign.' Steel committed a rare gaffe when he remarked publicly that he and Owen had been locked together in television studios looking like 'Tweedledum and Tweedledee' ('I could not believe', recalled Pardoe, 'an experienced politician had said this'), later compounding the problem by adding that 'two garden gnomes' was probably a more accurate description.

Mobile phones, large and unreliable though they were in 1987, also gave rise to media mischief, enabling journalists to put the comment of one David to the other very quickly, creating several 'split' stories in the process. Des Wilson grew exasperated at 'having two leaders in two buses in two different parts of the country with two different views on strategy, effectively conducting two different campaigns'. Michael Brunson, who covered the election for ITN, recalled one particular press conference:

> Both leaders emerged to board their respective campaign coaches … In full view of the cameras, Dr Owen turned right towards his vehicle, declaring, 'I'm off to Birmingham.' David Steel turned towards his, announcing, 'I'm off to Bristol.' The pictures, and the sound, of two leaders heading in different directions told the true story – that this was a deeply uneasy alliance.

Alec McGivan, the SDP's national organiser, later reflected that – in the glare of the media spotlight – the Alliance leadership simply had not worked, something he essentially blamed on the two party leaders. 'At the end of the day,' he said, 'they couldn't do it, they couldn't work together.' By the end of the campaign, concurred John Pardoe wearily, 'I was forced to admit to myself that I did not much want to be governed by either [David] and the thought of being governed by both was too appalling for words.'

In spite of all these problems, relations between everyone involved in the campaign were surprisingly good; no one, as Owen put it in his memoirs, 'was contemplating another Ettrick Bridge summit'. This relative harmony, however, probably owed more to the fact that those in charge of the campaign were resigned to defeat, the expected opinion poll rise having failed to manifest itself. In the final week Steel even acknowledged that Mrs Thatcher was likely to win, saying that 'any reading of the polls now suggests that the Conservatives are on course for victory. Any rational person would say that.' Rational, but hardly wise. 'DESPAIR FOR ALLIANCE AS STEEL SAYS: MAGGIE'S THE WINNER!' was one predictable headline in the *Mail on Sunday*, while 'STEEL ACCEPTS TORY VICTORY' was another.

Pre-election scenarios also crumbled. The two Davids had prepared a detailed seven-page memo identifying government portfolios and planning victory photo calls. Owen had also discussed the prospects for a hung Parliament with the constitutional expert Vernon Bogdanor (an informal adviser to the Liberals), who urged the Alliance to consider the prospect that Mrs Thatcher 'might resign as party leader, though not PM, and would stay on as caretaker until the Conservatives had a new leader'.[139] The Alliance, therefore, could offer to support a minority Tory government on the condition that Thatcher resigned as Prime Minister.

Steel, according to Des Wilson, had even lost enthusiasm for this slim chance of exerting influence, believing 'we will be the long-term loser from a power-sharing arrangement.' Rather, Steel 'would be more than happy to settle for a narrow Tory majority with the Alliance making an advance'. Although the Conservative

---

139   D 709 3/11/2/17, undated note.

campaign had not been without problems of its own, the natural party of government had provided the most coherent pitch to voters. Later, Conservative Party chairman Norman Tebbit admitted to making 'one tactical error'. 'We underestimated the capacity of the Alliance', he said, 'to make a mess of its own campaign.'

By 11 June all that remained were the declarations. In his memoirs, Des Wilson remembered watching television footage of Steel 'looking tired and unenthusiastic, speaking in a shabby hall in Scotland'. By contrast, 'at a school in his constituency in Plymouth, a defiant David Owen appeared on television still talking of his hopes of a coalition.' 'One had given up,' observed Wilson, 'one was fighting to the last breath.'

8

DEMOCRATIC FUSION

The 1987 general election saw the Alliance's share of the vote decline modestly from 25 per cent in 1983 to 23.1 per cent. On the face of it, this was disappointing rather than disastrous. Only five SDP MPs were returned (Roy Jenkins lost in Hillhead) but seventeen Liberals, including modest gains in Scotland. Interviewed during the BBC's election coverage, David Steel looked drawn and disappointed, later reflecting that 'we must undergo our internal debate about the future of the Alliance.' David Owen, meanwhile, appeared relatively robust, telling journalists on Friday morning that 'the endless examining of our own navels on whether or not we should exist is probably one of our greatest weaknesses. I have never doubted that we should exist.'

'We', of course, meant the SDP rather than the Alliance. Subsequent analysis suggested a combination of factors had led to the result: Owen's balance-of-power strategy, an apparent disagreement about which party the Alliance would favour if it held that balance but, above all, the two Davids. It was difficult to avoid the conclusion that – as in 1983 – having two parties pitching for power under a joint leadership was, as Ivor Crewe and Tony King put it, 'an experiment that had failed administratively, politically and electorally'. The logical response to that conclusion, therefore, was a full and speedy merger.

Certainly that was Steel's thinking as soon as the results started coming in. He spoke to Owen at around 4 a.m. by telephone and made clear his desire for an early merger. 'There is only one thing to do now and that is to get our two parties together,' Steel recalled saying, adding in his memoirs that Owen 'neither agreed nor demurred'. Contrary to subsequent accounts, however, it was actually Owen who made the first move, making it clear at a press conference in his Plymouth constituency that he would oppose merger if it was mooted in the wake of the election.

Steel was surprised, having taken Owen's pre-election statements – which appeared to accept the possibility of merger – at face value. Therefore he decided to act. Knowing the SDP's national committee was due to meet on Monday, Steel began to draft a memorandum that (in his usual style) identified a number of options while making it clear which he preferred. 'I do not regard the result of the general election as a disaster,' the memo began, 'though I readily acknowledge it was a setback.' He thought the media focus on the dual leadership was 'facile', while acknowledging that the UK's increasingly presidential politics made it unsustainable. 'Nevertheless I do believe that if either David Owen or I had been running the campaign as single leaders it would have had both a sharper image and strategy,' added Steel. 'David Owen, I think, would have wished a more assertive balance of power coalition focus, while I would have preferred a clear anti-Thatcher non-socialist alternative.'

He then set out the likely options:

1. Remaining separate parties;
2. The Liberals and SDP 'growing together'; and, Steel's 'preferred option',
3. 'democratic fusion' of the two parties, 'incorporating the best aspects of both'.

Steel continued:

I remain buoyant and optimistic about our prospects of creating an effective left of centre movement in time to replace this government at the next election. This is why I do not believe we should allow discussion of our internal future to drag on beyond the end of 1987. *I see it as my immediate task as party leader and co-founder of the Alliance to see this period of discussion through to its conclusion.* [Author's italics.] I will thereafter discuss my own position with colleagues and decide on my possible role when the decision of our parties on their joint future is clearer.[140]

Before he had finished writing the memo, Steel called Owen, who was out walking with Bob Maclennan. He told Owen's wife Debbie that he was arranging his thoughts on merger and wanted Owen to read it. On being told Owen was returning to London that evening, Steel said he would arrange for a copy of the memo to be in his office first thing on Monday morning. The next call Debbie took, as Owen recounted in his memoirs, was from the Press Association, which 'not only knew all about the existence of David Steel's memorandum but seemed to have a lot of detail'. 'Bob, Debbie and I had a good laugh about all this over lunch,' wrote Owen. 'It was so flagrant. David was mounting a clear take-over bid for the SDP, while trying too hard to protect his own back from Paddy Ashdown and showing his party that he was not about to resign or take a sabbatical as he had done after the last election.'

This was an overly cynical reading of Steel's motives, although the Liberal leader had invited television cameras to film him actually drafting the memo, pictures which, as planned, ended up on the evening news bulletins. 'It was all', sneered Owen, 'far too melodramatic.' But this was no mere publicity stunt. Steel wanted to make sure that Owen, and indeed everybody else, got the message: he wanted the two parties to merge, and merge quickly. If the SDP leader was isolated in the process, then so be it. Steel's tactics, however, allowed Owen to accuse Steel of trying to 'bounce' him into a merger, although that complaint, as Steel later wrote, 'came ill from someone who on the very same Sunday after the

---

140   David Steel Papers STEEL/A/5/1, 'The Future of the Alliance', 15 June 1987.

previous general election [1983] was arranging his own succession to the SDP leadership'.

On finally reading the full memo, Owen actually thought it 'a shrewd, well-crafted document', albeit 'predicated on a massive false assumption', chiefly that the Alliance consisted of two identical parties. Over the next few days Steel's constructive tone hardened. Any compromise along the lines of 'let's have two parties but one leader', he told one newspaper, 'would be doomed from the start'. Later, it hardened even more, Steel casting the choice in terms of 'merger or bust'.

There was undeniably a personal element to Steel's speedy response. Armchair psychologists had it that after several years of being perceived (mainly thanks to *Spitting Image*, which, after the election, depicted the two Davids crooning 'Goodbye' at a piano[141]) as Owen's junior partner, he was zealously exploiting an opportunity to gain the upper hand. As Crewe and King put it:

> It is impossible to prove – but also impossible not to believe – that the 1987–8 merger row took the form it did partly because Steel and the others were consciously or unconsciously out to 'get' the SDP leader. They would either tame him by forcing him to help merge the two parties; or they would break with him completely. In the case of many of them, dislike and impatience had long since given way to something approaching hatred.

Roy Jenkins had already proposed merger in a radio interview, swiftly followed by Shirley Williams and Bill Rodgers. Although Jenkins broadly approved of Steel's action ('The issue had to be faced, and there was a good deal to be said for striking quickly'),

---

141 Sportingly, the following year Steel guest-starred (as himself) in a *Spitting Image* special – *Bumbledown: The Life and Times of Ronald Reagan* – during which he introduced a segment on Irangate which, as Steel said, was 'beyond parody'. Roger Law and Peter Fluck, the show's creators, had written to Steel admitting their latex caricature was on their 'conscience'.

he felt the form it took – as he politely put it in his memoirs – was 'nonetheless unfortunate'. 'He made it look as though he were attempting to bounce Owen and the SDP as a whole,' while Sunday's news coverage had 'made the exercise look more like a media stunt than the advancement of a serious proposition between allies'. 'As a result it offended a lot of people within the SDP who were not opposed to merger,' concluded Jenkins, 'and who indeed eventually supported it, although more reluctantly than they would have done without that Sunday afternoon's activity.' Asked later if he had been bounced by Steel, Owen replied nonchalantly: 'Not really. I know it suited people to think that.'

In a reversal of moods from election night, Steel was surprisingly upbeat, reinvigorated by the task of seeing realignment through to its logical conclusion. There was no hint of the black dog that plagued him in the wake of the 1983 election; indeed, having been unable to publicly state the merger case for four years, Steel was finally free to speak his mind. Another illustration of this equanimity was the letter he sent Margaret Thatcher the day after composing his merger memo. It would, he wrote, be 'churlish of me not to recognise the very considerable *and personal* achievement which your election for a third term as our Prime Minister represents'.[142] Even Steel's animosity towards the Iron Lady had softened a little.

Owen, on the other hand, aged forty-nine and with no prospect of influencing events, was feeling bruised. As he later told the journalist Iain Dale: 'My political career was over on the Sunday of the 1987 election.' 'Hasty' was his public response to the memo as he reiterated his personal opposition to merger. However heavy handed Steel's tactics, Owen had behaved badly. To contrive the impression that the merger proposal had come out of the blue

---

142 STEEL/B/1/1/12, David Steel to Margaret Thatcher, 16 June 1987. Thatcher thanked Steel for his 'kind and generous letter' the following day. 'We all had a hard campaign – you no less than me. Thank goodness it is over,' she wrote. 'To adapt a phrase – three weeks is a long time in politics! Now for the exacting work of the session.'

was scarcely credible, while his decision to withdraw SDP MPs from their joint briefs with the Liberals was deliberately disruptive given the continued existence of the Alliance. 'The darling of social democracy had emerged as its Ahithophel,' David Marquand later observed, 'resolved to ruin what he could no longer rule'. But Owen realised this was untenable. 'I knew in my heart I couldn't block it,' he admitted in 2010. 'And in a way, I knew it was quite illegitimate to try and block it.'

On 20 June Steel set out his stall in a robust article for *The Guardian*. 'Surely it is right to get this right at the beginning of the new parliament rather than procrastinating and pussy-footing around for years,' he argued. 'To continue contemplating our navels well into 1988 would be to miss a great opportunity to capitalise on the great goodwill that exists towards us among the electorate.' Steel also raised the issue of leadership for the first time, observing that had it not been for David Penhaligon's death in December 1986, he would be saying to his colleagues: 'I've done my stint, let us proceed to the election of a fresh leader.' Although there was 'plenty of talent' among the Liberal group in Parliament, it lacked an 'obvious single successor established in the public mind'. Steel therefore felt bound, as he had said in his memo, 'to see through the next stage of development of the Alliance'.

Thereafter it would be

for my colleagues in the Alliance to ponder whether it would be better to go into the next election around 1991 with a fresh face at its head rather than someone who has appeared at three general elections already ... One possible candidate is obviously David Owen himself ... This is not an easy time for either of us, and neither of us is blind to the other's faults as well as attributes. All I will say is that I trust any development of the Alliance will be one in which he will feel comfortable in playing a crucial part regardless of who is the leader, as I intend to do.

It was a vain hope. At the end of June the SDP's national committee ordered a ballot of party members, giving them a choice between opening merger talks or Owen's plan for 'a closer constitutional framework ... short of merger'. When, on 6 August, it was announced that 57.4 per cent had supported the former and 42.6 per cent the latter (turnout was 77.7 per cent), Owen declared the result a tragedy and resigned as leader, while hinting he would not go quietly. 'I wish,' said Steel, taking the hint, Owen 'were with us in forming this new third force rather than, as it sounds, going off into a semi-wilderness to form a less effective fourth force'. Writing in *The Observer*, Roy Jenkins dismissed the idea of a new fourth party as nothing more than 'political self-indulgence'.

Steel had written to Owen on 13 July to suggest a private meal before they both departed for the summer recess. 'I don't expect to change your mind on your current course,' he wrote, 'but we could discuss how to get through the two conferences with minimum damage.'[143] Thus on 26 August the two Davids met for a 'private and pleasurable' lunch to mark the end of a four-year partnership. 'We still agreed to differ,' Steel said afterwards, 'but we're going to agree to differ pleasantly.' Thus a long-running show – the two Davids – ended with a fizz rather than a bang.

Three days later Bob Maclennan succeeded Owen as leader, the only candidate from among five SDP MPs. Although both were Scottish MPs, he and Steel were not exactly close. 'Basically we've both got a job to do and we're getting on with it,' Steel said later. 'We're determined to make it work.' Initially opposed to merger, Maclennan had since accepted the obvious desire of a majority of his party's members. Although only fifty-one, Maclennan appeared to belong to a more genteel political era; the 'ideal leader for a party whose time has gone' in the wounding words of one columnist. He consolidated his position, however, with a powerful speech setting out tough conditions for the merger at the SDP's Portsmouth conference on 31 August. Several members stormed from the

---

143 David Owen Papers D 709 3/11/5/3, David Steel to David Owen, 13 July 1987.

platform when a merger motion proposed by Shirley Williams was passed.

Liberals, naturally, were also split. Steel was encouraged by a steady stream of letters supporting merger, while Tony Greaves told the *Lancashire Evening Telegraph* there was no need for the SDP, merger or not. 'I do not think they have brought anything extra', he said, 'which would not have been achieved by the more Liberal-minded members of the SDP joining the Liberal Party.' Greaves also called upon Steel to resign, the first prominent Liberal to do so.

Having flagged up this possibility himself in *The Guardian*, Steel now had to fend off constant speculation to that effect. Asked if he wanted to lead the merged party in one television interview, he replied: 'To be quite candid I am ambivalent about it.' In reality, however, he had already resolved to resign once the merger of the two parties was complete. 'Basically I thought if I can get that through and settled,' recalls Steel, 'then I would bow out.' Alec McGivan, who still worked in the Liberal leader's office, says 'David wasn't interested really.' 'He just wanted to get it over with,' he remembers. 'I didn't ever get the impression he was likely to stay on as leader.' Steel, however, still received letters imploring him to stick it out. 'I am bound to say that, were you no longer to be leader of the centre in British politics,' wrote the academic Vernon Bogdanor, 'my own commitment to it would lessen very considerably … I appreciate the burden which you have to bear.'[144]

The historian Matt Cole identified three distinct phases in the merger process:

> [A] 'warm-up' phase; an intense negotiating phase during which the process came close to collapse; and the completion of the merger. It was a debate the parties would inevitably engage in at some point, but its conduct, the overall outcome, and its impact upon

---

144 STEEL/A/5/4, Vernon Bogdanor to David Steel, 18 August 1987.

the fortunes of the party which emerged, need not have been so
damaging as turned out to be the case.

As part of the 'warm-up' phase, Steel still had to secure the backing of his own party. 'This is to wish you every success in your
Assembly speech,' wrote Jeremy Thorpe towards the end of August,
'which will be one of the most difficult you will have to make.'[145]

Indeed, as James Naughtie observed in *The Guardian*, Steel was
in a paradoxical position, his strength apparently 'at its greatest just
at the moment when the talk about his leadership suggests it is at
its weakest'. Although widely assumed to be the natural leader for
the merged party, there was 'an insistent chorus beneath: Steel must
jazz up his act'. 'If third-party politics is really about vision, as he
has always claimed, he has to show it next week,' wrote Naughtie.
'The son of the manse must relax, and preach like fury.'

The merger debate at the Harrogate Assembly was certainly
memorable, although more for an impassioned speech (in
favour) from Sir Russell Johnston ('You don't change the taste of
the whisky', he said, 'by changing the shape of the bottle') than
Steel's contribution. 'Serious deliberations are necessary and valuable in setting up our new direction, but, I beg you, let them be
brief,' said Steel from the conference floor. 'Let the deliberators
be locked in a room for a month if necessary but let them get on
with it.' He would have no such luck and, although some delegates
expressed reservations about the pace and direction of the merger,
relatively few delegates opposed it outright. On 17 September,
by 998 votes to 21, the Liberal Assembly overwhelmingly backed
merger negotiations.

Having nurtured the idea of formal realignment between the
Liberals and Labour's social democrats for more than a decade,
for Steel it was a political triumph. His final Assembly speech as
leader, however, was a rather muted affair, undulating, as the sketch
writer Andrew Rawnsley put it, 'up and down the touchstones of

145   STEEL/B/1/1/9, Jeremy Thorpe to David Steel, 25 August 1987.

the contemporary Liberal Party: constitutional reform, common security and mutual care and concern'. 'The tour was familiar,' added Rawnsley, 'the guide seemed too tired to be bothered to make it very interesting.' 'We must move on from Thatcherism. We must set the new agenda. We must be the party of the future,' said Steel vaguely. 'To capture the goodwill towards us needs a clearer strategy, bolder themes and a sharper identity.'

Alas, the Assembly also decided – in spite of Steel's best efforts – to elect a negotiating team of seventeen that, after being matched by the SDP, meant formal negotiations were going to be anything but straightforward. Talks began on 28 September and were to last until the middle of January, taking place at Cowley Street (SDP HQ), the Reform Club and the House of Commons. As Ivor Crewe and Tony King put it in their history of the SDP, the merger negotiations resembled 'a cross between the Twilight of the Gods and Feydeau farce, with the farcical element increasingly to the fore as time went on'.

The ideal was to produce an agreement that retained the best attributes of each party. The Liberals had already recognised the need to abandon some elements of its constitution. Indeed, Steel relished the opportunity of ditching elements that had made his twelve years as leader more challenging than they might have been. This included the Party Council, although given Steel's roots he was keen to retain separate party structures for Scotland, Wales and the English regions. A party with a federal aim could hardly preach what it did not practise.

Bob Maclennan, meanwhile, was (according to Alan Beith) 'an awkward speaker, not an obvious leader, and a difficult and strangely emotional negotiator, but he was a natural Liberal'. Maclennan and his party were anxious to retain all-party ballots to decide major policy issues, something the Liberals wanted to remain firmly in the hands of Assembly delegates (Steel probably agreed with the SDP on this, for obvious reasons). Another sticking point, if only symbolically, was the new party's name; the Liberals wanted to keep the word 'Liberal' while the SDP, naturally enough, wanted to incorporate the term 'Social Democratic' (*Spitting Image* had anticipated such a spat a full year before). This, more than any other issue, dominated Steel's mailbag.

These splits were exacerbated by the respective negotiating teams, which included both supporters and opponents of merger (although Owen and his closest acolytes were not among them). Maclennan led a disciplined team, but the other side consisted of what one commentator called 'a leaderless organisation of diverse individuals'. 'The Liberal team, under David Steel's leadership, had sometimes not had prior opportunity to consider positions,' recalled Alan Beith in his memoirs, 'and would sometimes find that its leader was prepared to give ground in the full meeting without consulting his own team.' Steel, wrote Tony Greaves and Rachel Pitchford in their critical account of the merger negotiations, had a 'rather naïve ... view that if only everyone was reasonable everything would be all right'.

Although Steel was in the chair for the first meeting of the Joint Negotiating Team (JNT), he generally left others to the Liberal MPs Alex Carlile and Alan Beith. His impatience with such discussions was well known. 'We'll be here for week after week after bloody week,' Steel apparently exclaimed at one point. 'Why can't we just have a vote and get on with it?' One of the SDP negotiators, Willie Goodhart, believed both teams got the impression 'that David was as deeply bored by constitutional minutiae as Robert [Maclennan] was fascinated by them'.

The only thing Steel was directly involved with, at least initially, was Maclennan's desire for 'a great policy prospectus' to set out the new party's ideological stance as soon as the negotiations were concluded. Steel wanted 'a short document' which was generally 'anodyne and uplifting'. He was particularly anxious this should not be discussed during formal negotiation meetings, it having come up at one in mid-October. 'On our side I argued that this should be left as a kind of prospectus signed by the two leaders and inviting others to join with us in subscribing to it,' Steel wrote to Maclennan on 14 October.

My colleagues were prepared to accept this on two conditions: that I show them the draft for individual comment and that it reflects the general policy contained in *The Time Has Come* and *Britain United*. I regard this as rather satisfactory – the key to the document is obtaining someone who can draft in fresh, appealing language. We then have a free hand and I would not wish us to get bogged down in discussion round the table.

Maclennan agreed *The Time Has Come* and *Britain United* were the 'natural starting point', but believed a new party required a document 'fresh in content as well as in language'. He continued:

> I am clear, however, that the document in its final form will have to obtain the imprimatur of approval by the members of the joint negotiating team if we are to be in a position to say that the negotiations have been successfully concluded. At that point, the members of the team would be asked to endorse it as it stood without amendment, and the document should then be open for further signatures to give it the necessary weight.[146]

Thus what eventually became *Voices and Choices for All* was born. Its life would be brief, expiring in less than glorious circumstances three months later. Importantly, however, Steel had registered his concerns at its conception. He wanted a concise restatement of existing Alliance policy; Bob Maclennan wanted precisely the opposite.

Still the JNT meetings dragged on (*The Guardian* estimated there to have been 200 hours of them by December). At one stage in mid-November Maclennan had threatened to pull out, but on 15 December a new constitution was agreed with three notes of dissent from Greaves, Pitchford and that veteran member of the awkward squad, Michael Meadowcroft. Two weeks earlier the journalist

---

146 Robert Maclennan Papers Box 15, David Steel to Robert Maclennan, 14 October 1987; Robert Maclennan to David Steel, undated.

Peter (later Lord) Hennessy had asked Steel about his relationship with the Liberal Party. 'It's occasionally slightly strained,' he admitted. 'I think they find me rather exasperating and I can assure you the feeling is entirely mutual on occasions.' Citing the unwieldy negotiating team foisted on him at the Harrogate Assembly, Steel said he got 'quite openly irritated' by such things, 'and they in turn feel that I'm being unnecessarily autocratic so it's a very healthy, but acerbic relationship'.

Just how acerbic a relationship was demonstrated at a Northampton meeting of the Liberal Party Council on 15 December. Steel introduced the merger package on behalf of the negotiators, expressing some reservations but warning against irresponsible behaviour. 'Any stridency, any over-heated language,' he said (according to Greaves and Pitchford), 'any attempt to blow up matters of detail into exaggerated issues of principle will backfire on each and every one of us, and fatally damage the prospects for our new party.' If there was a row about the new party's name, added Steel, voters would 'see us as essentially frivolous and they would not be wrong'.

It was no use. Not only did the Party Council reject any mention of NATO in the constitution's preamble (insisted upon by the SDP), it also passed an amendment opposing 'The Alliance' as the new party's short title (the full title was verbose: 'The New Liberal and Social Democratic Party').

Maggie Clay, president of the Association of Liberal Councillors (ALC), suggested 'Liberal Democrats', which went down well with those present. Steel, however, had beaten her to it. 'The idea that there should not be a Liberal Party in British politics is too horrific to contemplate,' John Pardoe had told Steel on 7 December. 'Your original idea of Liberal Democrat was fine and seems to me a perfectly fair mix of the names of the two parties. The word "Social" adds nothing to either Liberal or Democrat.'[147]

Steel did not handle the Party Council's snub well, dismissing

---

147   STEEL/A/5/2, John Pardoe to David Steel, 7 December 1987.

the votes as 'no more than an irritation', indelicately adding that it would, in any case, soon cease to exist within the new party's structure. In his *Liberal News* Christmas message Steel added insult to injury, warning that 'we shall have to defeat the small groups of chauvinists who unhappily exist in both parties, who care more about their own party games than the broader purpose.' Greaves and Pitchford believed Steel had misunderstood the 'mood' at Northampton, which they said was one of 'constructive criticism' rather than 'straight opposition'. But then theirs was a losers' account of the process (both would soon abandon the talks), and even they conceded that Liberals remained 'overwhelmingly in favour' of merger.

Steel was also getting flak for not having stated clearly his personal position once the merger process was complete. 'One cast iron way to ensure that we do not have a leadership vacuum', wrote Adrian Slade (Des Wilson's successor as party president), 'is for you to declare your willingness to take on the leadership at least in the foreseeable future.'[148] At around the same time Peter Hennessy had pushed Steel on the same point, prompting an equivocal reply which amounted to both 'yes' and 'no':

> If it is the wish of my colleagues that I should continue to lead the party ... that is a very big question which I'm still discussing with all of them in both parties, then certainly I would have the appetite to do it ... [but] having carried out the sort of arduous chores of leadership for eleven years, it is not all that an appealing prospect to do another four year sentence if I put it that way.

Work on a joint policy document, meanwhile, had begun in late November, in parallel with the main negotiations on the new party's constitution. Having flagged up his desire for something short and sweet, Steel had then given Bob Maclennan a relatively free hand to formulate its contents. The SDP leader, however, had something

---

148 STEEL/A/5/3, Adrian Slade to David Steel, 4 December 1987.

very different in mind. Keen to provide a distinctive agenda for the new party, Maclennan was also looking over his shoulder – as were the wider negotiations – at David Owen. 'He was like a ghost at every meeting,' said one of those present, 'rattling his chains in the corner.' Thus the policy document was to depart significantly from previous Alliance positions.

The first serious engagement by Steel came at Ettrick Bridge on 22 December. Alan Beith and Alex McGivan, a former SDP official who was by then Steel's political adviser (an appointment contrived in the merger spirit), were also present, as were two young Maclennan aides, Hugo Dixon and Andrew Gilmour, both sons of Conservative MPs, who had been working on some ideas. Only defence was discussed in depth; the rest of the joint policy document existed only in a four-page outline. Maclennan also suggested that Steel consider a different name for the party, 'The Social and Liberal Democrats' or, in short, 'The Democrats', a US-inspired name Maclennan had floated a few months earlier.

In his memoirs, Steel said even 'with hindsight nothing in that first discussion should really have sent alarm bells ringing except that none of us really took on board the terribly short timetable we were setting ourselves.' Indeed, at this point he was preparing to visit Kenya (to work on a project constructing water tanks in rural areas), while Maclennan was heading to the United States to visit family (his wife, Helen, was from New England). This continued, as Robert Harris put it in *The Observer*, 'the fine old Alliance tradition of never letting anything interfere with a foreign trip'.

Before he left, however, Maclennan had asked Dixon and Gilmour to include proposals to extend VAT to food, fuel, newspapers, financial services and children's clothes, which Steel also saw via faxed drafts. On these he added a few comments before delegating oversight to Alan Beith as he headed to the airport on New Year's Day. 'The African trip showed either great confidence in being able to sell the document to the other Liberal MPs,' recalls Gilmour, 'or else relative lack of interest in that policy document and its finalisation. Quite possibly both.'

Motivating Maclennan and his advisers was a desire to demonstrate that far from representing the best bits of the two parties' policy agendas, this was a new party with a bold new prospectus. Maclennan was particularly keen that it be seen as 'reliable' on defence – particularly after the Alliance splits of 1984 and 1986 – by including a commitment to retaining Trident. Gilmour recalled:

> The aim was to prove that Owen was wrong – wrong in his belief that the Liberals were (in his view) hopeless impractical fuzzy-minded kooks, wrong that they could never be counted on to come up with a 'responsible' defence policy. We wanted to show that it was possible for the Liberal leadership to move away from that viewpoint; that they could come up with a credible set of policies, and therefore there was no reason to flounce off into the rump SDP.
>
> Bob was extremely interested in coming up with precise and clever new policies on various issues – which was why *Voices and Choices for All* contained a truly radical anti-poverty programme [to be paid for by the extension of VAT].

Indeed, *Voices and Choices* does not read at all badly nearly twenty-five years after it first appeared. Its central argument – that while Thatcherism had changed politics a better harnessing of its powers was necessary – anticipated Tony Blair's Third Way although, in fairness, it was much more radical.

On returning from Kenya on 10 January, Steel went through the document the following day but, probably still feeling tired, he remained unconcerned. Indeed, he congratulated Dixon and Gilmour for what he considered bold and imaginative work. Steel agreed to some redrafting on defence (he bore the scars of previous Liberal rows on his back), but not on VAT. With a press conference due on 13 January, attention then switched to signing off the party's name and constitution at a marathon negotiating session at Cowley Street. The final draft included a reference to NATO, which proved too much for Michael Meadowcroft, while at around midnight Maclennan threatened to call off the merger unless the

Liberals accepted the SDP's preferred name, 'The Social and Liberal Democrats', and dropped 'The Alliance', prompting three more Liberals, Greaves, Pitchford and Peter Knowlson, to walk out.[149]

All of this, however, was manageable. It is difficult to believe that Steel was upset about losing that particular quartet of Liberals, although the ticking time bomb was in another room. The Liberal policy committee, also meeting that evening, raised several major objections to the policy document and demanded major changes. 'We ended up trying to produce the document and finish the negotiations, and botched the document badly,' admitted Steel in his memoirs. 'At one point I was in two meetings at the same time in different buildings.'

The role of Alan Beith at this point is curious. He had been in possession of a full draft of the document since the beginning of the year, yet his objections were now – belatedly – much more vehement. 'We ended up discussing the policy document through the night,' he recalled in his memoirs. 'There were a lot of amendments agreed, but it remained a liability. At about four in the morning, when it was clear that the Leaders were insistent on going ahead, we broke up.'

But it was too late. Not only was such a tightly written prospectus difficult to amend at the eleventh hour, but its contents had been leaked to the press the previous evening (copies had been sitting in Steel's office for Liberal MPs to consult). *Voices and Choices for All* was certainly challenging. In addition to the Trident and VAT proposals, it also advocated an extension of nuclear energy, abolition of universal child benefit and the phasing out of mortgage interest tax relief. Although an ambitious plan to tackle poverty was certainly something of which any Liberal or Social Democrat could be proud, the press inevitably focused on the extension of VAT that would pay for it.

---

149   The alternative, 'The Liberal and Social Democrats' not only gave Liberals primacy (unacceptable to the SDP) but also had the potentially disastrous acronym 'LSD'.

Steel returned to the House of Commons after two hours' sleep and a bath unaware that the policy document had leaked. Jim Wallace, the Liberal Chief Whip, informed him the Parliamentary Party was in open revolt and would not accept it. Beith called Steel to make that clear, as did Alex Carlile and several others. Most of the criticism concerned what Beith called its 'distinctly Thatcherite rhetoric'. The whole document, wrote Tony Greaves, had the 'stench of Thatcherism about it, and ill-thought-out Thatcherism at that'. Some Social Democrats agreed. It looked, recalled Shirley Williams, 'like the work of a bunch of jejune neo-Thatcherites', although Roy Jenkins later praised its content and style, having come to appreciate its true intention. Hugo Young, meanwhile, reckoned it contained 'not a word that Dr David Owen could disagree with'. Des Wilson even sent Steel an open letter describing the policy declaration as 'barely literate' and 'politically inept'.

He got the message. With around an hour to go before the press conference unveiling *Voices and Choices for All* was supposed to begin, Steel asked to see Maclennan (they 'were in a fractious mood and dead tired') in order to tell him he was no longer prepared to go ahead, adding that he could not 'deliver his party'. 'Come on,' said an angry and shaken Maclennan, 'be a leader. You've got to be tough.' He even hinted that he might go ahead alone, telling journalists that Steel seemed to have been 'delayed'. Steel then cleared his inner office and spoke to Maclennan alone for ten minutes, who finally gave way. When they emerged from Steel's office, Maclennan looked as if he had been crying and both men, according to one witness, were 'as white as corpses'. Steel had made it clear he was prepared to resign should the merger founder in such circumstances.

Everyone present that morning, according to Crewe and King, agreed Steel appeared 'absolutely shattered'. They continued:

> He had been totally repudiated by his colleagues, and his very leadership was under threat. More than that, he had (as he must have known) been made to look a complete fool. Much of his

reputation was founded on his being a consummate political opera-
tor. It appeared that over *Voices and Choices* his much vaunted skills
had deserted him. He was supposed to be a magician, and he had
lost his magic.

Judy Steel remembered her husband calling her and his tone being
'one of defeat, of despair'. 'I don't think I'll still be leader by the
end of the day,' he told her. 'I don't think the merger's going to go
ahead. I'll have to resign.'

It then fell to Simon Coates, who worked for Maclennan, and
Alex McGivan from Steel's office to race to the Jubilee Room in the
House of Commons to try and stop distribution of the document
to journalists, but it was too late. Acutely embarrassed, McGivan
announced that the press conference had been postponed, while
Coates read out the following statement: 'We have not had the
chance to consider the final draft with our parliamentary colleagues
and wish to do that before this press conference is reconvened at
five o'clock.'

The Liberal and SDP MPs then gathered in Committee Room
6 for what everyone present remembered as a 'shocking' and
'deeply embarrassing' meeting. Not a single Liberal MP was
prepared to support the document, while Maclennan appeared
(according to Beith) 'uncontrollably distraught' and had to be
comforted by Charles Kennedy for nearly twenty minutes before
he was able to compose himself and rejoin the discussion. Steel too
was emotionally raw. As suggestions flew about how to rescue the
situation, he blurted out: 'I think I've let you all…' 'The word
"down" never came. His voice cracked,' recalled Menzies Campbell
in his memoirs. 'Nancy Sear [*sic*] held out her hand and placed
it comfortingly on his leg. David composed himself and moved
on. The moment had passed. I had never seen David cry before
or since.'

The meeting ended with an agreement to reconvene negotiations
over the policy document the following day. Steel and Maclennan
then headed over to the National Liberal Club, where the delayed

press conference was due to be held in the David Lloyd George Room. 'Although I could not escape my share of the blame,' recalled Steel,

> I decided that the moment should be treated as a minor setback which could be turned to advantage rather than some sort of final defeat. I did my best to rally the spirits of Bob Maclennan, who was deeply downcast by what he felt to be an exaggerated and unreasonable reaction to the paper. In a strange way, the joint calamity brought us closer together.

By this point Steel and Maclennan were ashen faced but composed, flanked by Jim Wallace and Baroness Seear, leader of the Liberal peers, to the left, and Charles Kennedy and Alan Beith to the right. Paddy Ashdown had also suggested that most other Liberal and SDP MPs 'ought to be there, standing behind them to show our support'. As Ashdown recalled in his memoirs:

> It was not a good suggestion. In the subsequent pictures Maclennan and Steel, with twenty MPs looking either menacing or melancholy behind them, didn't look much like two leaders in charge of events – rather, they resembled hostages, dragged from some dark dungeon by a new group of radical terrorists in lounge suits and forced to read out a prepared text just before being subjected to something indescribably horrid.

Maclennan said there would be a 'pause' in the negotiations, while Steel admitted they might have 'tried [to do] too much too soon'. When journalists asked the other Liberal MPs if they supported the document, Maclennan said with a hint of black humour: 'They will not be allowed to open their mouths.' Steel also denied the merger was off, although he admitted it was – at least for the moment – difficult to see a way forward. 'But give people three or four days,' he said, 'give people some sleep and there may be a way forward.'

Maclennan, however, had given no indication he was prepared to repudiate *Voices and Choices*. Interviewed that evening, he promised only to 'listen' to critical views, saying he remained 'enthusiastic' about the contents of what he regarded as a 'challenging' document (Hugo Dixon later wrote Maclennan a long letter urging him not to abandon it). Steel had also irritated some colleagues by appearing to stand by this aspect of the negotiations ('It's very exciting', he told ITN, 'and personally I'm proud of it'). The Liberal Party's National Executive, meanwhile, confirmed it wanted to press on with merger.

Newspaper headlines the next day were the worst for Liberals since the 1986 Eastbourne Assembly, only this time it extended to the SDP. The so-called 'third force', said one, had become the 'third farce', while a *Guardian* editorial said 'fiasco' was 'too mild a word' to describe the previous day's events. 'What should have been a major political moment,' reflected Des Wilson in his memoirs, 'the emergence of a credible alternative to the two old parties, became a humiliating shambles.' Later *The Observer* judged that even in retrospect, the performance of Steel and Maclennan 'seems so bizarre as to be almost unbelievable', while Hugo Young wrote that it 'revealed a failure of leadership on such a scale, to put to question whether Mr David Steel or Mr Robert Maclennan is the more incompetent politician. Neither of them, on this showing, is fit to run a whelk stall.'

Young's assessment was perhaps a little harsh, although correct in spreading the blame equally between the two party leaders. Steel had told Maclennan back in October to avoid lengthy statements of 'new' policies in favour of a short (but freshly written) restatement of existing Alliance policies. This, in retrospect, had been the correct call, but, keen to equip the new party with a distinctive identity, Maclennan had done precisely the opposite. The SDP leader had also resisted Steel's attempts to keep discussion of the policy document away from the Joint Negotiating Team. Had he succeeded, then much of the heartache of mid-January might have been avoided. Hugo Dixon agrees both leaders shared some of the blame but believes it 'really was David's responsibility to make sure that we had a document that was sellable to his side. Bob, of course, should have realised that David wasn't going to be able to do this. But I think that was a lesser failure.'

Had Steel actually read the document? It seems likely he had, both in outline at Ettrick Bridge and in draft at New Year. How closely, however, it is difficult to say. Aware of Steel's past form, Owen thought it 'was perfectly possible that he had done little more than give this policy prospectus a cursory glance'. When Steel left for Kenya, meanwhile, it had fallen to Alan Beith to keep on top of the document's progress. As Liberal policy chief he was best placed to raise serious objections, particularly during Steel's absence, but he did not do so, only disowning the document when it was already too late. Several on the SDP side (including Maclennan) believed Beith had deliberately set a trap in order to further his own leadership ambitions, although Steel rejects this interpretation.

Is it also possible that Steel had read the document and actually agreed with its contents? After all, 'sub-Thatcherite' ideology was not necessarily offensive to him (although the Prime Minister certainly was). He had hinted at aspects of Thatcherism in his 1975 pamphlet *The Liberal Way Forward*, and supported certain aspects of her first government's programme. But even if he had accepted the logic of the document's argument, Steel should surely have realised that its more controversial elements would not have been acceptable to his colleagues. Anything other than a close reading of the text would not have given him enough information to make that judgement.

Judy Steel remembered David coming back from his African trip 'exhausted, rather than refreshed, in no shape to be thrown into the final stages of the negotiations'. That, combined with a gruelling eight months of electioneering and merger negotiations (not to forget nearly twelve years as party leader), had knocked Steel's once perfect political antennae off balance. Never someone for detailed policy work, his lack of engagement also betrayed his intention not to linger as leader once merger had been signed off. After all, it would fall to someone else to sell such a 'bold' policy agenda to the party and public.

Maclennan had also been culpable. Although sincere in his desire to launch the new party on a distinct and imaginative basis, in doing so he had been guilty of over-reach. Furthermore, his political antennae proved as faulty as Steel's in failing to anticipate the reaction of Liberal (and indeed SDP) MPs to its contents. By 14 January Maclennan realised he had to give way; he and Steel issued a joint statement withdrawing *Voices and Choices for All* and appointing a new six-member team to come up with an alternative policy prospectus. It was at this point that Steel likened it to a 'dead parrot' (something for which Des Wilson also claimed credit), a Monty Python reference that was not only a gift to tabloid sub-editors but also a clear indication Steel considered *Voices and Choices* to have expired.

A new parrot, alive but not exactly kicking, appeared just four days later. *A Democracy of Conscience* was basically a reheated version of the 1987 Alliance manifesto (Steel called it 'sound and sensible') and, on 23 January, Liberals assembled in a snow-covered Blackpool to consider – and ultimately approve – merger at a Special Assembly.[150]

Determined not to repeat the mistakes of the 1986 Eastbourne Assembly, nothing was left to chance. As Steel spoke against David Alton's Abortion Bill (which proposed reducing the time limit from twenty-eight to eighteen weeks) in the House of Commons, Jim Wallace (the Liberals' Chief Whip) headed north having spent all week plotting tactics. On Saturday there was a breakfast planning meeting in Steel's suite at the Pembroke Hotel, where Alec McGivan and Richard Holme ensured that high-profile speakers

---

150 Robert Maclennan, meanwhile, made one last attempt to get Owen on board. 'The truth is that he is and always will be an Owenite,' observed Steel of the other David in *Against Goliath*. 'I do not decry that. The fact that what Owenites think on Monday may be different from what they think on Thursday is just something up with which lesser mortals will have to put.'

opposed to merger were immediately followed by high-profile Liberals in favour.

In a conscious rerun of the 1981 Llandudno Alliance rally, Steel also persuaded Jo Grimond (now Lord Grimond of Firth) and Roy Jenkins (now Lord Jenkins of Hillhead) to support merger during a five-hour debate, while his own bullish speech was also judged to be decisive. 'Opponents of merger sometimes talk as if the Liberal Party is going to be abolished,' he told delegates, 'that the new party will not be Liberal. If that were so, I should be voting against merger.' The Alliance, argued Steel, had not simply been a marriage of convenience, but the first step on the road to his and Jenkins's vision of a fairer and better Britain. 'I will be a Liberal to the day I die,' he said, adding that Liberalism had 'a noble past and, I believe, a noble future'. The SDP, meanwhile, had become their 'brothers and sisters in an enlarged family', while the 'assets of the two parties taken together' would 'provide the basis for a formidable force'. 'The choice is a simple one,' concluded Steel. 'Yes, for the chance to put Liberalism into practice, or no, for decades of division and a diminution of Liberalism. I say yes.'

Delegates backed merger by 2,099 to 385 and therefore voted the historic Liberal Party out of existence. A two-thirds majority had been required for it to pass, so such a high winning margin helped restore Steel's credibility after a harrowing couple of weeks. He hailed it as 'a tremendous pleasure and relief' after months of negotiation and years of waiting. 'When a politician achieves such a long-standing purpose, even if only imperfectly,' judged Geoffrey Smith in *The Times*, 'it is right to salute his persistence.' But should, wondered Smith, Steel be content with being the new party's architect rather than its leader?

In this respect, Steel was still hedging his bets. Although pleased with the outcome, it had not altered his 'general view that we should reflect on the wisdom of launching the new party with a new leader'. He asked for a 'close season' on the leadership question while he made up his mind, although colleagues suspected this was to allow Steel to gauge how much support he actually had. Grimond told the

BBC his protégé was the obvious choice,[151] although the ALC called for 'a change of style and a change of emphasis'. Names in the mix included the MP for Gordon, Malcolm Bruce (as a unity candidate), Sir Russell Johnston, Alan Beith and, of course, Paddy Ashdown.

Steel's immediate feeling, however, was one of relief. 'We took David and Judy to Ettrick Bridge and stayed for a celebratory dinner,' recalled Menzies Campbell in his memoirs. 'Judy pulled a large leg of lamb out of the freezer and David opened some very good red wine.' The following weekend, and after a bitter debate, the SDP backed the merger by 273 votes to 28 (with 49 abstentions). David Owen's attitude was one of good riddance to bad rubbish. Reflecting on the 'dead parrot' debacle in his memoirs, he remembered being 'told for months that I had been seen off by David Steel, that I had missed a historic opportunity to lead this grand new party and there they were, revealed to everyone as the "shower"'. 'I knew them to be incapable of fighting their way out of a paper bag,' added Owen bitterly. 'It was perfectly apparent that David Steel's leadership would not recover from this and he would have to step down before a new leader was chosen.'

Some Liberals agreed. 'There was no way David Steel could win Liberal support to lead the new party,' wrote Alan Beith in his memoirs. 'He was entitled to be regarded as a Moses, who had laboured long to bring the people to the promised land but would never, as leader, see it himself.'

> His speeches, his determination and his strategic vision had brought us to this point, but he had acquired far too much unwelcome baggage in the merger negotiations, and his mishandling over the policy document was the last straw, particularly for many of his parliamentary colleagues.

---

151 Grimond wrote to the leader's office with an alternative suggestion, 'making Roy [Jenkins] once again leader of the Alliance *as a whole*', with Steel and Owen remaining as leaders of their respective parties (STEEL/B/1/1/12, Lord Grimond to David Steel, undated).

Over the next few weeks Steel was bombarded with letters, some supportive, others discouraging. Bill Rodgers, for example, urged him to stay on, while the former Liberal MP Richard Wainwright – who had called publicly for Steel's resignation in advance of the 1987 Harrogate Assembly – initiated a long, bad-tempered correspondence with his leader, Wainwright indignant in tone, Steel typically unflappable and clearly demob happy. Now that Wainwright was no longer an MP, Steel clearly felt there was no need for diplomacy, ending one letter with the wounding line: 'Your letters are beginning to fall into the category of those underlined spasmodically in green ink and copied to the Queen.' Otherwise, Steel told Wainwright in another missive, he intended 'to inform colleagues privately of my own intentions after I have had a holiday at Easter week – my first week off in fifteen months'.[152]

Steel was still making up his mind when the new party was launched on 3 March 1988. As David Dutton observed, the Social and Liberal Democrats (SLD) was 'founded more on the ruins of its predecessors than as the beneficiaries of their respective political traditions', something symbolised by the presence of Steel and Bob Maclennan as joint interim leaders, in charge of a party with nineteen MPs (seventeen elected as Liberals, two as SDP), around 3,500 councillors and a declared membership of 100,000. The new party logo was a gold diamond with a black border (Steel had argued for something clean and simple, such as the SNP or CND symbol).

It was another personal triumph for Steel, the culmination of a decades-long dream, although it had hardly occurred in the best of circumstances. 'Rarely has an act of creation', wrote Hugo Young, 'been accompanied by so much destruction.' Young also thought it reasonably certain that Steel would not stand for the leadership of the new party, even though polling indicated – in the absence of David Owen – that he would have a reasonable chance of winning. 'None of this is made any less true', wrote Young, 'by the added fact

152 Richard Wainwright Papers WAINWRIGHTR/11/4, David Steel to Wainwright, 15 February 1988.

that Steel is a leader remarkably unencumbered by either affection or gratitude from his party.'

Still there were mixed messages. In mid-March Charles Kennedy told BBC Scotland that Steel ought to be the first leader. 'It's going to be the type of mainstream centre-left party that David Steel has always wanted to sit astride', he reasoned, 'and therefore I think he should sit astride it at the outset.' (Conversely, Steel privately urged Kennedy to stand, to put down a marker for the future.) In the *Radical Quarterly*, Gordon Lishman lamented Steel's 'lack of interest in political ideas … and his obsession with the tactics of politics to the apparent exclusion of political content'. Therefore, he wrote, the new leader had to 'lead from the front in terms of ideas and policy' and 'be interested in the content and goals of politics, as well as the strategy and tactics'. The former Scottish Liberal MP George Mackie, meanwhile, wrote that failing the emergence of 'a cross between Grimond and Gladstone', Steel was 'the only good choice for the new party'. Steel replied light-heartedly, saying, 'I thought I *was* a cross between Grimond and Gladstone!'[153]

Richard Holme informed Steel that the 'dead parrot' incident had seriously eroded his 'political capital' among party activists, so much so that he could only narrowly expect to win a leadership election. Most likely he already realised this. At Steel's fiftieth birthday party in Brussels, two or three close friends almost persuaded him to stand, against his 'better judgement'. He recalled:

> It was put to me especially strongly by Russell Johnston and David Alton that the prospect of yet another circuit of the same halls may seem an awful prospect, but what had I been working towards since my first leadership speech? One friend advised me not to stand, saying I should be 'the chrysalis that produced the butterfly, not the sow that rolled over in her litter'.

---

153 STEEL/A/5/3, Lord Mackie of Benshie to David Steel, 30 March 1988; David Steel to Lord Mackie, 6 April 1988.

In reality Steel, as Sir Graham Watson puts it, 'never had any intention of leading the new party'. 'All the stuff about him thinking about it was just for show. The whole point of his remaining leader had been to stop Owen.' Indeed, now that he had seen off the other David (not that *Spitting Image* had bothered noting the irony), Steel had achieved what he had intended in the wake of the election. 'Everything panned out after June 1987 but it had taken much longer than planned,' he says. 'It had also been much more traumatic than I'd planned. I didn't know the whole merger process was going to be so appallingly messy and long – it could have been done in a month with a bit of goodwill on both sides.'

Finally, during the Easter of 1988, Steel told his wife, 'in the unlikely setting of a car journey to Windsor Castle for a State banquet for the King of Norway', that he would not be contesting the leadership of the SLD, although this would not be made public until after May's local government elections. 'Someone else can take on the leadership,' Judy remembers him saying, 'someone fresh and energetic.' 'Political progress occurs step-by-step,' reflected Steel in a series of autobiographical pieces for *The Scotsman*. 'In uniting the SDP and the Liberals, we have taken a giant step, and I am proud to have been wearing the seven-league boots but now someone new should take the next step forward.'

Having made his decision Steel, according to Paddy Ashdown, 'seemed to waver for a bit' before informing a meeting of MPs discussing the rules of the forthcoming leadership contest that he would not be standing, a decision he repeated at an emotional meeting of his constituency party in Galashiels the following evening. There were tears in Steel's eyes as thirty Borders Liberals gave him a standing ovation, but later he made it clear his career was not over. 'If you can be President of the US at seventy-five,' he said, 'I obviously still have a long way to go in politics and I don't use an astrologer.'

Asked to comment at a press conference, David Owen said the SLD had 'launched its new aircraft with some of our spare parts and people. Now most of the leaders have parachuted out.' Former

Liberal colleagues were more charitable. 'I don't think it represents failure,' reflected Sir Russell Johnston. 'I think it's battle fatigue.' Steel was, agreed Menzies Campbell in his memoirs, 'exhausted by leadership'. 'I had come to see David', remembers Lord McNally, 'fall out of love with his party.'

Lord Rennard, however, believes Steel should have stayed on for at least a year or two longer. 'His was a strong brand,' he recalls, 'Some thought David was discredited after the dead parrot incident, but I don't agree. We even used his name on letters we distributed during one by-election, because voters still respected him.' Pondering Steel's next moves, meanwhile, was another former Liberal leader. 'Of course, politics and journalism can be combined,' Lord Grimond wrote in *The Scotsman*, 'but of late both have become more exacting and I would not think that David is ready to take on the rather inert role of a distinguished boy statesman.'

Still, the new party needed a new leader, and with Steel out of the running, the succession basically came down to a choice between Paddy Ashdown and Alan Beith. Steel did not publicly back either candidate but supported Beith. The result was announced on 16 July 1988. 'A significant factor', reflected Beith in his memoirs, 'was that Paddy was new, seemingly unconnected with the merger process or the leadership of David Steel, while I was seen as a continuation of what had gone before.' It was also a historic handover. Steel was photographed with Ashdown in front of a desk that had been used by every Liberal leader since H. H. Asquith, emphasising the point that Steel was departing as the last leader of a centuries-old party. A year later the journalist Terry Coleman put it to him that by advocating merger he had killed the party of Gladstone, Asquith and Lloyd George. 'Sentimentalists might say that,' replied Steel sharply, 'but I think Mr Gladstone was probably accused of killing off the Whigs.'

Steel, meanwhile, settled down to a less frenetic life, at least in terms of political activity. In April 1988, while still interim joint leader, he had received the freedom of Tweeddale District, a first in the burgh's history, and also the first of many honours – local and national – which came his way over the next few years. Indeed, at times over the next few months Steel behaved more like a media personality than a former party leader, covering the US Democratic convention for *The Guardian*, and imparting his talent for amusing, often self-deprecating, vignettes to journalists. He gave, for example, several frank interviews about his family.

Graeme, Steel's eldest son, had hit the headlines before the 1987 general election when he was fined £50 for assaulting a police officer outside a nightclub in the Borders, although by the following year he had settled in Galashiels with his partner, Lynne Turnbull. Catriona, the Steels' only daughter, was at college in London, where she lodged with her father. Billy, meanwhile, had taken up acting, got married and moved away. 'As he [Billy] receded in our lives,' reflected Judy in her memoirs, 'the chasm between ourselves and Graeme was gradually bridged.'

'I was the classic absentee father,' Steel told *The Guardian*. 'I've always felt guilty about that.' 'It's the one thing that I really regret,' he had told *Woman's Own* in September 1987. 'I missed my children growing up.'

> I've spent very little time with them in the eleven years since I became leader. They resented that and so do I, those missed years can never be recaptured. But for being away so much, I'm sure the children wouldn't have got into that sort of trouble, but they're through it now.

With a sense of wonderment, Steel told David Penhaligon's widow Annette that her son Matthew and his son Rory had 'suddenly become tall young men in place of little boys'. 'I am enjoying *not* being leader much more than I expected,' he added, 'except for having to get my book written; I'm already behind schedule.'[154]

---

154 STEEL/A/1/2, David Steel to Annette Penhaligon, 28 November 1988.

Indeed, Steel's memoirs – commissioned by George Weidenfeld before he relinquished the leadership – brought a significant advance but also a substantial commitment. David Thomson, who had worked for Steel in the House of Commons, was charged with organising his large collection of papers, while Steel did little else but write – on and off – over the next six months.

'The Steels do not have independent means,' a *New Yorker* profile had observed in 1984, 'and Steel clearly thinks a good deal about money.' He was certainly punctilious about expenses and refunds, the thrifty values instilled in him as a child having remained in place. 'I'm not good on money,' he reflected in 1989, 'or terribly interested in it so long as I'm comfortably off – which I am.' By the late 1980s Steel finally had the financial stability he craved. Not only was there the six-figure advance for his book, but a similar amount in libel damages as a result of the 1987 allegation about his private life. Also, freed from the burden of leadership, Steel was able to pursue additional income through journalism (he was, for example, a columnist with *Scotland on Sunday* when it launched in 1988). 'I earned less as leader', he told David Penhaligon's lawyer in October 1988, 'than either before or since!'[155]

Appearing alongside Steel on an edition of *Any Questions* the same month, the Conservative MP Edwina Currie noted that he was 'rather low key', adding cruelly: 'Now he's a nobody again, the edge, the fight, has gone.' The edge might indeed have been blunted, but not the fight. In February 1989 Marco Pannella, leader of the Italian Radical Party and a fervent Euro-federalist, invited Steel to contest the forthcoming European Parliament elections, taking advantage of a new law under which candidates were not required to be nationals of the country in which they stood. Initially, he refused, telling Pannella on 15 February that it was not a 'practical proposition' and he therefore had to decline. Some were concerned about the company Steel would be required to keep, including the Italian porn queen La Cicciolina. 'It is an invitation

155 STEEL/A/1/2, David Steel to David Blunt, 18 October 1988.

to which any respectable leader', wrote one, 'should not give even the remotest consideration.'[156]

In the absence of any SLD MEPs, however, Steel gradually warmed to the idea, encouraged by his former aide Graham Watson, whose wife Rita was Italian (she would later act as Steel's interpreter). Pannella was then informed that Steel would be delighted to contest the sprawling constituency of Central Italy (Tuscany, Umbria, the Marches and Lazio) under an alliance of three Italian centre parties. It was, at least, a novel undertaking and although eccentric, demonstrated Steel's desire to do something a bit different after twelve years as Liberal leader, while Watson believed it might provide 'closure' on his failure to secure PR for European Parliament elections back in 1977. 'The European dimension is very important to Liberals,' reasoned Steel. 'Why not be a pioneer?'

On his third campaigning visit to Italy in late May, there was little Steel would not do for the cameras, his campaign comprising a familiar mix of short press conferences, photo calls and gruelling bus journeys. British snappers were keen to secure one particular shot. 'Steel was astonishingly willing to march through Florence in rain,' wrote Martin Kettle in *The Guardian*, 'to stand beneath the more famous David in town, Michelangelo's statue in the Piazza della Signoria.' But while the campaign provided colourful copy for journalists, it also proved a bit of a farce. Not only did Steel speak hardly any Italian, but his attempt to transpose British campaigning techniques in a foreign country inevitably fell flat. 'I've learned during this campaign to shut up and just do what they tell me, Italian style,' he admitted to the *Wall Street Journal Europe*. 'Most of the time I haven't a clue what people are saying to me. I've given up worrying about making a big impact here.'

If Steel's intention had been to revive his flagging profile back in the UK, then it proved counterproductive. The press, more often than not, poked fun at his Euro ambitions, while his campaign received only token coverage in Italian newspapers. On the other

---

156 STEEL/B/8/16, undated letter.

hand, Steel livened up an otherwise uneventful campaign, and also made history by becoming the first British politician to deliver a national party political broadcast in another European country. He used it to attack Mrs Thatcher's record on Europe, calling her '*signora fuori tempo*', the woman out of step with others. The Prime Minister's retort was rather contrived. 'I've heard of a Spaghetti Western,' she joked, 'but never of a Spaghetti Scotsman.'

As polling day (or rather days) approached, *The Scotsman* carried an editorial in Italian wishing Steel well. 'I'm certain I won't make it,' he conceded after his final trip to Italy, 'unless someone who is elected backs out for some reason or another.' In the event, Steel did surprisingly well, polling 15,500 votes and coming fourth out of sixteen candidates. As several newspapers gleefully pointed out, not only was this more votes than Steel had managed in his own constituency at the 1987 general election, but more than most of the Democrats who had contested the European election in the UK (indeed, even the Greens polled more votes). Steel, meanwhile, insisted that his candidature had been 'symbolic' rather than serious, and hailed his share of the vote as '*di tutto rispetto*', or highly respectable.

'All politicians are ambivalent about publicity,' reflected Steel in 1989. 'We hate it when we want to go on holiday with the children without being pestered, but we'd be the first to complain if we didn't have it. All politicians, like actors, have a streak of vanity.' The European election of June 1989 could be seen as an attempt by Steel to regain some publicity, as could the publication of his memoirs a few months later, bringing further reflections on Steel's life and legacy.

Spitting Image had anticipated a reflective tome (which it called 'Man of Steel') as early as November 1987, and depicted Steel struggling to think of anything to put in it. This was unfair, for his twenty-four years in the House of Commons had certainly been packed with activity and genuine achievement, although Steel's natural reticence did not lend itself to confessional writing. In a series of autobiographical articles for *The Scotsman* in June 1988 he had given little away and *Against Goliath: David Steel's Story*, published in September 1989, was similarly unrevealing.

Most reviewers noted this gap, as well as the book's tendency to skirt over recent events (particularly those of 1987–8) in a few pages. 'I have always liked and admired David Steel, and wanted to know him better,' reflected David Marquand. 'After reading this book, I still like and admire him, and still feel that I do not really know him.' Book reviews, as any writer knows, often facilitate the public airing of petty rivalries and jealousies, and *Against Goliath* was no exception. In *The Times*, Ian McIntyre said it was 'scrappily written' and its style 'stilted' ('Could this possibly be the same Ian McIntyre', wondered Sir Russell Johnston, 'whom David Steel defeated in the 1966 election?'), while Steel took particular exception to a *Spectator* review by former Liberal president Des Wilson, which jettisoned literary criticism in favour of character assassination.

Others were kinder to a book that was both engagingly written and frankly acknowledged Steel's own failings. 'He is reasonably happy with David Steel's performance,' wrote Lord Grimond in *The Scotsman*. 'He is blissfully free of self-pity.' Also perceptive was the former Conservative minister John Biffen. 'This is a House of Commons book, not an ideological testimony,' he observed in *The Guardian*, 'part textbook and part travelogue.'

Indeed, a whole chapter of *Against Goliath* had been devoted to the 'wider world', travel having played a big part in Steel's life since his university days. He had briefly been Liberal Foreign Affairs spokesman in 1975 while, as leader, he had devoted a lot of time, as Des Wilson put it in his review of Steel's memoirs, 'meeting ambassadors and minor politicians from other countries and attending irrelevant receptions'. In July 1989, meanwhile, there had been talk about luring David Owen back into the fold by appointing him the SLD's foreign spokesman, although Paddy Ashdown realised Steel 'would not be too happy' if that were to transpire. Sir Russell Johnston also badly wanted the job, seeing it as a *quid pro quo* for having helped secure merger.

At the end of October 1989 Steel flew to Namibia for what he called the 'horrendous' task of monitoring elections in the southern African state. The visit also coincided with his appointment as Liberal Democrat shadow foreign affairs spokesman.[157] 'Every time Mrs Thatcher goes abroad her isolation and narrow nationalism become clear,' said Ashdown as he unveiled his new front bench. 'David Steel will map out an alternative course for Britain.' It had been a tricky appointment, not least because Ashdown himself had a strong interest in foreign affairs, but Steel was delighted, reflecting in a paperback edition of his memoirs that his appointment could not have come at 'a more exciting time of fundamental change in global politics'.

He revisited South Africa, the affairs of which had shaped his political outlook as a student, to find a 'quite astounding' transformation, and later met Nelson Mandela on his first visit to London. 'South Africa will suffer much turmoil in the transition,' Steel predicted, 'but the fight against apartheid was one of my earliest political commitments, and it is joyous to see the years of darkness coming to an end.' Within months of taking up his post the Berlin Wall also came down and the following year Germany was reunited as nations across eastern Europe held democratic elections for the first time.[158] And, in mid-1991, Steel visited Moscow just after a failed coup against Mikhail Gorbachev. He therefore concluded a postscript to *Against Goliath* with 'a greater sense of personal and political happiness than even I felt in concluding the first'.

The year 1990 had, for various other reasons, been 'a most

---

157 Since the merger, Steel had always referred to himself as a 'Liberal Democrat' and, when the SLD's short title of 'Democrat' failed to take hold, the party and media adopted the same terminology, which was formalised in the autumn of 1990.

158 Steel made an impression on foreign affairs in another respect. Having gifted one of his Labrador Jill's pups to President Ceaușescu of Romania after an official visit, by the late 1980s the dog still lived in the presidential palace in Bucharest and was, according to Steel, 'a favourite of the elderly autocrat'.

congenial year'. In January Steel had been knighted (Ashdown had wanted him to take a KBE in 1988 but Steel preferred a delay so it did not, in the words of Judy Steel, 'look like compensation for loss of office'), transforming him from – as a Borders newspaper put it – the 'Boy David to Sir David'. Writing to congratulate him, Lord Bonham-Carter wondered 'how much better it would have been – & we would have been – had it been office'.[159] The honour came just a few months before Steel celebrated twenty-five years as an MP, an anniversary marked with a 'seemingly endless series of events'. The National Liberal Club recreated its lunch to celebrate Steel's by-election win in March 1965, while there were also dinners in Melrose and on behalf of Borders Regional Council. 'Faced with this onslaught of continuous celebration and accolade,' joked Steel, 'Paddy Ashdown has threatened to organise an event to commemorate the first anniversary of my silver jubilee.'

Steel was also kept busy with a Channel 4 documentary on the 1843 'Disruption' of the Church of Scotland, while planning for the restoration of Aikwood, a virtual ruin conveyed to the Steels by the Duke of Buccleuch in 1989 (it had been part of his Bowhill estate), began in earnest. The roof, upstairs floors and every window in the tower had to be completely renewed, and electricity and water installed for the first time. The large chimney and the 'joggled lintel' of the Great Hall were also in danger of collapse, but gradually everything came together, Steel and his wife doing some of the work themselves in conjunction with local Selkirk firms. Begun in September 1990, Aikwood was complete by the summer of 1992, just in time for the wedding of Catriona, the Steels' only daughter.

As Aikwood enjoyed a new lease of life, meanwhile, the SDP finally died when its candidate in the May 1990 Bootle by-election secured only 155 votes (although it had come close to winning the Richmond by-election in February 1989), fewer than the Monster Raving Loony Party. David Owen finally got the message and

---

159   David Steel Papers TD 3431/56, Lord Bonham-Carter to Sir David Steel, 15 January 1990.

wound things up. 'Hello, David, it looks like we're merging at last,' Owen told Steel as the two Davids prepared to be melted down in a *Spitting Image* sketch, although Steel escaped that fate by playing a bit part in the following scene. 'The fact that two years were wasted', reflected Steel of Owen's decision, 'more than ever justifies my judgement that the merger issue should have been faced squarely after the 1987 general election and neither dodged nor delayed.'

The Liberal Democrats, however, were not exactly breaking the mould as Steel had predicted the merged party would in 1988. The low point had been the disastrous European elections of 1989, when the party polled just 6 per cent (the Greens managed 15 per cent). The former Leeds West MP Michael Meadowcroft even 'refounded' the Liberal Party using its old logo. By the local government elections of 1990, however, the SLD had bounced back with 17 per cent of vote while – as in the early days of the Alliance – a conveniently timed by-election came to the rescue. When the Liberal Democrat candidate David Bellotti won Eastbourne with a majority of more than 4,500 votes in October, it was a sign the new party had a future after all. And having pilloried the party's new Liberal Democrat 'bird' logo at the 1990 Conservative Party conference ('this is an ex-parrot, it is not merely stunned') the joke was now on Mrs Thatcher for having presided over the loss of a safe Tory seat. The *Evening Standard* covered the by-election result with a memorable headline: 'THE PARROT TWITCHED.'

The most significant feature of Steel's post-leadership phase, however, was the first of two Scottish postscripts to his long political career. In June 1988 he had spoken of his desire to devote more time 'to Scottish interests and to support those groups trying to seek unity of purpose to secure an assembly with real powers'. The push for Scottish devolution had grown in the wake of a third Conservative election victory in 1987 and, following a stunning SNP victory at the Glasgow Govan by-election in November 1988, the Labour Party was suddenly very keen to join a cross-party campaign to lobby for the creation of a Scottish Assembly – or Parliament – in Edinburgh.

Having long championed what he termed 'Home Rule' for Scotland, Steel, particularly now he had more time on his hands, was keen to play a high-profile role and ensure that this devolution scheme succeeded where others, most notably that in 1979, had failed, chiefly by ensuring any assembly was elected by PR to ensure representativeness and democratic legitimacy. Several high-profile Scots were keen to encourage him. The Liberal Democrat MP Ray Michie told Steel she had always been convinced that the true destiny of the 'Boy David' was to lead Scotland 'back to her own Parliament and a resolution of her future', while even the writer (and Conservative supporter) Allan Massie urged him to 'play a part in its creation'. 'It offers splendid opportunities,' he wrote, 'but if it is ill-made & – worse – ill-conceived, falsifying the hopes placed in it, the effect of whatever degree of independence we choose to take could be harmful.'[160]

Having initially pushed Steel in this direction too, Lord Grimond – himself a life-long supporter of Scottish Home Rule – began to have doubts. 'The politics of Scotland are rather like those of the Liberal Party,' he reflected when reviewing Steel's memoirs. 'Many of those active in the various movements for devolution or independence don't want to achieve anything.'

> They want to paddle their own small canoes and argue in the correspondence columns of *The Scotsman*. Like Liberals they endlessly debate their own affairs and latch onto bizarre schemes. Could anything be more peculiar than that a British government should decide what taxes are to be levied and that a Scottish government should spend them? The children are to be allowed to decide whether to spend the money which Daddy gives them on lollipops or toy trains but Daddy decides what money is available.

It was a prescient analysis from the Grand Old Man of Liberal

---

160 TD 3431/56, Ray Michie to David Steel, 30 December 1989; Allan Massie to David Steel, 6 January 1990.

politics but, in the cauldron that was Scottish constitutional politics in the late 1980s, rational debate frequently sank beneath nation-building. By January 1989 Steel had emerged as the favourite candidate to chair what became the Scottish Constitutional Convention (SCC), a cross-party movement which appealed to the co-operative politics he had long promoted.

Despite the Govan result, Steel still believed – as he had since the late 1960s – that most Scots desired greater self-government rather than full independence. 'They use the SNP as a sort of democratic battering ram to get what they really want,' he explained, precisely the sort of language which did not endear the former Liberal leader to Nationalists. 'He has not been identified with Scottish politics for fifteen years – he has been a UK politician,' the SNP leader Gordon Wilson complained. 'Now he wants to take up a Scottish job in his retirement.'

Writing to the academic (and future SNP politician) Christopher Harvie on 18 January 1989, Steel dismissed Wilson's objections ('He was at university with me and I have never held a high view of him'), while protesting that he was 'the media's candidate for the chairmanship but nobody else's!' He was, however, keen, adding that 'if enough consensus emerges for me to be chairman it is a challenge I would willingly accept.'[161] When the SNP dramatically withdrew from cross-party talks, however, Wilson's opposition evaporated and thus Steel's path was cleared.

On 30 March 1989 a hundred and fifty people, including more than fifty Labour and Liberal Democrat MPs (though not, impor-tantly, the SNP) queued up to sign the 'Claim of Right' at the end of the SCC's first meeting at the Church of Scotland's General Assembly Hall in Edinburgh. It had begun with the unanimous election of not one but two chairmen, the Labour MP Harry Ewing and Steel, who said Scotland had 'the right to insist on articulating its own demands and grievances rather than have them articulated by a distant government utterly unrepresentative of Scotland'.

---

161 STEEL/B/9/2, Sir David Steel to Christopher Harvie, 18 January 1989.

Steel, however, saw himself as a figurehead rather than someone who would provide day-to-day stewardship. He did not attend executive meetings and there is scant evidence among Steel's papers that he engaged directly with the detailed work of the SCC. He often missed meetings (because, as he frequently complained, he had not been notified in advance), generating clear tension between him and the SCC's secretary, Bruce Black. As noted earlier, Steel's primary interest was securing a PR electoral system for whatever devolutionary scheme the convention settled upon. 'Don't let's waste time drafting what would be the fine detail of a particular system,' he argued in *The Scotsman* on 15 March 1990, 'because there are 101 different proportional representation systems and I am using the words PR in their broadest sense.' Although Steel would, in the long term, be vindicated in this approach, at the time it created tension within not only his own party (Malcolm Bruce, the Scottish Liberal Democrat leader, wanted PR as a precondition for taking part in the SCC), but also Labour (naturally keen to preserve its majority status in Scotland).

By late 1990, the SCC had, as Steel wrote in the second edition of *Against Goliath*, 'confounded the sceptics and come up with a unanimously agreed blueprint [including PR] for Scottish self-government which removes many of the criticisms of the 1979 devolution proposals'. Steel, Harry Ewing and Canon Kenyon Wright, another leading light in the convention, also sent a copy of *Towards Scotland's Parliament* to the Prime Minister and asked for a meeting. But predictably, the Conservative government was not keen to engage, refusing to accept the SCC as 'as effectively representative of Scottish life'.[162]

In the face of continued Tory intransigence, Steel invoked Ireland's bloody history as a warning. 'I believe that if the government goes on resisting the sensible course for a parliament within the UK,' he told Scottish Television, 'they will actually fuel the flames of those who want to go a great deal further and want to

---

162 STEEL/B/9/13, John Major to Sir David Steel, 22 April 1991.

break up the UK.' But as the general election of 1992 drew closer, with Prime Minister John Major attempting to secure a fourth consecutive Tory victory, Steel and other devolutionists believed the result made the creation of a Scottish Parliament almost inevitable. Surveying three likely outcomes – a minority Labour government, a hung Parliament or a fourth Conservative win – Steel argued that every one would lead to devolution (even a Tory victory, he argued, would involve heavy losses in Scotland and, therefore, a return to 'the Home/Heath Tory policy on devolution'). 'The status quo is not an option,' declared Steel in a statement. 'Our convention's proposals are, and so your labour has not been in vain.'[163]

This, when polls closed on the evening of 9 April 1992, proved to be wishful thinking. Not only did John Major pull off a surprising, albeit narrow, election victory, but in Scotland the Conservatives, albeit modestly, increased their representation and share of the vote. Thus the third of Steel's scenarios had come to pass, although without heavy losses north of the border or, ultimately, any significant movement on devolution.

Nationally, the Liberal Democrats won almost six million votes and twenty seats, a loss of two on 1987 but hardly a catastrophe for a party established only four years earlier. In Tweeddale, Ettrick & Lauderdale (which the constituency had become in 1983), Steel's majority was down to just 2,520. It was possible that his involvement with the SCC had had an impact (devolution was less popular in the south of Scotland), while John Hein, who thereafter contested the seat at every election up to and including 2005, took a few hundred votes as a 'real' Liberal. Steel's campaigning methods, so fresh and new in 1965, had also grown rather stale. Although he had rightly built a reputation as a workaholic MP, constant absences in Italy, Africa and other parts of the world were bound to have had an impact.

The political atmosphere in the wake of the election result, meanwhile, was not a forgiving one. The SCC, having expected

163   STEEL/B/9/7, statement dated 28 February 1992.

swift implementation of its proposals by a Labour or (Labour–Liberal Democrat) coalition government, was thrown into disarray. When the SNP leader Alex Salmond attacked 'Sir David's pathetic attempt to allocate responsibility elsewhere for the convention's failure to turn even a majority of seats and votes into any action for Scotland', Steel responded privately, admitting that Salmond's critique of the convention's methodology was 'persuasive', although dependent upon 'securing the "right" UK result, or at least a crushing diminution of the Tories in Scotland'. He continued:

> Neither happened – but then nor did your thirty-seven seats materialise! I'm happy to have a constructive chat about 'thinking again'. I can assure you I bear no ill will towards the SNP, and still believe in the search for a united approach, nor am I suffering from 'paralysis of thought', simply dismay at the election result, a dismay which I assume you share.[164]

Steel considered this sort of private contact with Nationalists and sympathetic Tories as important while the SCC considered the best way forward. By July 1992, however, he had concluded 'the convention should wind up and if possible give birth to a more broadly based Civic Forum, open … to individual members, including the SNP and Tory dissidents'.[165] Canon Kenyon Wright and other convention founders were reluctant to let go. After a thinly attended meeting in St Andrews, Jim Wallace informed Wright in February 1993 that it had 'become more and more obvious that since the general election, the convention has lacked a clear sense of purpose'.[166]

In the absence of any progress in domestic Scottish politics, Steel continued to concentrate on international policy during the 1992–7

---

164 STEEL/B/9/14, Sir David Steel to Alex Salmond, 10 June 1992.
165 STEEL/B/9/14, Sir David Steel to Canon Kenyon Wright, 9 July 1992.
166 STEEL/B/9/16, Jim Wallace to Canon Kenyon Wright, 19 February 1993.

parliament. 'His views on foreign affairs were formed in the 1970s,' reflects Jeremy Purvis, who worked in Steel's office for some of that time. 'They developed in the 1980s and by the 1990s when all these issues were still in play, he felt he could play a valuable role.' An intriguing what-if had occurred as Steel flew home from the funeral of the former Indian Prime Minister Rajiv Gandhi in mid-1991. 'You should not be wasting your time as Lib Dem spokesman on foreign affairs,' the Labour leader Neil Kinnock told him, 'you should have a proper job – what about ambassador to South Africa?' 'Done,' replied Steel. 'The only problem was that he never became Prime Minister in 1992, and so the rest is history,' he recalled in 2012. 'I had to be content with chairing the Commonwealth Observer Mission at the second South African election.'

Indeed, Steel spent several years monitoring elections in Africa and was particularly involved in supporting multi-party democracy in Malawi when the long-serving Hastings Banda agreed to an election in 1994. He worked with Bakili Muluzi's United Democratic Front (a liberal party), developing campaigning material and even supporting the drafting of the first democratic programme of government from his Commons office. Steel not only enjoyed jet-setting, but appreciated the attention he received abroad, often more lavish than anything he experienced in the UK. The accumulated air miles, however, also served a broader purpose, helping the Foreign Office with low-level diplomacy (although Purvis remembers this coming to a halt when Labour won the 1997 election). Steel, noted Hugo Young following lunch in June 1993, 'feels he has more influence in Malawi than he does in England' [sic].

In the summer of 1994, Steel was also appointed president of Liberal International (LI), a London-based organisation that sought to promote liberalism and relations between liberal political parties around the world. Steel was the first Briton to hold the post, which – along with his constituency duties – was to dominate his final years as an MP (he stood down as Foreign Affairs spokesman the same year). Over the next few years he visited more than fifty countries accompanied by his Kenyan-born foreign affairs aide Dr

Atul Vadher, and helped to establish regional LI organisations in Asia and Africa. Vadher found his boss unflappable under pressure in even the most difficult countries, while Jeremy Purvis believes his LI presidency represented 'a bit of a peak'. 'The US Democrats were very open to us, Canada had a Liberal government and Liberals also held the balance of power in the European Parliament,' says Purvis. 'David was a bridge to all of that. As an international grouping, the Liberals had rarely been so influential.'

Purvis was also 'surprised by the seamlessness of his [Steel's] approach, from the constituency to ... international issues'. As a result, his boss took exception to implications – often made by newspaper diarists – that he was taking life easy. When the *Evening Standard* expressed envy at Steel's presence at a classic car rally (a passion since his schooldays) in Marrakesh, he was indignant in response. 'I have not held my Borders se[a]t in nine elections', he complained to the editor, 'by leading a life of idle pleasure.'[167]

Nevertheless, Steel remained uniquely capable of making time for a myriad of enjoyable activities. For a week in 1993 he guest-presented the Jimmy Young programme on BBC Radio 2, also leading a bid for the Central Scotland radio franchise in between accepting, as one journalist put it, 'every silly game show slot he's offered'. He also spent more quality time with Judy, preparing a second edition of their 1985 book, *Border Country*.

In Parliament, meanwhile, Steel's relations with his successor were occasionally brittle. During the first Gulf War in 1991 he had, according to Paddy Ashdown's diaries, become 'terribly wobbly', expressing concern that one of our demands is that the Iraqis must recognise Kuwait'. But, by June 1993, Hugo Young found Steel 'surprisingly unbitchy about Ashdown'. 'Says PA is much better than he ... was at the party machine: getting involved, making it work.' There was nevertheless tension over the foreign affairs brief (Ashdown liked to deal with big issues, such as Bosnia, himself) and, more surprisingly, realignment.

---

167   STEEL/B/13/19, Sir David Steel to the *Evening Standard*, 27 October 1993.

Prior to the 1992 general election the prospect of a hung
Parliament had seemed very real (indeed, Ashdown had earmarked
Cabinet posts for himself, Steel, Alan Beith and Menzies Campbell),
and thus Ashdown had been careful to cultivate an indistinct ideological identity. 'They [Labour] regard David Steel as a sort of "half
brother" – of the centre-left,' noted Ashdown in his diary, 'but
think I am probably "centre-right". Exactly what I want.'

When that prospect disappeared with Major's election victory,
Ashdown turned his attention towards Labour. Despite past form,
however, Steel was wary, telling Hugo Young that doing deals
with the Liberal Democrats was simply not on the agenda of John
Smith, Neil Kinnock's successor as Labour leader. 'Ashdown's
problem is that, with Labour not moving an inch towards him,
it is very hard for him to make clear what is in fact the truth: that
the natural alliance is between the Liberal Democrats and Labour,'
Steel told Young, who asked why Ashdown did not make that
clearer. 'Because', replied Steel, 'he will be left high and dry if he
concedes that clear identity and then finds that Labour won't give
him anything.'

His own dreams of realignment must have been in Steel's mind
as he gave a reading at the funeral of Lord Grimond a few months
later, although Jo too had cooled towards his own strategy in the
autumn of his years. When John Smith also died in May 1994,
the game changed completely. With an appealing new leader, Tony
Blair, 'New' Labour began to attract significant support. When
Ashdown extended feelers, however, he found the party nevertheless keen to engage lest it lack an overall majority at the next
election. Bob Maclennan and Robin Cook soon initiated what
became known, rather grandly, as the 'Cook–Maclennan' talks,
which focused on devolution for Scotland and Wales, as well as
wider-ranging measures of constitutional reform.

Steel, however, remained sceptical, wielding his experience
of the Lib–Lab Pact as evidence of the harm a close relationship
with Labour could do. When Ashdown consulted him in October
1995, Steel warned 'that a joint position with Labour before the

next election would not be wise', while a year later he pledged qualified support. 'It is a very risky move,' Steel told Ashdown, 'and I am not sure you can carry the party on it.' By December, however, Ashdown noted in his diary that Steel, who along with Menzies Campbell had tried to rein in his preoccupation with 'the project', was 'basically on board'. 'David Steel exhorted them to prepare for government,' observed *The Guardian* of the Liberal Democrats. 'Paddy Ashdown's best hope is to exhort them to prepare for influence.'

In the summer of 1995 Graeme, Steel's eldest son, and his partner Lynne were arrested for growing cannabis at their home in Galashiels. Through her 'theatre contacts' Judy had been aware of her son's use of the drug, but not David. 'He found it very difficult to take my worries over Graeme seriously,' she recalled in her memoirs, 'and our son's arrest came as a much bigger shock to him than it did to me.'

When the case came to court in October, Graeme got a nine-month prison sentence, a story well covered by the press (although the *Border Telegraph* simply reported 'Stow man jailed for growing cannabis'). Neither of his parents attended the hearing, although as an MP David was able to visit him at Friarton open prison in Perth without requiring a pass. Released after four-and-a-half months, Graeme gave a press conference restating his belief that cannabis ought to be legalised.

The incident, although embarrassing for Steel as he approached the end of his Commons career, also had a happy side effect. Not only did Graeme's days of what his mother called 'voluntary unemployment' come to an end as a result of his prison experience, but his relationship with Judy, 'which still suffered from the choice I had made ten years before when I had put Billy's interests before his, was at last healed'. Billy, although by this point estranged from the Steels, had been in trouble of his own. In 1991 he had been banned from driving for three years and fined £200 for failing to take a breath test.

Judy Steel, who had suffered from what she called 'dark times'
during her husband's period as leader, also became more confident,
shedding more than 5 stone, and acquiring contact lenses and a
different hairstyle. For a brief period, as she recalled in her memoirs,
she 'felt elegant and even beautiful'. (Later, to mark her seventieth
birthday, Judy had a jaguar – from David's heraldic arms – tattooed
on her shoulder.)

Steel, meanwhile, was once again preoccupied with Scottish
affairs. On St Andrew's Day in 1995, the SCC published
its final document, *Scotland's Parliament, Scotland's Right*.
A few months later Tony Blair U-turned and committed
Labour to a two-question (the second on tax-varying powers)
referendum on a Scottish Parliament, prompting Steel's
co-chair, Harry Ewing, to resign in protest at not having been
consulted. 'Blair's move bears all the smack of weak leadership,' commented Steel. 'It is one thing to hold a referendum
on the whole proposal for a Scottish Parliament, but it is down-
right silly to run scared before Michael Forsyth [the Secretary
of State for Scotland] and pick out the tax-varying powers as a
referendum question.'[168]

In another statement drafted, but not distributed, by Steel, he
said it was 'no good crying over spilt milk'. 'If there is a referendum
there should be a straight "yes" or "no" question in the package,'
he added. 'That is my view, and I hope that a future government
might yet see the sense of it.'[169] At around the same time, Steel
and Allan Massie exchanged correspondence on devolution in
the current affairs magazine *Prospect*. Steel had expressed scepticism (not unreasonably) at the strength of Blair's commitment to
a Scottish Parliament, and when the *Sunday Times* followed this up
with a story headlined 'STEEL DOUBTS BLAIR'S COMPETENCE', the

---

168 Labour had hitherto not accepted the need for a referendum at all. The
     Conservative Scottish Secretary, Michael Forsyth, meanwhile, had been
     raging against what he called the prospect of a 'tartan tax'.

169 TD 3431/44, press release dated 27 June 1996; statement dated 25 July 1996.

Labour leader was scathing. Steel, he told *The Scotsman* journalist Peter MacMahon, had 'never damned well delivered anything', whereas he was determined to deliver 'devolution'.

By this point, Steel was clearly winding down. In advance of entering his thirtieth year as an MP, he had announced his intention to retire from the House of Commons at the next general election, saying he wanted to do so while he was still young enough to contemplate 'doing something equally constructive and challenging with the remaining decades of my working life'. Having entered Parliament as the baby of the House, Steel told his constituency party, he harboured 'no ambitions to stay to become the father of the House'. Paddy Ashdown was generous in tribute. 'The role of an ex-party leader is one of the most difficult in politics,' he said. 'In contrast to some, David has been a model, always a valued background adviser, but never a back-seat driver.'

In February 1995, Steel welcomed the 29-year-old accountant Michael Moore as the 'young' prospect ('He's starting', he joked, 'a bit late in life') hoping to succeed him in a constituency almost abolished by the Boundary Commission the year before, while he returned to Ashdown's team in June 1996 as shadow Minister without Portfolio, ostensibly to help prepare for the general election. During his last years in the Commons, Steel was regularly deployed as an intermediary to prevent potential rows between Ashdown and his MPs.

In the early stages of Ashdown's leadership there had been plenty to resolve, but even when he came under sustained attack from MPs like Alex Carlile, Alan Beith and Malcolm Bruce, Steel never flinched from supporting his successor publicly, even when he agreed with the criticism. When Parliament dissolved in April 1997, Ashdown again praised Steel's qualities as an 'ex-leader'. 'You have been a brilliant one as far as I am concerned,' Ashdown wrote, 'always ready with advice and support when I needed it, but never criticising me in public, even when I deserved it.'[170] After thirty-two

---

170 David Steel Papers (private collection), Paddy Ashdown to Sir David Steel,
4 April 1997.

years as an MP, Steel inevitably found departing the Commons difficult. 'It was right that he was leaving,' reflected Judy, 'but it was hard for him as well.'

Membership of the House of Lords had, of course, been mooted, but Steel deliberately played down expectations. 'If I was asked,' he told a journalist in early 1997, 'I would say "It is nice of you to offer, but it is not for me".' But when John Major included Steel's name in his dissolution honours list, announced to the press on 18 April, he was hardly going to say no. As Tony Blair's 'New' Labour Party – changed almost beyond recognition by its 1981 split and four election defeats – was preparing for government, Steel was preparing for a new phase in his career.

9

CALL ME 'SIR DAVID'

Sir David Steel's years outside the House of Commons would represent the height of what Michael Foot had, back in 1979, called his 'elder statesman' period. During the election campaign Steel and his wife Judy had worked hard at ensuring Michael Moore held the Tweeddale, Ettrick & Lauderdale seat (which he did by nearly 1,500 votes). Then, after taking up his seat in the House of Lords on 11 June 1997, Lord Steel of Aikwood quickly set to work on becoming the great Pooh-Bah of Scottish and British politics, presiding over and commentating on Scotland, Liberal Democracy and 21st-century visions of realignment.

As soon as Steel's peerage had been announced, the businessman Sir Anthony Jacobs (who later became a peer himself) wrote expressing his desire to see him as leader of the Liberal Democrat peers. The present incumbent, Lord Jenkins of Hillhead, was also keen as he had a book to write (most likely *The Chancellors*, published in 1998). Steel, however, was reluctant to take on such a commitment so soon after leaving the Commons so agreed instead to act as Jenkins's deputy.

This was carefully chosen to give Steel status but not very much responsibility, freeing him up for two years of intense political activity ahead of the first elections to the Scottish Parliament in May 1999. Tony Blair's government (with its thumping majority) legislated quickly, not just to establish the devolved Parliament, but for a pre-legislative referendum the Prime Minister wanted held as quickly as possible.[171] The Liberal Democrats, Steel had written in the wake of the election result, could 'continue to act as guarantors of its [devolution's] fundamental delivery from an occasionally wobbly Labour Party'.

Steel's name had been floated as a possible leader of the cross-party 'yes' campaign in late 1996, but in the event a group (Scotland Forward) run by the businessman Nigel Smith took up the mantle. They were understandably irritated when Steel told the BBC they were 'well-meaning but politically inexperienced people'. He also lobbied Donald Dewar, the new Scottish Secretary and another friend since university days, to elect the Parliament via one nation-wide proportional list (something akin to the Israeli Knesset), arguing that eight 'wholly artificial' regions (based on Scotland's Euro-constituencies) would confuse the public, while presciently warning that 'an apparently grander MP in regional seats such as Glasgow or Edinburgh is bound to prove awkward'.[172]

No sooner had the two-question referendum been won on 11 September 1997, meanwhile, than Steel was plunged into a row about his involvement with the Countryside Movement, of which he had been chairman for eighteen months between October 1995 and the general election. Not only had his remuneration for two days a week been significantly larger than his salary as an MP (a total of £94,000), but Steel had tabled three motions on country-side issues without formally declaring an interest.

Steel protested that the position had been intended as 'retirement' income, his departure from the Commons having been announced in 1994. 'Throughout most of my thirty-two years in Parliament I had no significant outside interests,' he told *The Independent*, explaining that his principal role had been amalgamating

---

171 In December 1997, Blair also appointed Lord (Roy) Jenkins chair of an Independent Commission on the Voting System, which – in October 1998 – recommended an electoral system not unlike that planned for the Scottish Parliament. It was never implemented.

172 David Steel Papers TD 3431/43, Lord Steel to Donald Dewar, 25 June 1997.

three separate organisations into one called the Countryside Alliance (of which he remained deputy chairman). But when the Labour MP Dale Campbell-Savours referred it to the Commons' Standards and Privileges Committee, his complaint was upheld, Steel having failed to register details of his salary.[173]

It was a chastening experience for Steel so early in his Lords career, although a robust Liberal Democrat response helped limit the damage (Paddy Ashdown said he had been 'perfectly open about this from the word go'). Having secured an astonishing tally of forty-six seats at the general election (although share of the vote was down slightly on 1992), Ashdown's authority within the party was at its height. Relations between him and Steel, however, were occasionally rocky. When the BBC asked Steel to comment on Liberal Democrat inclusion in a joint Cabinet committee with Labour, he harked back to the Lib–Lab Pact, pointing out – accurately – that the Liberals had become tarred with Labour's difficulties even after the pact had ended. His point was that 'such tarring' could be even greater with a government sub-committee if Blair became similarly unpopular.

Ashdown, who had worked hard on forging relations with the Labour Party, was not amused, and accused Steel of failing to 'communicate' with the rest of the party. In a lengthy letter, Steel replied that 'concerned' did not adequately describe his response to that accusation, 'bloody angry' being closer to the mark. He then had a general rant about his 'overworked' assistant (Jeremy Purvis, who handled the transition between Steel's Commons and Lords offices) and the failure of the Liberal Democrat press office to promote his activities. 'David felt he had a standing, as well as Paddy,' recalls Purvis, 'which ought to be recognised.' Steel's letter concluded:

> I hope you can now understand my wrath at being accused of non-communication. Indeed you are not yourself immune. I can recall

---

173 During 1997 Steel also helped promote Charles Tyrwhitt shirts with the legend 'A liberal cut that suits all shapes and sizes'.

only one occasion since the election when you have consulted me
on anything. All other meetings between us – including that enjoyable dinner at your home – have been at my instigation.[174]

Ashdown moved quickly to appease Steel, sending him a semi-
apologetic letter and later dining with him at London's Gran
Paradiso in April 1998. 'A very enjoyable meal,' recorded Ashdown
in his diary. 'We got through two bottles of wine, which was probably half a bottle too much for either of us ... I let David into
about 80 per cent of my Blair meeting. He gave me his full support:
"This is what I have been after for so long."'[175]

Steel, however, 'most wanted to talk about Africa and his ambitions for the Scottish Parliament (he wants to be Speaker)', and
indeed the latter desire would preoccupy him for most of the
following year. He had written to Willie Rennie, chief executive
of the Scottish Liberal Democrats, on 26 November 1997 (and,
formally, on 10 April 1998) asking for his name to be registered as
soon as possible for both the European and Scottish Parliament
elections in mid-1999 (he was clearly hedging his bets). Steel's wife
Judy and daughter Catriona did the same, a potential triple salary
the press made much of. Usefully, Steel's membership of the Upper
House was not a barrier.[176]

Some Liberal Democrats, including Archy Kirkwood and

---

174 David Steel Papers (private collection), Lord Steel to Paddy Ashdown, 28
     December 1997.
175 When Ashdown's memoirs were published in 2009, he was rather more
     blunt about his predecessor. 'David Steel was always thought to be that nice
     wee David Steel – but he was a b****** behind the scenes,' he wrote. 'I use
     that in the best sense of the word. Complete political ruthlessness.'
176 When the John Wheatley Centre proposed standing orders for the Scottish
     Parliament in 1995, Steel wrote to them asking if they really intended
     to 'exclude' peers. 'If so, may I suggest a pause for reflection?' he added.
     'Pending reform of the Lords, I see no incompatibility, and indeed, some
     virtue in having an overlap' (TD 3431/44, Sir David Steel to Richard Norris,
     26 July 1995).

Menzies Campbell, cautioned Steel against standing at all, fearing his reputation would be at risk if he failed to be elected.[177] Indeed, his selection process was far from straightforward. After being interviewed by a panel of Scottish Liberal Democrats in Edinburgh, Steel was categorised as an 'approved' rather than 'commended' candidate, the latter accolade going to several applicants whose experience paled in comparison with a former UK party leader's. When others tried to exploit this perceived snub as a means of pushing him down the ranking for the Lothians regional list (he had been too late to apply for his home patch), Steel attacked them as 'small minded'.

There was, however, never any serious prospect of Steel failing to be selected, although his presence – and indeed his profile – certainly rankled with other Liberal Democrat hopefuls. In April 1998 he went public with what the press called a 'return to frontline politics', while appealing for other senior Westminster figures to do the same. 'There is need for a sprinkling of experience,' he declared in a mildly patronising manner, 'to balance the inexperience of newcomers.' Steel also fended off speculation about becoming the Scottish Parliament's first Speaker (although he had, that same month, told Ashdown of that ambition) by saying there remained 'many bridges to cross' before he considered any such role. He said that since the referendum he had been 'like a man with a pair of whispering birds, each perched on a shoulder', one saying leave it to others, the other saying 'Stop dithering and get stuck in.'

On 6 July 1998 it was announced that Steel had topped a postal ballot of Liberal Democrat members for the Lothians regional list with more than 50 per cent of the vote. The party hoped that with such a high-profile name in first place it would be able to 'piggy back' one or two more Members of the Scottish Parliament (MSPs) as a result. Steel, meanwhile, was obviously pleased to be

---

177 Before Steel was firmly committed to the Scottish Parliament, his former aide Stuart Mole sounded him out about becoming the first British secretary-general of the Commonwealth, for which Mole then worked.

on the cusp of returning to elected politics. 'Scotland is about to embark on redressing a wrong committed in 1707,' he had said in April, 'when, in the course of sensibly entering the Union, the Scottish Parliament was abolished. Liberal leader Gladstone's vision of Home Rule all round is coming nearer. Our hour has at last come.'

Steel was fully involved in the 'long' campaign. 'We need heavy concentration of human and material resources in the first four months of 1999 if we are to secure fifteen to twenty seats in the 129-person parliament next May,' he told colleagues in October 1998. 'We are not committed in advance to coalition with either party.'[178] Indeed, in what the journalist Benedict Brogan called a 'superbly judged' pre-election conference speech in Aberdeen, Steel's self-deprecating humour had been deployed to good effect. 'I am not going to end this speech', Steel told delegates, 'by saying go back to your constituencies and prepare for coalition.'

By the beginning of 1999 Steel was no longer denying his ambition to be the new Parliament's first Speaker. '[I]f the question's put to me, "Would you be willing to accept the role?" then the answer is yes,' he told the *Scottish Sun*. 'I'm determined to give politics five years and the end of this first parliament will coincide with me reaching sixty-five – so I'll be picking up my bus pass.' When campaigning began in April 1999 Steel stressed his enduring support for devolution and international standing, his election leaflet featuring a picture of him with Nelson Mandela under the legend 'A statesman for Scotland'.[179] He also chaired the Scottish Liberal Democrats' morning press conferences, although this gave rise to at least one gaffe. 'Whether it's a coalition or a minority government,' Steel declared two days before polling day, 'tuition fees will go. Tuition fees are dead as of Friday.' This infuriated party

---

178 TD 3431/49, memo dated 28 October 1998.
179 The picture had featured Jim Wallace, but when Steel was told he was not allowed party endorsements, he opted for Mandela instead.

managers, who feared having their hands tied in advance of negotiations with Labour.

As for Steel's designation in the new Parliament, he had used
his *Edinburgh Evening News* column ('The Voice of Experience') to
affect disdain for his peerage. 'You read it here first,' he wrote, 'I am
going to give up being a "lord".' 'For nearly two years I have lived
with the cumbersome name Lord Steel of Aikwood,' explained
Steel and, having eschewed this title on his passport (he continued
to travel as 'Sir David Steel'), he indicated his intention to do the
same as an MSP. 'Being addressed as Lord Steel sounds pompous,'
he wrote. 'Lord David Steel is incorrect – I am not the younger son
of a duke – while Sir David is warm and friendly. So, Sir David
Steel it was, is now and evermore shall be.' There was a certain
degree of irony in this, but the invitation to 'call me Sir David' was,
perhaps surprisingly, taken up by both journalists and MSPs.

Steel was elected one of seventeen Liberal Democrat MSPs in the first
elections to the Scottish Parliament on 6 May 1999. In the Lothians
the party attracted 47,565 votes, or 14.4 per cent of the vote, which
was enough to return just one Liberal Democrat out of eight elected
in that region. For an hour or so it was not clear if he had actually
been elected, prompting Steel to remark, half-jokingly, 'Whoever
thought up this PR system?'

When the Parliament met for the first time on 12 May, there
were just two nominations as its Speaker, or Presiding Officer: Steel
and George Reid (an SNP MSP), who had known each other for
forty-four years. Steel won eighty-two votes to Reid's forty-four
(with three abstentions), and immediately undertook 'to set aside
party affiliation and to be the servant of the whole Parliament'.
He had been a Liberal Democrat MSP for just six days and, given
his perceived fast-tracking to top the Lothians list, Scottish Liberal
Democrat HQ fielded calls from several indignant activists.

In his first speech as Presiding Officer, Steel quoted a poem by
William McIlvanney which spoke of the Scottish lion becoming
a kitten again, a kitten he said ought to be cherished. 'We must

cherish this Parliament,' said Steel. 'This is the start of a new sang.'[180]
But while Steel undeniably brought experience to his second
Scottish postscript (the other having been his co-chairmanship of
the Scottish Constitutional Convention), the Scottish Parliament
would rarely be cherished over the next few years, either by the
media or many of those who had just voted.

The following day, Steel presided over the election of a 'First
Minister' (he had first proposed such a title in the 1970s) and also
wrote to his old Alliance colleague Lord Rodgers of Quarry Bank
(Jenkins's successor as leader of the Liberal Democrat peers) to resign
as his deputy with immediate effect, although he looked forward to
'continued participation in the Lords on a more occasional basis'.
He added: 'May I add my thanks to you and colleagues for a most
enjoyable and not exactly strenuous two years as your deputy.'[181]

Steel's first official engagement as Presiding Officer was to
address the General Assembly of the Church of Scotland, which
was meeting in alternative accommodation so that the Parliament
could meet in its Mound Assembly Hall. Twenty-five years before
his father, the Very Reverend David Steel, had moderated Kirk
proceedings, and indeed his son's new office was the very room
he had used.[182] Given Steel's repudiation of party ties, he was not
present when the Liberal Democrats ratified a coalition agreement
with Donald Dewar's Labour Party. He approved, of course, that it
meant Liberals would be in government for the first time since the
Second World War. Jim Wallace, once Steel's Defence spokesman
and Chief Whip, was to become Deputy First Minister.

Having had his fingers burned by the Countryside Movement
affair, Steel moved quickly to relinquish his remunerated post as a
director of Border Television in order to avoid potential conflicts

---

180 This was a reference to the words of the Chancellor of Scotland, the Earl
      of Seafield, who had signed away Scotland's independence in 1707: 'There's
      ane end of ane auld sang.'
181 Steel Papers (private collection), Lord Steel to Lord Rodgers, 13 May 1999.
182 In the autumn of 2000, Steel's father would also lead 'Time for Reflection'
      in the Scottish Parliament.

of interest. Nevertheless, in the run-up to the new Parliament's official opening ceremony the press went to town with stories alluding to Steel's outside interests, his desire for ornamental gowns for himself and his deputies (George Reid and the Labour MSP Patricia Ferguson), an official residence, that he had been given an official limousine, that he had fallen out with First Minister Donald Dewar, and so on, none of which was actually true. Steel was even accused of stuffing the opening ceremony with 'Borders cronies', although he had no control over invitations.

Steel was not amused, and it did not augur well for the rest of his term as Presiding Officer. Paddy Ashdown, meanwhile, had decided to call it a day as Liberal Democrat leader and, on 11 August, the former SDP MP Charles Kennedy was elected his successor with Steel's support. Steel had come to admire Ashdown as leader, particularly his 'detailed interest in policy', not least because he had always acknowledged that as a weakness of his own leadership. Kennedy, believed Steel, would follow his big-picture style.

A few weeks later Steel announced his intention to stand down after just one four-year term as Presiding Officer (although he had made this clear from the start). 'I came into politics when I was very young,' he explained, 'and I have every intention of leaving it when I am reasonably young.' Steel then hit back at what he called the 'recent trend of bitch journalism'. He alluded in particular to the Labour-supporting tabloid *Daily Record*, which he had referred to the Press Complaints Commission 'in the hope that those who run the paper may be persuaded to return to the standards of decent journalism' (the newspaper had criticised the long summer recess and the awarding of a commemorative medal costing £56 to every MSP). Although controversial (the SNP leader Alex Salmond demanded to know if he was speaking in a personal or official capacity), Steel's remarks resonated with most MSPs, who were sick of what they saw as relentlessly negative coverage.

In November Steel also criticised the Scottish Executive when details of plans to scrap motorway tolls (not yet announced to Parliament) were leaked to a newspaper. 'It's a question of courtesy, good practice and the observing of the founding principles of this Parliament,' he told MSPs, 'openness and account-ability.' Steel, however, also faced criticism himself, for continuing to sit as a Liberal Democrat peer at Westminster (while carrying out an impartial role on the Mound), for missing first-anniversary celebrations in favour of a three-day trip to Iceland, and for a week-long guest appearance on Channel 4's *Countdown* game show.

The criticism – some fair, some not – irritated Steel, and also his wife Judy, who complained in her memoirs that younger MSPs and journalists 'seemed to know nothing of his radicalism and his pioneering work during his years in the Commons'. 'They simply saw him as an establishment figure,' she wrote, 'one, moreover, with a couple of titles and a "castle".' This was true, although Steel's pronouncements on how he ought to be addressed ('call me Sir David') and propensity for dressing up (he was particu-larly fond of his privy counsellor's uniform) hardly helped. He was also quick to remind everyone of his neutrality while often accepting media invitations that required a partisan viewpoint. Appearing alongside Steel on the BBC's *Any Questions*, Tony Benn was surprised to hear him protest that 'he wasn't political any more and couldn't comment on political questions'. As a result, accusations of pomposity also came from older MSPs who were well aware of Steel's political provenance. The Independent MSP Dennis Canavan, for example, thought he 'could be rather full of his own importance'. Others, meanwhile, poked fun. Rab McNeill, then *The Scotsman*'s sketch writer, referred to the 'Presiding Orifice' or 'Dame Hydrangea Steel', while the *Daily Record*, aggravated by Steel's official complaint, often used his *Spitting Image* puppet (which the newspaper had purchased) to tease him in print.

Looking back on the Scottish Parliament's first year, Steel claimed it could 'hold its head high and claim a successful start', although surveys of public opinion often told a different story. Although he would later describe the first session as 'a pale imita-tion of Westminster', when MSPs returned from their summer recess in September 2000, Steel praised their behaviour in the debating chamber, saying he never had to keep order by 'bellowing like a fishwife', unlike his equivalent in the House of Commons.

He took a constructive attitude, meanwhile, towards the Parliament's minority members, particularly the firebrand Socialist MSP Tommy Sheridan. Steel often allowed Sheridan to intervene in debates (including one, to Labour's chagrin, on the fiftieth anniversary of the Queen's coronation) and was particularly helpful when he introduced a member's Bill to abolish warrant sales (a means of collecting debt) in Scotland, perhaps because it reminded Steel of his own youthful radicalism and his abortion legislation. Sheridan's Bill (drafted by Mike Dailly of the Govan Law Centre) also prompted Steel to establish a special parliamentary unit to help draft future backbench legislation.

In some ways, Steel was generationally out of place in the new Parliament, as were the half-dozen or so other MSPs who had served at Westminster (most MSPs, including Sheridan, were in their early forties). This was underlined when Donald Dewar, who was just months Steel's senior, died of a brain haemorrhage on 11 October 2000. When Steel called Judy to tell her about the First Minister's terminal illness, she remembered his voice sounding 'shocked and sullen'. 'It is cruel how Scotland has been robbed in recent years of so many able politicians in their prime,' reflected Steel when the Scottish Parliament convened to pay tribute.

> John P. Mackintosh, Labour; Alick Buchanan-Smith, Conservative; Allan Macartney, SNP; John Smith; and now Donald Dewar. Donald, however, at least had the satisfaction of leaving behind the completion of what he described as first a hope, then a belief, then a promise and then a reality … Under his leadership, this new Parliament had already found its head, its energy and its skills. Today, as it meets to mourn his death, it has found its heart.

Not only had Steel known all those he listed personally, but some were direct (Smith and Dewar) or near (Macartney) contemporaries. 'With the death of Donald Dewar, the only old friend he had in the Parliament was George Reid,' recalled Judy Steel in her memoirs. 'It was a lonely time in some ways, and there was some personal hostility to him.'

In April 2001 Steel too had a reminder of his own mortality. Although initially given the all-clear following tests for suspected prostate cancer, after a second biopsy on 24 May he was told he would, after all, require treatment. Having enjoyed generally good health throughout his life, it came as a 'hell of a blow' ('I didn't even know', admitted Steel, 'what the prostate was'), although he was stoical in the circumstances. Initially Steel opted for a new treatment called brachytherapy (his brother Michael, a cancer specialist, had dispensed advice), but when this proved unsuitable he had to fall back on conventional radiotherapy. Diligently, he managed to have his treatments scheduled to minimise disruption to his Chamber duties.

The burden on his deputies George Reid and Patricia Ferguson, however, still increased, and Steel was frustrated that no provision had been made in the Parliament's standing orders for absence through illness. In February 2002 Steel had an intensive three-week course of radiotherapy and, at the end of that month, began to make a gradual return to his full duties. In April he was given the all-clear and thereafter campaigned for middle-aged males to have regular checkups, agreeing to become patron of the Scottish Prostate Cancer Support Groups.

By the time Steel returned to the Scottish Parliament in early 2002 he had witnessed the death of one First Minister (Dewar) and the resignation of another, Henry McLeish, following a row about undeclared sub-letting of his constituency office. Indeed, prior to McLeish's resignation, Steel had ruled questions about his office expenses out of order as they dated from McLeish's time as an MP. Although technically correct, Steel could have been more flexible in the circumstances. Otherwise he kept a low profile during the 'Office-gate' affair, which added further to the fledgling institution's woes.

Steel's contacts, meanwhile, proved useful in raising the new Parliament's international profile. His biggest coup came in June

2001 when he invited the South African President, Thabo Mbeki, to address MSPs on the Mound. Mbeki, who Steel had known since the 1970s, embraced the Presiding Officer warmly as he arrived in Edinburgh. Having campaigned against apartheid and for devolution since his student days in the Scottish capital, it was clearly a significant moment for an emotional Steel. He could, however, also be critical of the institution he now presided over. When the Procedures Committee conducted an inquiry into the founding principles of the Scottish Parliament, he let off steam by criticising the weekly First Minister's Question Time ('not healthy'), the Scotland Act (which he thought needed revising) and his own job title ('bizarre'), although Steel continued to believe that the two-year-old Parliament had become 'central to Scottish life'.

Central to Steel's term as Presiding Officer, meanwhile, was the infamous saga surrounding the Holyrood building project, an ambitious scheme to equip Scotland's new Parliament with state-of-the-art premises opposite the Palace of Holyroodhouse. This was not something he had factored into his likely duties before the 1999 election, being the sort of technical work expected of a chief executive rather than a Presiding Officer. It was also not the sort of role to which Steel was suited. As the Liberal Democrat official Andy Myles put it early in his tenure, Lord (Sir David) Steel was simply 'too grand for the detail'.

Steel had actually criticised a bold design by the Catalan architect Enric Miralles during the election campaign, commenting that the shape of the debating chamber ('like theatre seating in rows') would not lend itself to proper debate. Confronted with the design again as Presiding Officer, Steel remained unhappy, although by then it was too late to do anything other than 'tweak' the design owing to the building's 'footprint'. He did, however, persuade Miralles to bring the seats round into as much of a horseshoe shape as possible.

As Secretary of State for Scotland, Donald Dewar had rejected a scheme – favoured by Steel – to renovate Edinburgh's old Royal High School (along with two other buildings) to house the new Parliament.

At one of the regular dinners Steel and Dewar would enjoy until the latter's untimely death, Steel asked Dewar why he had ruled it out. 'Don't you think, David,' replied Dewar, 'that a new Scottish Parliament after an absence of 300 years merits a new building and not just a jumble of old ones?' 'He had', as Steel came to believe, 'a point.'

Following the choice of the Holyrood site and an international architectural competition (won by Miralles), the project, initially controlled by Dewar as Scottish Secretary, was handed over to the Scottish Parliament Corporate Body (SPCB) under Steel's ex-officio chairmanship. The estimated cost at that point, importantly, was £109m. By December 1999 Steel admitted that amount would probably increase 'marginally' to provide more office space for MSPs. In April 2000, meanwhile, Steel dramatically informed the Chamber that Miralles was seriously ill as MSPs voted by a majority of nine to press on with the project. He took the unusual step of personally proposing the motion during a debate he found, according to his wife, 'especially dispiriting'.

An Audit Scotland report in September 2000 concluded that the SPCB should have commissioned an independent review of the building project as soon as responsibility had been transferred from the Scottish Office, a point endorsed by the Scottish Parliament's Audit Committee. And when a new 'progress group' was established in mid-2000 (the main recommendation of a review by John Spencely), Steel apparently resented the group's remit to make sure the building was delivered on time and within budget. A statement issued by the Parliament called it an 'advisory' body, while the Presiding Officer was accused of trying to retain 'a Steel grip' on the project, one source explaining that it was 'a pride thing'; Steel did not want to appear as if he had relinquished control.

The projected cost, meanwhile, kept on rising, first to £195m (with a completion debate of December 2002), while another 'final' estimate in early 2002 put it at £260m. Frustrated by a stream of negative press coverage, Steel protested that it was 'not exceptional for expenditure on such a complex and unique building', citing the £235m cost of Portcullis House, a new office block for MPs at Westminster. When three MSPs criticised a mocked-up office, meanwhile, Steel responded tetchily, ticking them off as 'irresponsible and juvenile'. He repeatedly stressed the building's potential as a long-term investment. 'That is of small comfort to me,' he said, 'but it is important to emphasise that the value for money for something to last over 200 years must be assessed over that time frame.'

When, during the 2003 Scottish election, First Minister Jack McConnell announced an inquiry (to be chaired by the Tory peer Lord Fraser of Carmyllie) to try and draw a line under the issue, Steel lobbied to have it referred to the Auditor-General for Scotland instead, while offering a lengthy defence of his own involvement during a Donald Dewar memorial lecture at the Edinburgh International Book Festival. He blamed, among other factors, an inherited 'construction management' approach which involved an expensive tendering process, the rising cost of – and delays arising from – renovating the seventeenth-century Queensberry House (soon to be incorporated into the Scottish Parliament complex) and post-9/11 security measures. He also denied that the true cost (which rose by another £37m after George Reid became Presiding Officer) had been hidden prior to the election for political reasons.

Steel even revealed that he had asked 'senior figures' at the Bank of Scotland to contrive 'a method of paying off the costs over the lifetime of several parliaments as with a house mortgage', but although sympathetic, they cited 'Treasury rules' and were not able to help. 'What we will have, admittedly at great expense,' Steel concluded optimistically, 'is a building of international renown which the people of Scotland will enjoy for very many generations to come.' But when Lord Fraser began taking evidence for his inquiry in early 2004, Steel did not emerge from the process untarnished.

Called to give evidence himself, Steel tried to read out a prepared statement and persisted despite being rebuked. Later, he admitted MSPs had been given censored minutes of meetings concerning a row between Miralles and his Edinburgh architectural partners, RMJM. 'If this had come out in public we would probably not have got a resolution,' Steel explained under questioning. 'As it was we got it resolved.' When Lord Fraser published his report in September 2004 he concluded there had been 'no single villain of the piece'. 'With the honourable exception of Sir David Steel on behalf of the Scottish Parliament Corporate Body accepting some responsibility for increased costs,' said Lord Fraser, 'the ancient walls of the Canongate have echoed only to the cry of "it wisnae me".' Steel and the SPCB, however, were criticised by Lord Fraser for failing to 'take the initiative' on controlling the soaring cost of the project.

Steel continued to protest that he had done everything possible to keep building costs down although, in hindsight, he later admitted the project should either 'have been left to the new parliament to decide, or the originators of it – the Westminster government through the Scottish Office – should have completed the task rather than passing the buck'.

While it was true that Steel had inherited an unenviable logistical nightmare, it was also the case that he had never really got to grips with the detail of the project, while his public pronouncements frequently jarred with the public mood. Another problem had been wishful thinking on the part of Steel and others involved with the building project, a tendency to convince themselves that everything was under control, even when it self-evidently was not. 'There was also a lack of openness about the project,' recalls Ian Swanson, who charted every twist and turn in the saga for the *Edinburgh Evening News*. 'Every setback came as a fresh blow and added to the impression that it was out of control.'

As early as December 2000 the SNP MSP Margo MacDonald had come close to hitting the nail on the head with the following observation:

> The lack of rigorous management by the project team, the inexperience of its key members and the misplaced trust in it demonstrated by the late First Minister [Donald Dewar] and later, the Presiding Officer [Steel], conspired to produce a situation in which politicians and civil servants had a vested interest in being other than transparent in their reporting to MSPs.

From Steel's point of view, what he had envisaged as a largely
ceremonial retirement job had quickly turned into something very
different. 'The problems of the building never left David, and ...
really bedevilled and haunted those four years,' Judy Steel later
reflected. 'Otherwise it would have been a wonderful four years,
creating a new institution.'

Steel's term as Presiding Officer was more positive in other respects.
Early on in his tenure he had argued for additional staff, chiefly a
special adviser (who would have been Jeremy Purvis), to help him
act as a counterbalance to the Scottish Executive. And although this
was vetoed, it eventually occurred under Steel's successor, George
Reid. More widely, he also applied serious thought to the Scottish
Parliament's strengths and weaknesses while considering possible
improvements. Although some of these were misunderstood (Steel's
proposal for an 'external review panel' to consider legislation was
widely interpreted as an exercise in self-aggrandisement) others,
mainly set out in his Donald Dewar lecture, were both practical
and far-sighted.

He called for the post of Scottish Secretary to be abolished, a
move away from the Additional Member System ('It was a terrible mistake,' he later admitted) to the Single Transferable Vote in
multi-member constituencies, citing his experience of 'infighting'
between regional and constituency MPs (as he had warned Dewar
would happen in 1997), and, most importantly, a degree of 'fiscal
autonomy' for the devolved Parliament. 'Frankly no self-respecting
Parliament should expect to exist permanently on 100 per cent
handouts determined by another Parliament,' he argued, 'nor
should it be responsible for massive public expenditure without
any responsibility for raising revenue in a manner accountable to
its electorate.' It was a theme to which Steel would return a few
years later.

In March 2003 Steel had presided, a little tearfully, over his last
full session of the Scottish Parliament. Tributes from party leaders
were generally warm and witty, with David McLetchie imploring

him to 'go back to your constituency and prepare for retirement'.[183] Steel, reckoned the *Daily Telegraph*'s generally unimpressed Alan Cochrane, had 'done a good job'. 'He is not the best chairman of proceedings this parliament has had; George Reid of the SNP takes that prize ... But he has undoubtedly given a veneer of respectability to an often unruly bunch of second-raters and tried to show them the way to better things.' The journalist Matthew Spicer concurred, reflecting that he had 'kept the show on the road by a mixture of experience, wisdom and invention'.

Above all, Steel had tried to steer attention back to the bigger picture. 'I do not pretend that the early days of the Parliament's existence have been without hiccup or stooshie,' he once reflected, 'but it seems almost easy to overlook the magnitude of the shift in balance of power from Westminster to Scotland.' And, from the personal perspective of a long-standing champion of devolution, to have presided over the Scottish Parliament in its first term was 'an honour and an experience' of which Steel 'could not have dreamed ... [as] a young [Liberal] candidate espousing the cause of Scottish Home Rule'.

Steel had already learned of his next role while still Presiding Officer, having been appointed Lord High Commissioner (the Queen's representative) to the General Assembly of the Church of Scotland in February 2003.[184] He took up the post shortly after retiring from the Scottish Parliament, donning his privy counsellor's garb and telling the Kirk of his fond memories of past Assemblies, 'once as

---

183 Steel briefly reprised his role as Presiding Officer in order to oversee the election of his successor (George Reid) and the swearing-in of MSPs after the 2003 election. He even gained an unlikely kudos for commenting *sotto voce* 'I have to say, the view is certainly going to improve in this Parliament' as a casually dressed female MSP was sworn in. Steel's remark was picked up by a live microphone and widely reported.

184 The author recalls a press statement to the effect that once he had retired as an MSP his salutation should revert to Lord, as opposed to Sir David, Steel.

a commissioner and once sitting in the gallery ... with my mother, brothers and sisters when my father became moderator in 1974'.

There was another family connection, Steel's great-great-uncle James Brown (also the Labour MP for South Ayrshire) having been Lord High Commissioner in 1924, and again in 1930/31, 'the first commoner in modern times to be appointed to the office'. Steel hoped to invite Malawian President Bakili Muluzi to attend the Assembly (whom he had worked with in 1994), although the British High Commissioner in Lilongwe warned it 'would be highly risky for the Church of Scotland to issue an invitation as [sic] such a sensitive time'.[185] Nevertheless, Steel reprised his role as Lord High Commissioner the following year.

In March 2005 Steel marked the fortieth anniversary of the Roxburgh, Selkirk & Peebles by-election by having a quiet meal with his wife and a stroll along Jedburgh High Street, down which he had been carried shoulder high four decades earlier. A few days later Riddle Dumble, who had helped Steel get elected before acting as his agent for more than two decades, died aged seventy-three. 'He was the eyes and ears of the MP,' commented Steel in tribute, 'more often than not solving constituents' problems before they ever got to me.'

Reflecting on Scottish politics in a lecture at around the same time, Steel spoke of what he saw as a 'dangerous narrowing' in public life. 'When I was first elected there were people on the green benches who had worked down pits and in steelworks,' he said. 'There were senior bankers, rural estate owners, managing directors of companies. We even had a rear-admiral and more than one general. They have almost all disappeared.'

Steel was describing another political era, although he seemed perfectly content to gather more Establishment honours. In July 2006 he was installed as one of sixteen Knights of the Thistle at a ceremony in Edinburgh's St Giles' Cathedral. His specially designed crest included a Border Reiver and a Masai warrior.

---

185   TD 3431 Acc/58, British High Commissioner to Lord Steel, May 2003.

Earlier that year he had watched as Charles Kennedy had been compelled to resign as Liberal Democrat leader following rumours of alcoholism. Nevertheless, Steel had been 'irritated' by the way the Kennedy affair had been handled, later suggesting that he and Paddy Ashdown could have taken him 'by the scruff of the neck and [told] him to go off and sort himself out' particularly as, unlike so many politicians, he had 'the gift of coming across to people as a fully paid-up member of the human race'.

Although Steel believed his friend Sir Menzies Campbell was making a mistake by standing in the leadership contest that followed, Steel praised his 'unimpeachable integrity'. And when Campbell's brief tenure ended badly in October 2007, Steel backed Chris Huhne, another former Social Democrat he had known for more than twenty years. Nick Clegg, however, won the leadership by a narrow margin. Huhne had served on the Steel Commission in 2005–6, a Liberal Democrat body that came up with a cogently argued report (largely drafted by David Paterson) – *Moving to Federalism: A New Settlement for Scotland* – which was interpreted in some quarters as a coalition pitch to the SNP. Steel, who of course had toyed with such a Liberal–Nationalist pact in the 1960s, said his report did not, as some claimed, amount to independence, but a 'new, modern settlement for Scotland in the UK based on more federal principles'.[186]

In March 2008 Steel celebrated his seventieth birthday with three parties, one in London, a formal dinner at the local village hall and a lunch for friends and family at Aikwood.[187] Two years later he campaigned on behalf of his daughter Catriona Bhatia (a Borders councillor since 2003) when she contested the Dumfriesshire, Clydesdale & Tweeddale constituency, part of which had once been

---

186 http://www.scotlibdems.org.uk/files/steelcommission.pdf
187 In late 2010 the Steels would move out of Aikwood, realising, as Judy put it in her memoirs, it was not 'a sensible home for septuagenarians'. Instead their younger son Rory turned it into 'a boutique accommodation and events venue' which opened in the spring of 2011.

in his own constituency. Although Bhatia lost out to Scotland's only Conservative MP, David Mundell, and 'Cleggmania' (which brought to mind the Alliance's peak in 1981–2) failed to translate into seats, the first 'balanced' Parliament since February 1974 finally produced the opportunity Steel had hoped for since entering politics. 'David's call to his party to "Go back to your constituencies and prepare for government"', observed Judy Steel, 'was nearly three decades premature.'

After four days of negotiations and a 'big open offer' from David Cameron, the Liberal Democrats agreed to form a full coalition government with the Conservatives, the only outcome that ensured a workable majority. While it was not the sort of realignment Steel had ever anticipated (he had, he later admitted, 'an instinctive horror of collaboration with the enemy'), he realised Nick Clegg had little option other than 'to sit in opposition, watch a minority Tory government struggling with declining sterling and share indices, head for a second election in the autumn armed with buckets of [Michael] Ashcroft-type cash and annihilate our party as useless hand-wringing debaters'. Although Steel had made it clear during the negotiations that he favoured a deal with Labour, equally he realised the 'folly' of being seen to sustain a defeated Prime Minister, be it Edward Heath in 1974 or Gordon Brown in 2010. 'We have not only to hope this coalition works,' concluded Steel, 'we have got to make damn sure it does.'

Having steered the Liberals through the Lib–Lab Pact in the 1970s and the Alliance in the 1980s, however, Steel was under no illusions as to what lay in store, later warning that when public spending cuts started to bite, the party should brace itself for a rough ride, advising Clegg to prepare an 'exit strategy' (as Steel had done in 1978) before the next election. Steel also criticised the formation of the coalition in such an 'unseemly rush', having concluded from his experience of March 1977 (with James Callaghan) and 1999 (when Scottish negotiations had taken weeks rather than days) that politicians had to have time and space to negotiate complicated agreements.

Over the next year, however, the Liberal Democrats experienced exactly the sort of bumpy road Steel had anticipated back in 1976. The key moment as far as Steel was concerned had been the U-turn on tuition fees (a 'terrible mistake') while in May 2011 a UK-wide referendum on electoral reform was heavily defeated. Steel had 'warmly' supported the Alternative Vote ('not strictly speaking a proportional system,' he argued, '[but] it could pave the way for more fundamental reforms'), although it must have brought back uncomfortable memories of similar battles over direct elections to the European Parliament on a cold, disappointing night in December 1977.

Steel believed the coalition could survive but needed to become less 'lovey dovey', acknowledging that it was not a 'meeting of hearts and minds' but a 'business arrangement' to facilitate a solution to the UK's economic problems. He also favoured having a referendum on Scottish independence (something else he had put to Callaghan in 1978) sooner rather than later, perhaps amending the Scotland Bill – which went some way to implementing the 'fiscal autonomy' advocated by the 2006 Steel Commission – to that end. Later, Steel gave his backing to another cross-party constitutional campaign, this time for so-called 'devo-plus', whose public face was Jeremy Purvis, a former Steel aide and Liberal Democrat MSP between 2003 and 2011.

Steel's principal focus in the 2010–15 parliament (fixed terms having been another coalition innovation), however, was House of Lords reform. On this, Steel's views had moderated significantly since he had first proposed – in a university essay – an all-elected senate. By 2005 he had 'come round' to the view (as had Tony Blair) that 'an appointed, not elected, House of Lords' was essential in order 'to inject wider expertise into our parliamentary processes'.[188] Between 2006 and 2012 Steel introduced four reform

---

188   Tony Benn had once speculated that Steel might end up as the first Speaker in an elected Upper House. '[H]ow they'd deal with that,' he noted in his diary, 'I don't know.'

Bills comprising four main elements: a retirement scheme for peers who wished to relinquish their duties; the gradual phasing-out of the remaining ninety-two hereditaries; an appointments process genuinely independent from No. 10 ('to end the abuse of political patronage'); and a mechanism to disbar members, such as Lord Archer, who had served lengthy prison sentences.

In July 2010 the deputy leader of the Lords, Lord McNally (who had worked with Steel, as Callaghan's political secretary, on the Lib–Lab Pact), refused to grant Steel debating time because the coalition was committed to a cross-party committee and draft Bill of its own. Not unreasonably, Steel pointed out the dangers of ministers trying to bite off more than they could chew; much better, he argued, to 'revise' the status quo before attempting more fundamental reform. By mid-2011 Steel's various Bills had been debated three times and attracted cross-party agreement, but still the government refused to budge.

Steel considered the coalition's proposals, finally unveiled in early 2012, to be muddled and potentially dangerous. 'I am old enough to recall the defeat of Lords reform proposals through getting bogged down in the Commons in a war of attrition led by Michael Foot and Enoch Powell,' wrote Steel, 'and I fear the same may happen to these. There is no public clamour for the changes; indeed, they are seen as a distraction from the main task facing the coalition government – rescuing our economy.' When rebel Conservatives pushed for a referendum on Lords reform, Steel told *Newsnight* it would 'put the kybosh on the whole thing; people aren't going to vote for 400 more elected politicians'.

His approach to Lords reform could be termed cautious, but equally it could be described as realistic. To an extent it reflected his proposals for Scottish Office reform in his 1968 pamphlet *Out of Control*, which urged consolidation as a precursor to more radical reform. Whatever the case, Steel's approach to the House of Lords neatly encompassed his political style, a combination of compromise and tenacity. By mid-2012 Steel had demonstrated plenty of the former, dropping the hereditary and appointments elements of

his proposals and instead limiting a fifth version of his reform Bill
to three purposes: a retirement scheme, removal of inactive peers
and removing those convicted of serious offences.

Even those modest measures appeared to irritate Steel's colleagues
but then, aged seventy-four, the Boy David confessed to being 'semi-
detached' from the party he had once led. Although he continued
to try and persuade Nick Clegg of his Bill's merits ('He sees it as a
halfway house,' said Steel, 'and I accept that'), Steel also grew more
frank about the coalition's electoral prospects, pointing out that
while the Liberal Democrats had certainly made 'impressive' gains,
they were nonetheless 'all details'; there was nothing big enough
to 'carry over in the public mind'. He could trace contemporary
opposition to Trident back to Jo Grimond's opposition to Polaris,
but even now that Grimond's cherished vision of realignment had
occurred not once (1988) but twice (2010), that Liberal opposition
appeared no closer to actually achieving anything.

Meanwhile the coalition government embodied realignment,
just not as Steel knew or had intended it. But then ideology had
never much interested him; he just knew instinctively that the 2015
general election would, in Steel's understated phrase, 'be tricky'.
He saw that as the natural point at which to withdraw from frontline politics and, assuming his Bill had become law (rather than the
coalition's proposals), retire from the House of Lords. After all, that
year would also mark the fiftieth anniversary of Steel's stunning
by-election victory. 'I would quite like to leave at the end of this
parliament,' he said in early 2012. 'We shouldn't go on forever.'

10

BREAKING THE MOULD

It is always difficult to assess the lives of governing men, particularly when they have never governed. Shorn of ministerial records, initiatives and the internal machinations of high politics, the biographer is instead left with the strategies, speeches and – in essence – wishful thinking of opposition politicians. David Steel, of course, was also a party leader, and perhaps one of the most significant in post-war British politics.

Although he never held ministerial office, Steel's career was one of solid achievement out of all proportion to his status as the leader of a small (later larger) third party. As a young backbencher in the 1960s he effected a lasting and important reform to Britain's abortion laws; during the Lib–Lab Pact of 1977–8 he wielded influence if not power; while in the 1980s he was a central figure in a political realignment that came close to breaking the mould of UK politics. And, later in life, Steel helped guide a new Scottish Parliament through a difficult birth. Not a bad balance sheet for someone outside the political mainstream.

Steel's political career can also be seen as a proxy for significant changes in post-war British politics: the relative decline of two-party dominance, the growing influence of modern campaigning and media techniques and, less positively, the steady drift from ideology towards less dogmatic, and arguably more opportunistic, politics. All were features in Steel's life and times. Indeed, his has also been a remarkably consistent biography, with little change in his character and central political beliefs between his undergraduate career and his semi-retirement in the House of Lords.

Four years spent in colonial Africa fundamentally shaped Steel's political outlook, equipping him not with a detailed agenda but an instinctive liberalism in relation to individual liberty, human rights and internationalism. He recognised those values in the inspirational Jo Grimond and was savvy enough to become the then Liberal leader's protégé, his reward being a fast-tracked political career. Having learned the game of politics at university, Steel barely had two-and-a-half years' practice in the real world before transferring those skills to the House of Commons.

While undoubtedly talented, Steel ended up playing some aspects of the game better than others. Having never actually implemented any policy, even on a parish council, his carelessness with policy detail – although not evident at first – became well known. Aware that his agile mind would usually extract him from the tightest intellectual spot, he made little attempt to remedy this weakness. His brief acquaintance with the Scottish Liberals, meanwhile, left him largely ignorant of the English party, which he never really made any effort to win over. Steel instinctively preferred the intimacy and camaraderie of the Scottish Liberal scene.

Steel was at his best during his early years as an MP, as Des Wilson put it, 'a genuinely liberal and humane campaigner, combining courage with charm and intelligence'. Radical in his views on race relations and abortion, he nevertheless sought to effect change by orthodox political means. Politics to Steel was the art of the possible, ideological purity held no interest for him; realism combined with dogged persistence did.

Ecumenically minded both theologically and politically, Steel relished working with politicians from other parties, on his Abortion Bill, on race relations and immigration, and later on Europe and Scottish devolution. Furthermore he *liked* people in other parties and wanted to draw disparate progressive strands together for the greater good. Grimond had called this 'realignment', and Steel applied it both at home (in Scotland) and abroad (in the political salons of Westminster). His and John Pardoe's Radical Action Movement may have amounted to nothing, but it hinted at the direction in which he intended to travel.

Therein lay the source of Steel's growing detachment from the party he would soon lead. During the 1970s he was rarely in sympathy with the growing 'community politics' section of the Liberal Party. While they worked hard to build Liberal support from the bottom up, Steel appeared to favour a top-down approach which stressed strategy over policy and, as those at the bottom saw it, a distressing tendency to see potential allies in other parties. To them Steel could be a little *too* realistic, casually admitting that Liberals did not have to fight *every* constituency for the Liberals were never likely, in their own right, to actually *form* a government.

Indeed, after the disaster of the 1970 general election and the relative triumph of those in 1974, Steel became even more convinced that realignment, coalitions and pacts were central to Liberal prospects. But to an extent, Steel had misread the electoral runes. In 1970 the Liberals had done badly without a strategy, while in February 1974 the party polled more than six million votes having not corrected that deficiency. Rather support for Liberals in general and by-elections waxed and waned depending on the fortunes of one or both the main parties, and not according to a rational assessment of third party prospects.

Steel was correct to state that the party could not survive with such a small base of consistent supporters, but nor was he particularly interested in identifying a solution by mending cracked pavements and establishing local government bases, even when such techniques produced tangible results in 1972–3, and again in 1979. Instead, he continued to rely upon protest votes, which remained the case even under the Alliance from 1981 to 1987. Nevertheless, Steel arguably salvaged the Liberal Party's reputation in the wake of the debilitating Jeremy Thorpe affair that dominated the first half of 1976. Young, articulate and free of personal scandal, he saved it from possible collapse and imbued it with a new sense of purpose. To some degree it was ironic that what Steel's first biographer called a 'rugged realist' should have ended up in charge of such a romantic, rag-bag party, but although he accepted (as Steel put it in 2000) that leadership involved 'taking knocks ... both personal and political', it also provided 'an opportunity to point a course, to stamp a platform and to gather others to one's cause'.

As Stuart Mole has written, Steel saw his leadership as 'an odyssey – stretching over the course of a decade and more – building upon the ideas of cross-party cooperation developed at the time of the European referendum, the experiment of the Lib–Lab Pact and, in particular, the creation of an Alliance' with moderate left-wingers. To that end, Steel was much more interested in the mechanics of his very personal 'agreement' with Prime Minister Callaghan than any specific policy it might deliver. He lacked, in the words of Alistair Michie and Simon Hoggart, a 'revolutionary vision of a new Liberal society'; rather

> Steel's ideal Britain would perhaps be a rather more agreeable version of the present one. Workers would work harder, encouraged by profit-sharing schemes; the end of economic dogmatism by the two major parties would bring a steady increase in prosperity; Steel's own virtues and the qualities he admires most, decent moderation and tolerance in all things, would determine the shape of society and the standards of living.

The Lib–Lab Pact could be seen as having continued Grimond's realignment strategy without having added anything new philosophically. As Lord Grey said of Asquith, Steel had used 'the machine of a great political brain to rearrange old ideas', but in sustaining an agreement with a minority Labour government for more than a year, Steel had punched above his political weight while achieving something that had eluded both his immediate predecessors.

As Duncan Brack observed, unlike Grimond and his eventual successor Paddy Ashdown, 'Steel was never fascinated by ideas.' 'He was primarily a strategist, determined to show that Liberals could exert influence by working with others,' he wrote. 'As the leader of a small third party, this was not an unreasonable approach, but his neglect of details of policy that mattered to his party activists was a serious weakness.' Indeed, the experience of the Lib–Lab Pact served to make many Liberals even more suspicious of their leader's motives and style.

Given what Steel now envisaged – a formal 'alliance' between the Liberals and a breakaway wing of the Labour Party led by his mentor Roy Jenkins – the areas in which he was weak, policy development and party management, became even more important, particularly as what became the Social Democratic Party (SDP) was perceived as superior in both respects. Although impressive – perhaps even decisive – in managing the course of what Jenkins called 'two rivers ... with a common delta', Steel's weaknesses became more pronounced, particularly after the 1983 general election.

During that campaign Steel blinked first. There was certainly a case for a coup against Jenkins at the Ettrick Bridge summit, and equally there was a case for retaining the SDP leader as 'Prime Minister designate'; but there was a relatively weak case for a coup both attempted and abandoned in the course of a Borders morning. Whether a Steel-led Alliance campaign would have beaten Labour in terms of the Labour vote is a moot point – it did not – and the two rivers then had to choose between merging and charting their own independent course.

With miserable hindsight, Steel was full of regrets: regret that he had tried to sideline Jenkins and therefore hastened his demise as SDP leader; and regret, as he later put it, at not having 'merged the two parties after the 1983 election rather than wait another four years'. 'The delay', he added, 'lost us a lot of momentum.' Acutely aware that the high hopes of the Alliance had been dashed by a combination of bad luck (the Falklands), hubris (unrealistic expectations) and a deeply unfair electoral system (first past the post), Steel even tried to resign, arguing in a parting shot (later withdrawn) that 'having spent seven years largely on Liberal strategy', he wanted to 'devote more time to writing and speaking on Liberal philosophy and policy'.

Steel, of course, changed his mind and instead spent another five years talking and planning strategy rather than 'philosophy and policy'. Events, of course, also conspired to thwart the best-laid plans of realignment: David Owen's reluctance to sacrifice the SDP's independence, Thatcher and Kinnock's continued dominance of two-party politics and the inability of the Alliance to build a more solid electoral base. But, even so, it is difficult to refute Hugo Young's 1988 assessment that the 'climax of David Steel's political life occurred in the 1983 election'.

Of course, it did not look that way at the time, and for a while by-elections gave a misleading impression as to the Alliance's continued electoral virility. The 'two Davids' kept the show on the road, a tribute to Owen's intellectual energy and Steel's media prowess, but they were not *progressing*. Steel's obvious integrity (although he was, like any human being, fallible) and considerable stamina, not to forget his stirring platform oratory, equipped him with wide popular appeal. Even after his political peak in 1983, polling revealed approval ratings Nick Clegg or Danny Alexander would die for.

And whatever the faults of the Liberal Party, which included poor discipline and a tendency to dance on the head of a pin, they were mirrored by faults in the SDP, unquestioning loyalty to Owen's leadership coupled with unimaginative policy-making. If the Liberals were nothing more than a debating society (as Steel had once put it), Social Democrats, in the words of Simon Hoggart, were 'London intellectuals surveying a declining Britain from the comfort of Holland Park'. With Owen, Steel also lacked a close political relationship, a dynamic so crucial to his early career (Grimond), early leadership (Callaghan) and electoral peak (Jenkins).

And while it is fun for historians (and indeed biographers) to indulge in games of 'what if?', most alternative scenarios crumble, as Ivor Crewe and Anthony King argued in their history of the SDP, upon closer analysis. Even had the Gang of Four joined the Liberals instead of creating their own party, the short-term boost would never have achieved a lift-off akin to the Alliance, fuelled by novelty and big personalities; and even had the two parties merged after 1983 and chosen a single leader – perhaps even Steel – there is limited evidence it would have made a tangible difference at the 1987 election.

Had the framework of two separate parties in an uneasy Alliance been quixotic? As the Liberal psephologist Michael Steed put it:

> Pretending to an equality of status whilst the form of their relation-ship made for clear mutual suspicion; pretending to the total agree-ment of a common manifesto but not trusting each other enough to allow a common process of policy making; not even able to trust their members to choose a single leader – did we not end up with the most difficult way of bringing together the people who make up the Liberal and Social Democratic parties into a force strong enough to break the mould?

Without PR, meanwhile, however impressively the Alliance polled it remained electorally meaningless. 'Thus the Alliance had failed to remedy the weaknesses from which the Liberal Party, standing alone, had long suffered,' was the judgement of Liberal historian David Dutton. 'The Alliance, like the Liberals, enjoyed no solid ideological or geographical base.' Indeed its vote, as Crewe and King noted, came 'from everywhere in general and nowhere in particular'.

Steel, to be fair, was acutely aware of his political weaknesses and strengths. 'I do not think I will ever be awarded full marks for either party management or pioneering policies,' he reflected in his memoirs. 'Where I believe I made a contribution was in articulat-ing our values and attitudes in a way which brought a huge public response.' This was a fair assessment and, indeed, Steel later recog-nised a little of himself in Charles Kennedy, the Liberal Democrat leader from 1999 to 2006. 'There is an apparent diversity between the broad appeal to the electorate,' Steel told Kennedy's biographer

Greg Hurst, 'mainly on television and at public meetings, and the detailed management of the team in Parliament ... Ideally you want someone who combines both.'

Steel's relationship with his party was indeed remote and often pained. As Geoffrey Smith wrote, in exercising his leadership Steel had not always paid 'sufficient regard to the sensitivities of his party'. In this regard he anticipated the Blairite style of leadership, promoting an ideology-lite agenda while bouncing his troops into strategic positions many did not much like, then trying to make it all better with a barnstorming speech. And like Blair, Steel was not unusual in not liking the party he led. Its obsessions irritated him, and worse, its internal structures sent him to sleep. 'He wanted order, his kind of order,' judged *The Economist*, 'they preferred, or behaved as though they preferred, an aimless anarchy – politics as street theatre.'

The terminal phase came after the 1986 Eastbourne Assembly, at which Steel took his eye off the ball, found himself humiliatingly rebuffed on defence policy and, in response, turned bitterly on his party. By then he had been leader for more than ten years – longer than Thorpe and Grimond – and it showed. If Eastbourne was the inevitable consequence of Steel's weakness in terms of party management, then the joint policy declaration of 1988 (the so-called 'dead parrot') was the inevitable consequence of his lack of policy engagement. With some exceptions, such as 'industrial partnership' and African affairs, Steel's interest was not in the policies themselves but the overall mood he was trying to generate. He always had more sympathy than feel for big domestic issues, particularly on economics.

Des Wilson's critique, that Steel's radical instincts were dulled by his absorption 'with the machinations of politics rather than its purpose' also contained an element of truth. It was easier, in some ways, to be radical while unencumbered by leadership or government office, while as political trends waxed and waned Steel showed little sign of revising the view of the world he had first imbibed as a young man in Africa and Edinburgh. While Owen and the 'dead parrot' acknowledged the impact of Thatcherism, Steel stuck to his script about PR, devolution and workers' councils. Although sincere and consistent, by the late 1980s it had become a rather limited political vision. As Hugo Young judged in 1988, Steel had 'failed to produce any compelling vision of a Liberal or any other kind of non-Thatcherite Britain'.

Nevertheless, as Liberal leader Steel possessed a number of thoroughly admirable qualities, not least an anti-authoritarian instinct – he consistently stood up for underdogs at home or abroad – while displaying remarkable steadiness under fire. Much of this could be traced to his background as a 'son of the manse', a spiritual provenance that also gave Steel a natural reserve seemingly at odds with his public persona. As James Naughtie put it, 'His appearance is that of the outsider, but his instincts drive him to try to be the insider.' He added: 'We have the paradox of a man who, whilst essentially reserved and shy, save with close friends or convivial cronies, could nevertheless find the magic, in word and tone, to touch the heart of a Party Conference or, on television, to move the minds of millions.'

Thus Steel derived satisfaction from his status as a Privy Counsellor (and indeed the uniform that went with it), his membership of the Other Club (London's most exclusive dining club) and his presence at international conferences in Europe and Africa. He needed – as John Newhouse of the *New Yorker* noted in 1984 – 'the separate worlds of Ettrick Bridge and London' to keep him grounded. Crucial in this respect was his wife Judy, an unfailingly loyal political wife who maintained a comfortable local base while providing an essential political counterpoint to the Westminster bubble.

Steel was certainly no saint. He could be ruthless, ruthless in his fight against John Pardoe (and, fleetingly, Russell Johnston) in 1976, ruthless in refusing the campaign on behalf of Jeremy Thorpe in 1979, ruthless in dispatching David Owen in 1987 and, above all, ruthless in dealings with his own party. Such steeliness was necessary for any leader, particularly that of a small third party, but one cannot help feeling that Steel could have done more to address his

weaknesses. Jo Grimond thought he could have appointed someone to 'explore and co-ordinate the many new ideas sprouting all
over the place and weld them into a structure which people would
instantly recognise as the core of Liberalism', while Des Wilson
believed he could easily have maintained a closer relationship with
his party. Steel was a good and effective Liberal leader but, had he
engaged a little more with party and policy, he might have been a
formidable one.

Inevitably, on his withdrawal as leader in 1988, it was often put
to Steel that the 'Goliath' later alluded to in the title of his memoirs
was still standing. 'I fought against the two-party system – and
that is more questioned than when I began,' he protested. 'The old
idea that you have to be either Labour or Conservative has gone.
Voters are more fluid and open to argument.' Again, this was a fair
assessment of Steel's own achievements, however modest.

Having completed an odyssey comprising the Lib–Lab Pact, the
Alliance and finally the 1988 merger, Steel forced his party to shape
up and confront the prospect of holding power in a way none of
his immediate predecessors had. And while the new party (with its
many names) had a difficult birth, the result was a tighter organisation with a more coherent political philosophy. By 1997 the Liberal
Democrats were making gains that would have been unthinkable in
the 1970s and 1980s. Although its share of the vote did not change
radically – the same proportion delivered fourteen Liberal MPs in
February 1974 and forty-six Liberal Democrats in 1997 – it became
a lot better at targeting, and indeed winning, seats. The 1983 high of
more than 25 per cent, meanwhile, has never been bettered.

Outside the House of Commons, Steel may have been guilty
of trading on past glories, but then he could be forgiven that
after twelve years as leader. Even so, the autumn of his years was
not devoid of achievement. The Africa that had crept under his
skin during those four years in Kenya continued to preoccupy
his attention, and even in his late sixties Steel thought nothing of needling the Kenyan and Malawian governments when
he felt it was required. In Scotland, too, he helped steady the

devolutionary ship when a new Parliament initially struggled to find its way.

'The proper province of the historian lies in the past – its elucidation and its explanation,' wrote David Dutton. 'But when history is brought to the present, the historian may be permitted a few speculative observations about the future.' So how does Steel's political legacy – particularly in terms of realignment – look in the cold light of early 21st-century coalition politics?

In one sense it is positive. It seems likely that Nick Clegg opted for a full coalition in 2010 because of his predecessor's experience during the Lib–Lab Pact (responsibility without power, to reverse Baldwin's aphorism); the Liberal Democrats had finally faced up to the reality of power, just as Steel had predicted they would. On the other hand (as Steel often said), this particular realignment involved sharing power with the Conservatives, which, even under the modernising influence of David Cameron, were not perceived as natural bedfellows in the 'progressive' centre ground.

In other respects it was negative. While the Liberal Democrats negotiated a cast-iron agreement and timescale (unlike in 1977), their experience thus far has not been an edifying one. The Scottish experience, however, demonstrated that governing in coalition with another party *and* retaining a distinct political identity *was* possible, provided that the junior partner was seen to win concessions (in Scotland, most notably, the Single Transferable Vote for local government elections).

This does not mean Steel's realignment strategy was necessarily wrong; purist schemes such as those pursued by Michael Meadowcroft (whom Steel called 'that self-appointed and wholly destructive keeper of the Liberal conscience') were just as unrealistic as David Owen's determination – post-1987 – to preserve the SDP as an independent force. Although the Liberal Democrat vote might easily crumble at the next general election, that will be down to misjudgements and events, dear boy, events, rather than any failure in strategy or vision.

As Vernon Bogdanor wrote in the *New Statesman* in May 2010:

> The decision by the Lib Dems to form a coalition with the Conservatives brings to an end the project of realignment on the left, begun by Jo Grimond in the 1950s, and continued by David Steel in the 1970s and by Paddy Ashdown, with support from Tony Blair, in the 1990s … it seems the Labour Party and the left do not yet realise what a catastrophe has hit them. It is comparable to 1983, though then the left could at least hope that Labour and the SDP–Liberal Alliance might come together.

The point is that in 2010 the mould was finally broken, and all the hopes and aspirations of 1983 and 1987 fulfilled – at least in theory. PR could have followed, as intended, but the scheme (the Alternative Vote) was half-hearted and its implementation (a referendum) an ill-advised political gamble, but, even so, the UK took to coalition politics with alacrity. The strategy, therefore, will outlast Steel and Clegg, just as it outlasted Grimond and Thorpe. To borrow an aphorism from Mrs Thatcher: There Is No Alternative.

Indeed, in 2012 there was already talk of another realignment post-2015, between a Vince Cable-led wing of the Liberal Democrats (assuming a left–right split) and Ed Miliband's Labour Party. But if it was David Steel's mission to take Jo Grimond's fine words about realignment and make them a reality – even if he only partially succeeded – it must be doubted whether anyone else could have done better than the Boy David. As Hugo Young concluded, he was 'a manoeuvrer not a dreamer, a brilliant maximiser of small positions rather than a Field Marshal who might transform the course of war'. And, furthermore, he was always realistic. As John Pardoe puts it, 'David Steel achieved a significant amount of what he was *trying to achieve*,' and that is not a bad political legacy. In 1981 Steel implored his party to 'prepare for government' and while he did not personally strike the penalty, he did more than most to prepare the Liberal team for the premier league. Eventually, Steel got them into the arena – where they have remained ever since.

BIBLIOGRAPHY

Published Works

Addison, Paul, *No Turning Back: The Peacetime Revolutions of Post-War Britain* (Oxford: Oxford University Press, 2010)

Adonis, Andrew and Thomas, Keith (eds), *Roy Jenkins: A Retrospective* (Oxford: Oxford University Press, 2004)

Ashdown, Paddy, *The Ashdown Diaries Volume One 1988–1997* (London: Allen Lane, 2000)

— —, *The Ashdown Diaries Volume Two 1997–1999* (London: Allen Lane, 2001)

— —, *The Autobiography of Paddy Ashdown: A Fortunate Life* (London: Aurum Press, 2009)

Barberis, Peter, *Liberal Lion: Jo Grimond – A Political Life* (London: IB Tauris, 2005)

Barnett, Joel, *Inside the Treasury* (London: Andre Deutsch, 1982)

Bartram, Peter, *David Steel: His Life and Politics* (London: WH Allen, 1981)

Beith, Alan, *A View from the North: Life, Politics and Faith Seen from England's Northernmost Constituency* (Newcastle: Northumbria University Press, 2008)

Benn, Tony, *Conflicts of Interest: Diaries 1977–80* (London: Arrow, 1991)

— —, *More Time for Politics: Diaries 2001–2007* (London: Hutchinson, 2007)

— —, *Free at Last!: Diaries 1991–2001* (London: Hutchinson, 2002)

Bessell, Peter, *Cover-Up: the Jeremy Thorpe Affair* (Wilmington: Simons, 1980)

Bochel, John, Denver, David and Macartney, Allan (eds), *The Referendum Experience: Scotland, 1979* (Aberdeen: Aberdeen University Press, 1981)

Bogdanor, Vernon (ed.), *Liberal Party Politics* (Oxford: Clarendon Press, 1983)

Boothroyd, Betty, *The Autobiography* (London: Century, 2001)

Brack, Duncan (ed.), *President Gore ... and Other Things that Never Happened* (London: Politico's, 2006)

Bradley, Ian, *Breaking the Mould? The Birth and Prospects of the Social Democratic Party* (Oxford: Martin Robertson, 1981)

— —, *The Strange Rebirth of Liberal Britain* (London: Chatto & Windus, 1985)

Brunson, Michael, *A Ringside Seat: The Autobiography* (London: Hodder & Stoughton, 2000)

Butler, David and Kavanagh, Dennis, *The British General Election of October 1974* (London: Macmillan, 1975)

— —, *The British General Election of 1987* (Basingstoke: Macmillan, 1987)

Butler, David and Kitzinger, Uwe, *The 1975 Referendum* (London: Macmillan, 1976)

Callaghan, James, *Time and Chance* (London: Fontana, 1988)

Campbell, John, *Margaret Thatcher Volume One: The Grocer's Daughter* (London: Jonathan Cape, 2000)

Canavan, Dennis, *Let the People Decide* (Edinburgh: Birlinn, 2009)

Clarke, Peter, *A Question of Leadership: Gladstone to Thatcher* (London: Hamish Hamilton, 1991)

Cole, John, *As It Seemed to Me: Political Memoirs* (London: Weidenfeld & Nicolson, 1995)

— —, *The Thatcher Years: A Decade of Revolution in British Politics* (London: BBC Books, 1987)

Cole, Matt, *Richard Wainwright, the Liberals and Liberal Democrats* (Manchester: Manchester University Press, 2011)

Cook, Chris, *A Short History of the Liberal Party: The Road Back to Power* (Basingstoke: Palgrave Macmillan, 2010)

Crewe, Ivor and Harrop, Martin (eds), *Political Communications: The General Election Campaign of 1987* (Cambridge: Cambridge University Press, 1989)

Crewe, Ivor and King, Anthony, *SDP: The Birth, Life, and Death of the Social Democratic Party* (Oxford: Oxford University Press, 1995)

Currie, Edwina, *Diaries 1987–1992* (London: Little, Brown, 2002)

Day, Sir Robin, *Grand Inquisitor: Memoirs* (London: Weidenfeld & Nicolson, 1989)

Donoughue, Bernard, *Downing Street Diary: With Harold Wilson in No. 10* (London: Jonathan Cape, 2004)

— —, *Downing Street Diary: With James Callaghan in No. 10* (London: Jonathan Cape, 2008)

— —, *Prime Minister: The Conduct of Policy under Harold Wilson and James Callaghan* (London: Jonathan Cape, 1987)

Douglas, Roy, *Liberals: The History of the Liberal and Liberal Democrat Parties* (London: Hambledon and London, 2005)

Duff, Andrew (ed.), *Making the Difference: Essays in Honour of Shirley Williams* (London: Biteback, 2010)

Dutton, David, *A History of the Liberal Party in the Twentieth Century* (Basingstoke: Palgrave Macmillan, 2004)

Freeman, Simon with Penrose, Barrie, *Rinkagate: The Rise and Fall of Jeremy Thorpe* (London: Bloomsbury, 1996)

Grimond, Jo, *Memoirs* (London: Heinemann, 1979)

Harris, Kenneth, *David Owen: Personally Speaking to Kenneth Harris* (London: Weidenfeld & Nicolson, 1987)

Harrison, Brian, *Finding a Role? The United Kingdom 1970–1990* (Oxford: Clarendon, 2010)

Healey, Denis, *The Time of My Life* (London: Michael Joseph, 1989)

Hindell, Keith and Simms, Madeleine, *Abortion Law Reformed* (London: Peter Owen, 1971)

Hurst, Greg, *Charles Kennedy: A Tragic Flaw* (London: Politico's, 2006)

Ingham, Robert and Brack, Duncan (eds), *Peace, Reform and Liberation: A History of Liberal Politics in Britain 1679–2011* (London: Biteback, 2011)

Jenkins, Alice, *Law for the Rich: A Plea for the Reform of the Abortion Law* (London: Victor Gollancz, 1960)

Jenkins, Roy, *European Diary 1977–1981* (London: Collins, 1989)

— —, *A Life at the Centre* (London: Macmillan, 1991)

Jones, Sir Hugh, *Campaigning Face to Face* (Brighton: Book Guild, 2007)

Jones, Tudor, *The Revival of British Liberalism: From Grimond to Clegg* (Basingstoke: Palgrave Macmillan, 2011)

Josephs, Jeremy, *Inside the Alliance: An Inside Account of the Development and Prospects of the Liberal–SDP Alliance* (London: John Martin, 1983)

Kennet, Wayland, *The Rebirth of Britain* (London: Weidenfeld & Nicolson, 1982)

MacCormick, Neil (ed.), *The Scottish Debate: Essays on Scottish Nationalism* (Oxford: Oxford University Press, 1970)

Macdonell, Hamish, *Uncharted Territory: The Story of Scottish Devolution 1999–2009* (London: Politico's, 2009)

MacIver, Don (ed.), *The Liberal Democrats* (Hemel Hempstead: Prentice-Hall, 1996)

McManus, Michael, *Jo Grimond: Towards the Sound of Gunfire* (Edinburgh: Birlinn, 2007)

Marquand, David, *The Progressive Dilemma: From Lloyd George to Blair* (London: Weidenfeld & Nicolson, 1999)

Michie, Alistair and Hoggart, Simon, *The Pact: The Inside Story of the Lib–Lab Government 1977–8* (London: Quartet, 1978)

Mole, Stuart (ed.), *The Decade of Re-Alignment: The Leadership Speeches of David Steel 1976–1986* (Hebden Bridge: Hebden Royd, 1986)

Morgan, Kenneth O., *Michael Foot: A Life* (London: HarperPress, 2007)

Oaten, Mark, *Coalition: The Politics and Personalities of Coalition Government from 1850* (Petersfield: Harriman House, 2007)

Outwin, Dennis, *The SDP Story* (Maidenhead: Hartswood, 1987)

Owen, David, *Time to Declare* (London: Michael Joseph, 1991)

Parris, Matthew, *Great Parliamentary Scandals: Four Centuries of Calumny, Smear and Innuendo* (London: Robson Press, 1995)

Penhaligon, Annette, *Penhaligon* (London: Bloomsbury, 1989)

Radice, Giles, *Diaries 1980–2001: From Political Disaster to Election Triumph* (London: Weidenfeld & Nicolson, 2004)

— —, *Friends & Rivals: Crosland, Jenkins and Healey* (London: Little, Brown, 2002)

Rhodes, Mandy (ed.), *Scottishness: Reflections on Identity* (Edinburgh: Holyrood, 2006)

Rodgers, Bill, *Fourth among Equals: The Autobiography of Bill Rodgers* (London: Politico's, 2000)

Sandbrook, Dominic, *Seasons in the Sun: The Battle for Britain 1974–1979* (London: Allen Lane, 2012)

Shea, Michael, *A View from the Sidelines* (Stroud: Sutton, 2003)

Short, Edward, *Whip to Wilson: The Crucial Years of Labour Government* (London: Macdonald, 1989)

Sisman, Adam, *Hugh Trevor-Roper: The Biography* (London: Weidenfeld & Nicolson, 2010)

Smith, Cyril, *Big Cyril* (London: WH Allen, 1977)

Spicer, Matthew (ed.), *The Scotsman Guide to Scottish Politics* (Edinburgh: Edinburgh University Press, 2002)

Steel, David, *Against Goliath: David Steel's Story* (London: Weidenfeld & Nicolson, 1989)

— —, *Against Goliath: David Steel's Story* (paperback edition) (London: Pan, 1991)

— —, *A House Divided: The Lib–Lab Pact and the Future of British Politics* (London: Weidenfeld & Nicolson, 1980)

— —, *Labour at 80 … Time to Retire* (London: Liberal Publication Department, 1980)

— —, *The Liberal Way Forward* (London: Liberal Publication Department, 1975)

— —, *No Entry: The Background and Implications of the Commonwealth Immigrants Act, 1968* (London: Hurst, 1969)

— —, *Out of Control: A Critical Examination of the Government of Scotland* (Edinburgh: Scottish Liberal Party, 1968)

— —, *Sharing Profits: The Partnership Path to Economic Recovery* (Hebden Bridge: Hebden Royd, 1986)

— —, *The Story of James Hogg and of Aikwood Tower* (1994)

Steel, David and Holme, Richard (eds), *Partners in One Nation: A New Vision of Britain 2000* (London: Bodley Head, 1985)

Steel, Very Rev. David, *A Very Happy Life: A Memoir for the Family by David Steel 1910–2002* (privately published)

Steel, Judy, *Tales from the Tap End: The Memoirs of Judy Steel* (Edinburgh: Birlinn, 2010)

Stephenson, Hugh, *Claret and Chips: The Rise of the SDP* (London: Michael Joseph, 1982)

Thatcher, Margaret, *The Downing Street Years* (London: HarperCollins, 1993)
— —, *The Path to Power* (London: HarperCollins, 1995)
Thomas, George, *Mr Speaker: The Memoirs of Viscount Tonypandy* (London: Century, 1985)
Thorpe, Jeremy, *In My Own Time: Reminiscences of a Liberal Leader* (London: Politico's, 1999)
Torrance, David (ed.), *Great Scottish Speeches* (Edinburgh: Luath Press, 2011)
Trewin, Ion (ed.), *The Hugo Young Papers: Thirty Years of British Politics – Off the Record* (London: Allen Lane, 2008)
Turner, Alwyn, *Rejoice! Rejoice! Britain in the 1980s* (London: Aurum, 2010)
Walker, Peter, *Staying Power: An Autobiography* (London: Bloomsbury, 1991)
Watkins, Alan, *Brief Lives* (London: Hamish Hamilton, 1982)
Weeks, Jeffrey, *Sex, Politics and Society: The Regulation of Sexuality since 1800* (London: Longman, 1989)
Whitehead, Phillip, *The Writing on the Wall: Britain in the Seventies* (London: Michael Joseph, 1985)
Williams, Shirley, *Climbing the Bookshelves: The Autobiography* (London: Virago, 2009)
Wilson, Des, *Battle for Power: The Inside Story of the Alliance and the 1987 General Election* (London: Sphere, 1987)
— —, *Memoirs of a Minor Public Figure* (London: Quartet, 2011)

Periodicals
Reference was made to various editions of the following newspapers, magazines, journals and official reports:
Big Issue
Border Telegraph
Daily Telegraph
Democrat
Edinburgh Evening News
Glasgow Herald (later *The Herald*)
The Guardian
Hansard (Commons and Lords)
Honey
The House
The Independent
Journal of Liberal Democrat History
Liberal News
New Outlook
New Yorker

Official Report (Scottish Parliament)
Penthouse
Phoenix
Radical Quarterly
Scotland on Sunday
The Scotsman
Scottish Daily Express
Signature
Southern Reporter
The Student
Sunday Post
Sunday Telegraph
The Times
The Universe
Wall Street Journal Europe

Broadcasts

Analysis (BBC Radio 4), 3 December 1987
Empire's Children: David Steel – Kenya (Channel 4), 16 July 2007
Face the Press (Tyne Tees Television), 23 August 1987
Newsnight (BBC2), 23 April 2012
Newsnight Scotland (BBC Scotland), 7 May 2011
Not While I'm Alive He Ain't (BBC Radio 4), 14 April 2002
The Pursuit of Power (BBC2), 11 June 1981
Scotland Today (STV), 14 October 1991
Spitting Image (Central Television) 28 September 1986, 5 October 1986,
    29 November 1987, 18 June 1989, 3 June 1990
Spitting Image: Bumbledown – The Life and Times of Ronald Reagan
    (Central Television), 29 October 1988
This Week: The Liberal Dilemma (Thames), 11 May 1978
VIP (Scottish Television), 1994
The Week in Politics (STV), 2002
World in Action: The Fight for the Centre (Granada), 27 March 1982

Archives

Abortion Law Reform Association Papers (Wellcome Library)
Sir Alan Beith Papers (private collection)
David Owen Papers (University of Liverpool)
David Steel Papers (London School of Economics)
David Steel Papers (National Library of Scotland)
David Steel Papers (private collection, being transferred to LSE)
David Thomson Papers (private collection, research notes for Steel's
    memoirs, *Against Goliath*)
Hugo Young Papers (*Guardian* Archives)
James Meade Papers (London School of Economics)

Liberal Party Papers (London School of Economics)
Margaret Thatcher Papers (Churchill College, Cambridge)
Michael Meadowcroft Papers (London School of Economics)
Neville Sandelson Papers (London School of Economics)
Richard Wainwright Papers (London School of Economics)
Robert Maclennan Papers (University of Essex)
Scottish Television/STV (Pacific Quay, Glasgow)
William Rodgers Papers (University of Essex)

Interviews
Jim Archer, 24 July 2011
Lord Ashdown of Norton-sub-Hamdon, 14 June 2012
Sir Alan Beith MP, 16 May 2012
Sir Malcolm Bruce MP, 24 April 2012
Sir Menzies Campbell MP, 23 April 2012
Simon Coates, 24 April 2012
Hugo Dixon, 8 July 2012 (by email)
Andrew Gilmour, 2 May 2012 (by email)
Philip Goldenberg, 17 April 2012
Lord Greaves, 27 June 2012
Hugh Kerr, 2 July 2012 (by Facebook)
Lord Kirkwood of Kirkhope, 25 April 2012
Alec McGivan, 14 May 2012
Lord Maclennan of Rogart, 18 May 2012
Lord McNally, 13 June 2012
Michael Meadowcroft, 24 April 2012
Stuart Mole, 15 May 2012
Lord Owen, 4 July 2012
John Pardoe, 3 July 2012
Willis Pickard, 7 May 2012
Jeremy Purvis, 30 April & 2/3 July 2012
Lord Rennard, 29 May 2012
Lord Steel of Aikwood, 29 May, 21 June & 3 July 2012
Lord Wallace of Saltaire, 14 June 2012
Lord Wallace of Tankerness, 9 December 2011
Sir Graham Watson MEP, 28 May 2012

INDEX

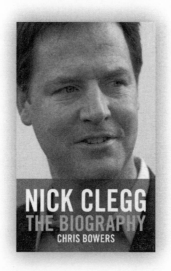

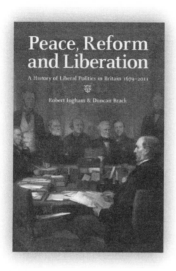